DECADES

BRITPOP

Peter Richard Adams and Matt Pooler

sonicbondpublishing.com

Sonicbond Publishing Limited
www.sonicbondpublishing.co.uk
Email: info@sonicbondpublishing.co.uk

First Published in the United Kingdom 2022
First Published in the United States 2022

British Library Cataloguing in Publication Data:
A Catalogue record for this book is available from the British Library

ISBN 978-1-78952-169-6

Typeset in ITC Garamond & ITC Avant Garde
Printed and bound in England

Graphic design and typesetting: Full Moon Media

Peter Richard Adams   Matt Pooler

Acknowledgements
With thanks to our wives, Donna and Rosie,
for all the hours we ignored them.

Foreword

I'm not sure why I emerged from the weighty grunge duvet I'd been festering under around 1992/1993, but I somehow found myself elevating from the *Friday Rock Show* with Tommy Vance to the bright and enthusiastic sounds of the *Evening Session* with Jo Whiley and Steve Lamacq. It was a new world. Minor chords and self-loathing were replaced by clean, shimmering guitar, lyrics filled with quirky observations and an overwhelming sense of optimism.

My world continued to expand, as every Wednesday afternoon, I'd march to my local newsagent and purchase the music papers, hoping for a cover-mounted cassette tape. Whilst devouring the pages of the *NME* and *Melody Maker*, it felt like every week there was something exciting: a new band or subgenre. It was hard to keep up. Going to live shows soon became a priority, and the gig pages were full of opportunities. I was lucky enough to have at least three venues within bus-ride distance, so I attended as many as I could. It felt like I was part of a unique musical movement – one tailored for me – and I fully embraced it. As this book shows, the music from that era has largely stood the test of time – the anthems stirring the emotions like a two-fingered call-to-arms. Long Live Britpop.

Chris Olden
Back To Britpop / the indie alternative podcast
September 2021

DECADES | BRITPOP

Contents

Introduction

Britpop. What was it?

Although interpretations may vary, for us, the term Britpop is a banner term for the huge number of (mostly) guitar bands that came to prominence in Britain during the 1990s. Although at the time, the title was interchangeable with 'indie' (and many of the groups given the label initially sought to distance themselves from it to remain edgy), few were truly independent of major labels and even less felt any indifference or embarrassment about the success they achieved – something which had so defined the 80s alternative scene. In fact, it's telling that the rejection of the title in the 90s was due to the ambition of many to continue to have careers once the media bubble burst, and it's now slightly ironic to see such bands wearing the tag as a badge of honour given their musical careers now take place largely on the revival and anniversary tour circuit.

Although a number of groups certainly did go on to have hugely successful careers, many others were mere flavours of the week. However, if they found themselves under the media-created Britpop big top, then there were two things for sure:

One: They were British.

Two: They played pop.

The clues were in the name.

But this was a very different type of pop music to that being forced down our throats by Saturday morning TV. It wasn't about four boys sat on stools, doing complex dance routines and singing about soppy stuff like love and following your dreams (although such subjects did creep in here and there). This was music created by bands building on the musical landscape that we had come to recognise from our parents' record collections and, rather than that being inherently uncool, seemed to kick start something deep within us in the same way that The Beatles and Stones had for their generation. It gave us a slightly alternative air, a tribe of our own and, as the whole thing built and built, allowed us to believe that by following this (slightly) alternative music, we were *right*... and what teenager doesn't want to feel like that?

Oh, how smug we were.

Most of all, though, these were songs that seemed to be about us and the lives we led... or at least the lives we'd like to lead. The truth was, that in 1990 we were both ten years old, hanging out together at middle school, avoiding the bullies and trying not to get told off by the teacher in music class. If we're being brutally honest, we weren't paying a huge amount of notice to rave culture or to taking E. We regret this decision (noticing things, not taking E), if only because it would have made the early chapters of this book easier to write.

The decade covered by this book very neatly covers the course of our lives from children growing up in deepest, darkest, rural Worcestershire to young adulthood. Bands mostly didn't visit us on tours (although there was a brief period) and you could only hear songs on the radio or a select few TV music shows across the four British channels. You were actually far more likely to read about a band in the press than to hear them.

This book chiefly concerns itself with what we believe to be the most important Britpop albums of the decade, although we've also made a note of all the single releases and our favourite deep cuts, just in case you don't fancy wading through 100 hours of music, year by year. We've chosen to write about albums for three reasons. Firstly, they allow us to delve deep into the music being created by the key artists while also giving an overview of the other gems from each year – something that has never been before done as most books concentrate on the personality and stories of the period. Secondly, it was a time when genuinely amazing albums were being created that would rival everything that preceding generations had produced. Thirdly, however, it's because if you were a teenager in the 90s, then you simply didn't have a lot of money to spend on the long players. This was a time before streaming, before Youtube, before mp3s and before easy access to the internet. Even when we were able to access the digital revolution in the late 1990s, life wasn't easy. A three-minute song could take hours to download and cost a fortune in phone bills. Songs, bands and albums were shared through a huge and illicit black market trade in school taping of which we were willing participants – each new release doing the rounds until your version was a copy of a copy of a copy. It's come as quite a surprise in revisiting some of the records that many don't intentionally come complete with warping or crackles.

Ultimately, this is a very personal book – we are, and always will be, fans of this era. We've done all we can to give you the detail and descriptions that you have come to expect from other publications of this type and hope we can be forgiven for the inclusion of our own personal memories about each release and band. The intention is to give the reader a flavour of the time – the excitement, the exhilaration and occasionally the crashing disappointment. To chart the period, we have split the book into three sections and what follows is a brief description of who we were during these periods.

All references to chart placings are British unless stated otherwise.

1990-1992: The Britpop Birth

In 1990, all the cool kids seemed to be into Iron Maiden or AC/DC. Bedroom posters of an ugly brute called Eddie or a duck-walking schoolboy with a guitar were all the rage, and, in order to fit in, you had to have some hair rock album or other in your Walkman, even if you never actually listened to it. Not necessarily being cool kids ourselves, however, even at this young age, it seemed clear that this wasn't the music we wanted. In fact, it seemed like something more fundamental just wasn't *right*. Britain seemed dull, grey and past its prime. The whole world around us was increasingly Americanised (although it would be many years until we understood the term), while the history we were both obsessed with at school only talked of our own country's achievements. It felt disappointing… as if the culture our parents had obsessed over in 60s and 70s had come to a grinding halt in the 1980s. Had we been born too late?

And then the drip began…

Slowly at first, we began to get glimpses that something else was happening, something that had been slowly brewing out of the alternative movements of the 80s. Top Of The Pops gave us glimpses of another world where rock bands played home-grown music delivered by people with names and teeth like our own. Occasionally some of these would even make it as far as the radio on the school bus, which for reasons that completely escape us, only seemed able to pick up Long Wave Radio Atlantic 252.

And then the drip became a river.

1993-1996: The Britpop Boom

There *was* other music out there. A recommendation from a schoolmate here, a 'wow what was that?!' moment listening to the radio there, and before we knew it the Britpop marketing machine had done its work and we were obsessed teenagers. We were hungry for input and far more interested about learning facts about the latest guitar bands from the NME and Melody Maker than anything our GCSE or A-level textbooks had to offer.

The height of Britpop covered our high school and college years. They say these are the best days of your life and, while we've never been entirely sure of that, they were incredible. There was always something new and exciting to discover, and not just in music. All areas of British culture – art, fashion, film, even football – contributed to a golden period marked by hot summers and star-filled nights. Although we were never at the heart of the action, it still finally felt we were at least in the right *country* at the right time. Anything seemed possible and it's no coincidence that, as we sat in a field drinking cider and listening intently to a tinny radio to discover who had won the Battle of Britpop between Blur and Oasis, we should instantly decide to form our first school band (even though we couldn't actually play any instruments).

And then the river burst its banks.

1997-1999: The Britpop Bust

Suddenly school was over and we were at university. It was bleak, damp and the only music that seemed to be pumping out of the dorms was Gomez's first album. Something had flipped and no attempts by the government to brand everything we loved and felt proud to call our own, as 'Cool Britannia' really cut the mustard. It was like some sort of mass sci-fi mind wipe had hit the whole country simultaneously. Everyone had forgotten all about the fun of the last five years, including most of the bands themselves.

What we didn't understand at the time was that nothing lasts forever. In order to exist, popular music goes through cyclical periods of refreshment and the media are as sure to pull down your gods as they were to have built them up in the first place. We had lived through the birth, boom and bust of one of the most exciting musical movements of our nation's history, but it would take decades for us to realise.

Britpop would go on to inform the years that followed, just as the scenes that had come previously had informed it in turn. To this day, the stars it created remain heavy chart hitters and cultural figures, while many of the smaller bands and personalities continue to play to packed houses on the nostalgia circuit. As for us, we moved on, got into different music and even had a stab at making some of our own.

We're now 30 years distant from where the book begins. We're not the people we once were. But on cold nights, when the pressures and responsibilities of the modern world are bearing down upon us, at least we can switch on the record player and reflect on our glory days. Our Britpop.

Peter Richard Adams & Matt Pooler
January 2022

Part One. 1990-1992 – The Britpop Birth

1990 - There could be success outside of dark rooms with sticky floors.

As Grunge broke in the Seattle underground – barely noticed by the world at large, and still some time from its all-conquering domination of the western world as the alternative music of choice – the UK was basking in the afterglow of the Second Summer of Love. Rave culture fuelled by the drug Ecstasy, had broken down the barriers within youth culture, and had begun a fruitful cross-pollination within the arts. It felt like something was afoot and change was coming, even if it might be at a glacial pace.

After a decade-long reign, Prime Minister Margaret Thatcher had finally lost the support of her cabinet and unwillingly resigned, giving way to the sleepwalker-like tenure of John Major (under whose proprietorship much of this book takes place). Britain was physically joined to the continent now that the Channel Tunnel had broken through. Internationally, the end of the Cold War continued – relationships between the USA and the Soviet Union thawing as communist parties dissolved and borders opened. However, the world we know *now* – or even the world of 2000 – still seemed unimaginable.

Although 1988 had seen the height of rave and the acid house movement, its MDMA-enabled smiley face had now sunken its way deep into youth culture. Even the Italia-90 World Cup song 'World In Motion' by New Order with lyrics by Keith Allen, got in on the action. Not only a massive chart hit, it was also a lyrical in-joke featuring a raft of drug-culture references for those in the know, and offered an inclusive British sense of humour to these previously separate spheres.

It was time for the indie scene to take notice. Throughout the majority of the 1980s, this had been an unusual place – dominated by Manchester's The Smiths – where ambition was sneered at, even by the ambitious. But now, one scene and one band above all others, were firing up the engines. The only issue was that they didn't have a driving licence, and were probably on too many drugs to know how to find the steering wheel.

The Madchester scene and its 'baggy' sound that combined jangling indie with dance-orientated rhythms, was primarily focussed on Manchester and – under the Factory and Creation labels – had given birth to a crop of bands that began to make waves as the decade drew to a close. Standing head-and-shoulders above them all – both musically and in terms of sales – were The Stone Roses. They'd broken the indie mould and successfully brought the two cultures of dance and indie together. Most importantly, though, they were not ashamed about what they wanted to achieve. The top-and-tail titles of their 1989 debut said it all: 'I Wanna Be Adored'/'I Am The Resurrection'. As if to prove the point, in May 1990, the band brought 28,000 people together at Spike Island to proclaim them the greatest band of a generation.

All the 'baggy' scene needed to do now was build on this success and follow it up.

The albums representing 1990 have been chosen to show both where music had come from (see the indie-tastic Inspiral Carpets) and where it could potentially go (see the clattering proto-Britpop of The La's). Ultimately though, it's about all the bands that in one way or another, broke through, got on *Top Of The Pops*, annoyed your parents and showed that there could be success outside of dark rooms with sticky floors.

Key Album: Inspiral Carpets – Life (1990)

Personnel:
Clint Boon: keyboards, vocals
Craig Gill: drums
Tom Hingley: vocals
Graham Lambert: guitars
Martyn Walsh: bass
Recording sessions: Out Of The Blue, September 1989
Mixing: Square One, December 1989
Producers: Inspiral Carpets and Nick Garside
Record label: Mute
Chart position: UK: 2
Release date: 23 April 1990

Pete: I feel ashamed to admit it, given that we're dealing with the opening album of the book, but I came to the Inspiral Carpets through the now time-honoured tradition of the Britpop fan: through Noel Gallagher. I'd read in the press about this band he'd been a roadie for, and I was greatly amused that on occasion, he'd get interviewed as a sub for Tom Hingley. There was this awesome quote dug up later, with him explaining why it was good that Blur were in the charts.

Matt: This was a band that you always heard about either through association with Stone Roses and Happy Mondays or, later, due to their famous roadie. At the time, I was never really aware of them other than the spaced-out cow logo. It was only later that I actually went back and listened.

The Band

Formed in Oldham, Manchester, in 1983, Inspiral Carpets quickly became linked to the growing Madchester scene, which helped raise their prominence. In their early years, the band released a number of demos, before being invited to record a radio session for John Peel in 1988. Shortly afterwards, they formed their own label – Cow – and then signed with Mute Records in 1990. Band personnel changes would occur right up to the recording of their debut album and – following the release of *Life* – the band would release a number of albums before being dropped by Mute and splitting amicably in 1995. In 2003, the band reformed, with original vocalist Stephen Holt returning to replace

Tom Hingley in 2011. They continued to actively tour and record until 2016 and the suicide of drummer Craig Gill.

The Album

Despite independently putting out two albums and various EPs before the Mute label came calling, *Life* is still considered as Inspiral Carpets' debut. With a sound more indebted to post-punk and 1960s garage than what would come to define the Madchester sound, The Stranglers were a particular influence (as will become clear). It's interesting to note, the band that created this album were almost a fresh proposition, with original members Stephen Holt (singer) and Dave Swift (bassist) having left in 1989 to form The Rainkings, when *Life* was only half-written. Swiftly recruiting new blood in the form of singer Tom Hingley and bassist Martyn Walsh, the band managed to capitalise on their independent success, attracting Mute's attention and leading them into the top 40 (which, in fairness, they'd only missed by a whisker under their own steam). A mix of raw instrumentation – including Clint Boon's 1960's Farfisa/Hammond Organ experimentation – dark verses and upbeat sunny choruses are often undercut by their raw subject matter. *Life* may at times be a somewhat jarring listen, but it's always exhilarating and is the sound of a band ready for success. As an interesting footnote, it was in the run-up to the release of *Life* that a young Noel Gallagher made an attempt to become the band's singer, but instead had to make do as their technician and roadie. Somewhere, in a parallel world, this might've meant that – come the mid-1990s – Blur would've been battling it out with Shed Seven in the great Battle of Britpop.

'Real Thing' (Inspiral Carpets)

Beginning proceedings with a subdued keyboard line, 'Real Thing' bursts into life shortly after the 30-second mark, with a full-on blast of the album's trademark sound – the entire band all going full pelt, clattering over each other in a manner that feels like it could fall apart at any moment, and, by simple virtue of *not* doing so, creating an exhilarating effect. An early call-to-arms, and often used to open their gigs, it lets the listener know for sure that the Inspiral Carpets are indeed 'the real thing'.

'Song For A Family' (Inspiral Carpets) [Deep Cut]

A darker, slower song about the daily life of a working-class family, with a keyboard line that feels reminiscent of The Stranglers' 'No More Heroes' (which is itself a motif of the entire *Life* album), the song employs the quite unusual technique of having verse and chorus at different tempos. In many ways, this song sets out the stall for the band in mixing dark verses with upbeat choruses to mesmerising and bombastic effect: almost as if The Doors had a punk rock chorus injected into one of their hits.

'This Is How It Feels' (Inspiral Carpets) [Single]

For many, 'This Is How It Feels' is the early apex of the band's powers. It was released as a single in March 1990, one month before the album's release, albeit in a version that has (slightly) less depressing lyrics removing the hints to suicide. In either version, the key subject-matter of 'This is how it feels to be lonely/This is how it feels to be small' remains at its core. Unusually for a single, the song never really takes flight like you might expect, and remains amongst the band's more subdued offerings. Two years later, the song was covered by Carter The Unstoppable Sex Machine (More on them later).

'Directing Traffik' (Inspiral Carpets) [Deep Cut]

Kicking off with an almost disco beat before a post-punk riff gets involved, the accidentally misspelt (or Germanic tribute) 'Directing Traffik' is a wonderfully bass-heavy song showing off some great work by Walsh. It continues with a central section again reminiscent of The Doors, in which Boon takes his keyboard for a walk (if such a thing is even possible). The entire song has a somewhat spooky feeling, thanks to its lyrical skeleton motifs, monotone backing vocals and angular keyboard breaks.

'Besides Me' (Inspiral Carpets)

Subverting the album's template so far, 'Besides Me' instead uses super-fast verses against a slow chorus, incorporating a mid-verse keyboard break that feels like the whole affair is about to come crashing down at any point and adequately imitates the classic 1960s garage sound that Boon admired. Though lyrically very simple (based on how you can outgrow some people), this does have an air of filler about it.

'Many Happy Returns' (Inspiral Carpets)

It's your birthday! Happy birthday! To celebrate, Inspiral Carpets have decided to do something rather unusual with this track inspired by the 1960s series *The Prisoner*. Of course, there's no rule book that says a song has to be all at one speed, and if there is, then this is an album that tears that rulebook to shreds. However, this is their most interesting twist on it. Despite being essentially a classically-framed sort of tune, there is a marked increase in tempo from the beginning up to the end of the first chorus, at which point it returns to its original speed. This creates a real sense of drive, while also agitating the ear somewhat, as we're not culturally attuned for such shifts. The end of the song changes again, using a hooky, washed-out guitar line, which is again reminiscent of 'No More Heroes', which is odd, because...

'Memories Of You' (Inspiral Carpets)

This song had been kicking around for a long time and is essentially a note-for-note recycling of The Stranglers tune, albeit with some psychedelic reversed voices at the beginning and end, delivered courtesy of an inebriated homeless individual outside the studio. As psychedelia goes, this fits more into the Rolling Stones ...*Satanic Majesties*... style than the Beatles mould. However, the truly interesting thing about the use of 'No More Heroes' here is that it's incredibly blatant. But – to the best of our knowledge – never resulted in court action, which is incredible given the fate of similar steals by Elastica (which will be covered later).

'She Comes In The Fall' (Inspiral Carpets) [Single]
Perhaps the album's best song, for being both a perfect representation of Inspiral Carpets at this point, and a really radio-friendly anthem. It was released in June 1990, following the album by two months. Though not as successful as 'This Is How It Feels' – peaking at 27 (again in a slightly different version) – this is a wonderful song, introduced by military-style drums that give way to some great vocal interplay in the bridge and choruses.

'Monkey On My Back' (Inspiral Carpets)
And from the best to possibly the record's worst song. This is thankfully the shortest cut here, at 1:59, though even then, it seems to slightly outstay its welcome. It's poppy and fun and was almost certainly a heck of a lot of fun live. But on record, it quickly gets a bit boring due to its repetition.

'Sun Don't Shine' (Inspiral Carpets)
Coming across as a great lost single, yet almost naïve in its lyrical content and simplicity, this is a charming song that had been written years before and was reminiscent of 'Scarborough Fair' and early R.E.M. With a stunning (yet possibly dated-sounding) Pink Floyd keyboard line, this is basically a good old-fashioned breakup song. 'We had something good, we can't take away/Will you see me tomorrow, well who can say?' sings Hingley, which pretty much sums up the mood with or without accompaniment.

'Inside My Head' (Inspiral Carpets)
Like 'Monkey On My Back', this is another somewhat by-the-numbers song, shooting for the goal at 100 miles per hour and only pausing for a great instrumental breakdown bridging section. The album's second-shortest song, it supplies one last burst of post-punk energy before coming to an abrupt end.

'Sackville' (Inspiral Carpets)
By far, the album's longest song (6:43), 'Sackville', feels a little like a missed opportunity. With Smiths-like verses about the local area, the prostitutes who walk there at night, and the band's thriving t-shirt business which also funded many of their early recordings (yes, really), these never really catch the ear. In contrast, the chorus soars with such a classic 1980s-style pop-hit melody that

it could've been a massive single if only the song had been about half as long. Possibly a slightly disappointing end to the album, this is still quite wonderful stuff, with a minute and a half of spooky sound collage, including whale noises, to round things off. Turn the end up, and it's quite unsettling, even if it doesn't feel exactly necessary.

Optional Extras

In 2013, an extended edition of *Life* was released, including the single 'Move', two EPs, the John Peel Session and a live gig. Furthermore, in 2014, *Dung 4* was released, containing a number of demos – recorded in December 1987 – of songs from the album and the EPs included on the extended edition. *Dung 4* is a band finding their feet, and as such, has a rough, amateur quality, many of the songs being recorded better subsequently. The 1988 *Planecrash EP* and the 1989 *Trainsurfing EP* continue the band's journey, and though the songs are interesting in showing their development, they're often devoted to the band's harder, punkier side, and follow similar musical themes to 'Monkey On My Back' and 'Inside My Head'. In fact, few if any of these songs would be a worthy addition or replacement for songs on the album, and arguably should continue to be considered as separate recordings in their own right. Only the single 'Move' – recorded a few months before the rest of the album – has a similar feel to the *Life* songs, and though it's not equal to the album's singles, it does have a catchy chorus.

James – Gold Mother (1990)

Recording sessions: Mid-1989
Producers: Tim Booth, Larry Gott, Jim Glennie, Nick Garside
Record label: Fontana
Chart position: UK:16
Release date: 4 June 1990

Pete: In the early 1990s, 'Sit Down' was just everywhere, wasn't it? At the time, I could never quite get my head round James; were they too popular with my Nan at weddings, to be cool? Obviously, in later years I reassessed this, and felt like I'd been rather unfair to them.

Matt: For me, they're summed up by two singles. You had 'Sit Down' and then 'She's A Star' during the Britpop heyday. Then, seemingly nothing before the singer bizarrely turned up in *Batman Begins*. When you do manage to get past the overplayed 'Sit Down' though, this is a band with a huge back catalogue to get lost in: *Gold Mother* being one of the best.

The Album

One of the UK's most enduring bands, yet so very often overlooked, James' 1990 album *Gold Mother* was the group's third and most diverse work to date. Though essentially a baggy album at its core, folk, world music and some surprising experimental elements also featured in the recipe that – when cooked up and left to simmer delivers a great alternative pop record that's the stepping stone between the 1980s and the 1990s. An expansive album, where even its tightest singles feel as if they have room to stretch their legs, played some 30 years later, it has all the feel of a greatest hits collection. 'Come Home' had indie dance floors full, while 'Sit Down' has experienced remarkable multigenerational appeal as the song that can get entire weddings to... well... sit down on the floor and still attempt to awkwardly dance. Successful on its initial release, the album was an even bigger hit on its 1991 reissue, when key singles were added and it peaked at number two.

Standout track: 'Gold Mother'.

Key Album: The La's – The La's (1990)

Personnel:
Lee Mavers: lead vocals, backing vocals, guitars
John Power: bass, backing vocals
Peter 'Cammy' Camell: lead guitars
Neil Mavers: drums, tambourine
John 'Boo' Byrne: electric guitar on 'There She Goes'
Chris Sharrock: drums and tambourine on 'There She Goes'
Paul Hemmings: electric guitar on 'Way Out'
John 'Timmo' Timson: drums, tambourine and bells on 'Way Out'
Recording Sessions: July-September 1988: 'There She Goes' recorded at Woodcray Studios, Wokingham, UK with producer Bob Andrews (Remixed by Steve Lillywhite for the album)
December 1989-February 1990: The rest of the album was recorded at Eden Studios, London, UK by producers Steve Lillywhite and Mark Wallis
Producers: Steve Lillywhite, Mark Wallis, Bob Andrews
Record label: Go!
Chart position: UK: 30, USA: 196
Release date: 1 October 1990

Pete: I find it hard to imagine that there could've been any time in my life when the whole world didn't seem to know 'There She Goes'. It just seems unfathomable to me – it's less a song and more a collective race memory. Which I suppose is a pretty neat way of summing up the whole album, really. I wish there were more records by The La's, but, if there were, it would probably dilute how special this one truly is.

Matt: The La's get unfairly dismissed as one-hit wonders with 'There She Goes', often followed by the statement that Mavers disappeared into eccentric obscurity. The reality is more complicated – Yes, Mavers has kept a very low public profile, but The La's had so many great songs. It's just a shame that it wasn't realised at the time.

The Band

Mike Badger formed The La's in 1983, with Lee Mavers joining the following year. The band maintained a fluid lineup throughout its existence, with Lee Mavers as their most enduring member, although John Power was also a long-standing member. Arguably, The La's have never split up, with various one-off gigs, tours and many rumours flying around over the last 30 years. However, their most active period by far remains their 1986-1992 heyday.

The Album

Frankly, it takes less time to make an elephant. Liverpool's The La's eponymous and only studio album was three years in the making after the band signed on the dotted line to Go! in 1987. The initial hope that the band would release their debut in early-1988 was scuppered by the unrealistic ambition of band leader Lee Mavers, who continually chased a sound heard only by himself, like a drunk chases an eye-floater. The number of studios, producers and sessions that The La's' debut went through, was only matched by the number of band members they also went through in this period, although one man stayed true to the cause throughout – bassist John Power, being Mavers' ever-dependable wingman right through to 1992, when even he finally had enough and went on to form Britpop stalwarts Cast.

Despite the group actively disowning the final album upon its release – being a label construct mostly utilising the final sessions with producer Steve Lillywhite – the record's impact still proved to be enormous. Noel Gallagher later declared that his plan was 'to finish what The La's started', even later inviting the drummer on 'There She Goes' (Chris Sharrock) to join Oasis. But that was all in the future. Back in 1990, Mavers and co – despite their disgust at the finished article – had created something truly special. A mixture of Merseyside mysticism, trademark 'rattle n roll', and packed full of incredible tunes, *The La's* deserves its place as a cornerstone of what would become Britpop.

As for Mavers himself, he became something of a Syd-Barrett-like recluse, willingly playing his new songs to those who sought him out but never entrusting them to tape again, despite various La's reformations in the decades to come: a true lost talent of British music.

'Son Of A Gun' (Lee Mavers)

A slab of pure La's, this mixes jagged acoustic strums with call-and-response picks, along with a chorus melody that owes more than a little debt to The Monkees' 'A Little Bit Me, A Little Bit You'. As with so many La's songs, this shows Mavers' singular talent for being able to make a song flow so naturally that you don't realise the chorus has begun until it's washing right over you. As the album's lead track, this acts as something of an unwitting manifesto for

Mavers himself, beginning with the prescient lines, 'If you want, I'll sell you a life story/About a man who's at loggerheads with his past all the time', who was 'burned by the twentieth century'.

'I Can't Sleep' (Lee Mavers) [Deep Cut]

An absolute rip-roarer of a track, with a crashing bridge and call-and-response vocals with bassist John Power. This is The La's displaying their 'rattle and roll' sound to full effect with a stop/start guitar that Wilko Johnson would be proud of. Sadly, this was never released as a single, when by rights, it should've been a prime contender.

'Timeless Melody' (Lee Mavers) [Single]

A single released one month before the album was, it reached 57 in the charts. It may not actually have a timeless melody (try humming it 20 minutes later), but it is a beautiful, swirling, wistful track that is both undercut and enhanced by the ragged lead vocal delivery, while Cammell delivers some great lead guitar lines. This song, again, shows Mavers' unique skill at allowing a verse to drift into a chorus with the same grace of waves overlapping on a gentle sea.

'Liberty Ship' (Lee Mavers) [Deep Cut]

Did we mention the sea? Well, here's The La's doing their own version of a shanty. Coming across as an update on the seafaring ditties of old, it's easy to imagine this being sung aboard a ship in the 1800s. However, it also manages to mix in a touch of modernity, especially in the 'Sail away on an ocean wave/ Sail away on the airwaves' outro.

'There She Goes' (Lee Mavers) [Single]

The big hitter of The La's is undoubtedly 'There She Goes' – a song so big and ubiquitous that it seems impossible to imagine a time when it wasn't pumped out of radio stations since the switch was first thrown at Ally Pally. Even if people don't know the band's name or have never heard the album, they know this tune, and with just cause: it's beautiful, upbeat and anthemic, but never brash.

Originally released in 1988 and then again in 1989 – but not touching the top 20 until its third outing in 1990 – the song finally hit its peak at 13, thanks to a Steve Lillywhite remix. Urban myth would have you believe it's an ode to heroin – a *fact* the band often disputed; Mavers himself admitting he never tried the drug until after the album's release. Often cited as one of the greatest songs ever written, and a founding cornerstone of what would become Britpop, it's an amazing piece of work given that it doesn't even have a verse. Mavers once again uses his quite incredible writing skill, making the listener believe they've listened to far more than a chorus repeated four times with a bridge section.

'Doledrum' (Lee Mavers)

Despite its title, 'Doledrum' isn't boring, and has a certain deep south-inspired jangling blues. However, it also isn't the record's most exciting song. It rattles along at a fair old clip, and has some enjoyable swelling harmonies, plus an *a cappella* bridge that ends the song in one of the album's most sublime sonic moments.

'Feelin'' (Lee Mavers) [Single]

Rattling, upbeat and joyous, 'Feelin'' was the album's last single, released in early-1991, reaching 43. It's the record's second song to owe a debt to The Monkees: this time with Cammell's 'Last Train To Clarkville'-like lead line. At only 1:45 in length, this is not only the album's shortest song but its most lightweight offering.

'Way Out' (Lee Mavers) [Single]

A much more interesting choice of single, this song piles on hook after hook, building into an earworm that's next to impossible to not hum all the way through on your way to work. Probably displaying the album's best guitar work, 'Way Out' was the band's debut single in 1987, reaching 87 in the charts. The album version is a re-recording rom the Lillywhite sessions.

'I.O.U.' (Lee Mavers)

It's probably fair to say that 'I.O.U.' is the album's worst song. Ultimately saved by its 2:13 length (the album's second-shortest), the rhyming of 'knowledge' with 'porridge' is either inspired or atrocious, depending entirely on your level of fandom. We're inclined to plump for the latter, though Noel Gallagher may have been taking note in understanding just how low a lyrical bar can be when writing pop masterpieces. And this *is still* a pop master class, heavily indebted to The Beatles, especially in the early-Harrison/Carl-Perkins-style lead lines.

'Freedom Song' (Lee Mavers)

'Freedom Song' has a different feel to any other track on *The La's*, partly due to its unexpected Klezmer styling and the room to breath given to each instrument. Despite coming in at less than two and half minutes, this song is in no hurry, unlike…

'Failure' (Lee Mavers)

Employing the same southern-fried noisy blues that Jake Bugg would utilise on his 2013 hit 'Lightning Bolt', 'Failure' blows away the cobwebs of the album's second half, and, in its latter third, employs sneakily subdued vocals in the mix that grabs the ear and drives the whole beast forward to a conclusion.

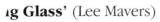

...g Glass' (Lee Mavers)

..., in at almost five minutes longer than any other track on the album, this ...al realisation of Mavers' elusive quest for perfection. 7:51 of lush swell and build with a chorus comprising as much instrumental as vocal hook, Mavers deploys a different singing style here, using a higher register than elsewhere, while the mesmeric pounding drums – speeding up into a machine gun roll before ultimately falling apart – really do give the impression of smashed glass. Again employing The La's' trademark ebb and flow, 'Looking Glass' is a crowning achievement for any album, especially one that also contains 'There She Goes'.

Optional Extras

For a band with only one album, there are a number of official and even unofficial albums of the multitude of sessions that took place in the long journey to produce it. On average, each song was recorded in different studios with different recording teams and equipment four or five times, with 'Doledrum' winning hands down with at least eight attempts to reach perfection. A number of these are included on the deluxe edition of *The La's*. The differences between versions are often more in the recording techniques and sounds achieved than in the songs themselves, and as such, offer interesting alternatives. However, ultimately it all comes down to personal preference, and they're not always worth repeated listening. The songs that didn't make the album vary, and show some interesting alternative sides to the band. 'Clean Prophet' has a rhythmic guitar sound, like mid-period Yardbirds or The Kinks, depending on which recorded version you listen to. 'Come In Come Out' is the riff from Ian Dury's 'Sex & Drugs & Rock & Roll' crossed with the harmonies of 'Marrakesh Express'. 'Man I'm Only Human' is a different beast altogether, with a chanting vocal and a dominating bass guitar leading the song, accompanied by a pounding drum and occasional bursts of sitar, which deliver a Velvet Underground feel. The sitar continues on the slowed-down 'Paint It Black'-like 'Endless'. 'Who Knows' and 'All By Myself' meanwhile are nursery-like lullabies, while 'Knock Me Down' and 'Over' are hidden gems that could easily have found a home on the album.

Lush – Gala (1990)

Recording Sessions: July 1989-August 1990
Producers: Tim Friese-Greene, Robin Guthrie, John Fryer
Record label: 4AD
Chart position: N/A
Release date: 13 October 1990

> Pete: I came to Lush really late, with their 1996 Britpop album *Lovelife*. At that point, I suppose I didn't quite understand the huge body of work they had behind them or how important they'd been in paving the way for indie bands, including women. It's not fair, but they were simply part of the Britpop wash by that point. They deserve more.

Matt: It's amazing how a slight tweak of sound and vibe can change how you perceive/notice a band. Their previous albums were indebted to the American alternative rock scene (even being Pixies-esque) or sounded indie/shoegaze (and more). Then when *Lovelife* appeared (with its Britpop-influenced bright pink logo and an arrangement of cactus in what looked like a garden shed), their past combined with an altered Britpop sound, meaning that all of a sudden they were being noticed by a whole new audience while unfortunately alienating some of their existing fans. It's only when you work backwards, you hear the band's other aspects/styles.

The Album

Enthusiastically received by critics upon release, Lush's debut album is actually anything but. Essentially a compilation – consisting of all their released work to date in one long-playing format chiefly for the attention of the US market – this is by no means a cohesive statement of intent. However, though it may be difficult to pigeonhole into any one simple category (despite elements of shoegaze and jangly guitar pop; 'Thoughtforms' essentially taking the Stone Roses template and levelling up) – the real power of *Gala* is in its rich assortment. Some elements may be too sweet, some too sour, but taken as a whole, the balance is enough to satisfy. Always a hard-touring band, not afraid of tackling international markets, it's an album notable for Lush, due to the glacial and ethereal – but still notably English-accented – voices of Miko Berenyi and Emma Anderson, which bring a washed-out coolness to proceedings.

Standout track: 'Thoughtforms'.

Ride – Nowhere (1990)

Recording sessions: Spring 1990
Producer: Marc Waterman
Record label: Creation
Chart position: UK: 11
Release date: 15 October 1990

Pete: Ride are just great. A strong statement perhaps, but they're the only band that matters when it comes to the shoegaze genre, which is a funny title in itself, as *Nowhere* is an absolute powerhouse, and I find it hard to believe that this could ever have been delivered live in a bored, concentrated manner.

Matt: Shoegaze – and Ride in particular – is definitely a mood music, and if you are not ready to go on that sonic journey, you will get left behind. For a band so young, producing a debut album with so many parts to it, is just amazing. There's something new to hear every time you listen to it.

The Album

In the year The Byrds reunited, it must've been vaguely fortuitous that a British band was busy laying the ground for new listeners. Ride's debut – full of fuzzy semi-psychedelic guitars, Indian-sounding harmonics, woozy trips and noisy wig-outs – also employed subdued chanting Byrds-like harmonies, and is pretty much the masterpiece moment for the whole genre. An album best experienced by laying back and allowing the universe to wash over you, there's a great juxtaposition here between its stunning wall-of-sound guitars and the way it often seems it's the drums that are actually playing the song. With accents gloomily unaffected by pretence, the Creation label unknowingly already had its first member of Oasis on the roster: in the form of Ride-founder Andy Bell, who would later join the Gallagher brothers on bass.

Standout track: 'Polar Bear'

Key Album: Happy Mondays – Pills 'N' Thrills and Bellyaches (1990)

Personnel:
Shaun Ryder: vocals
Paul Ryder: bass
Mark Day: lead and rhythm guitar
Paul Davis: keyboards
Gary Whelan: drums, programming
Bez: dancer
Rowetta: guest vocals
Tony Castro: percussion
Simon Machan: original programming
Recording sessions: 'Step On': February 1990 at Eden Studios in West London
The rest of the album: Summer 1990 at Capital Studios, Los Angeles; mixed at Eden Studios
Producers: Paul Oakenfold, Steve Osbourne
Record label: Factory
Chart position: UK: 4, USA: 89
Release date: 5 November 1990

Pete: Along with The La's, Happy Mondays are one of the bands that managed to seep through into my ten-year-old awareness. Obviously, I didn't actually *get the* band's ethos; I didn't even know what *drugs* were then! But I had enough about me to realise a blinding single or two when I heard them.

Matt: Happy Mondays always made me think that no matter what, if you couldn't play an instrument or sing, or could only hop from foot to foot or pretend to swim/drown roughly in time with music while occasionally shaking some maracas, you would still be okay. Even better if the band could write some of the catchiest party anthems around.

The Band

There seem to be differing views on when Happy Mondays actually formed. With an initial emergence in 1980, it took a number of years for them to get a manager and start making headway. We can only guess at the reasons why, but it probably didn't have a lot to do with perfecting the sound. Eventually signing to Factory Records in 1985, and as a major part of the growing Madchester scene, the band's rise was swift, with an output of albums, EPs and singles, culminating with *Pills 'N' Thrills and Bellyaches,* and headlining Glastonbury in 1990. By this time, the band had grown, with the addition of Rowetta supplying an extra vocal dimension. Unfortunately, success didn't last, and the follow-up album was a disaster – recording being disrupted by the band members' well-documented drug problems, while the recordings had replaced the trademark sound with something that alienated fans and saw significant critical backlash. This led to not only the band splitting, but also Factory Records going bankrupt.

The Album

Okay, we know what you're thinking: Happy Mondays aren't Britpop. However, as key contributors to the Madchester scene (which is a whole other book altogether), their importance as a stone to step on (ha!) in the road to Britpop, can't be overlooked.

By 1990, the band were still fully engrossed in their quest to stretch the first three minutes of Can's 'Halleluwah' over a whole career, at the same time consuming as many mind-altering substances as possible. Led by Shaun Ryder – Factory's answer to Shane MacGowan – *Pills 'N' Thrills and Bellyaches* was the band's third album and by far their most successful in terms of sales and artistry. Part-indie/part-house-music, producer DJs Paul Oakenfold and his collaborator Steve Osbourne had already successfully remixed previous singles and were now chosen to piece together the best of two worlds to create the Mondays' defining statement. Although the band would never again scale such heights, they had tipped over the edge into the mainstream, something which would later set Ryder up perfectly for his Britpop adventures in Black Grape.

'Kinky Afro' (Shaun Ryder, Paul Ryder, Mark Day, Paul Davis, Gary Whelan [Single])

Out of the starting blocks at an absolute gallop, 'Kinky Afro' is a strong contender for the album's best song. As funky as you like, with Ryder's drawling vocals at their least drawled, it gets its hooks into you simply by piling on the hooks, and maximising acoustic guitars and lush synth strings. Initially called 'Groovy Afro' and swiftly changed due to a similarly titled offering by The Farm, it was released as a single one month before the album, reaching number 5 in the UK. The song was also the band's biggest hit in US, where it staggeringly hit number-1 in the *Billboard* Modern Rock Tracks chart: not bad for a song about someone who isn't a very nice person. All together now, 'Yippee-ippee-ey-ey-ay-yey-yey!'

'God's Cop' (Shaun Ryder, Paul Ryder, Mark Day, Paul Davis, Gary Whelan)

For a song written about a hard-line local Chief Constable with strong moral views (that didn't align with the band's), and built around the central notion that Ryder believes 'God made it easy on me', 'God's Cop' suffers somewhat from a strained vocal. It's Happy Numbers by numbers, really. This is largely built on a loop, with some surprisingly dated keyboard solos and a siren-like guitar.

'Donovan' (Shaun Ryder, Paul Ryder, Mark Day, Paul Davis, Gary Whelan)

The most stripped back song in the pack, 'Donovan', provides a steadily rolling groove built from programmed drums and accordion samples. The band kick in proper at the two-minute mark with an angular post-punk-style riff which does step things up a gear, but the song never really goes anywhere. In addition to the 'Sunshine Superman' lyric influence, there's also a cheeky touch of the Cockney Rebel in the 'Come up and see me, make me smile' outro.

'Grandbag's Funeral' (Shaun Ryder, Paul Ryder, Mark Day, Paul Davis, Gary Whelan)

The award for the record's most lightweight song certainly goes to 'Grandbag's Funeral'. Harking back to their earlier sound, this is structured around repetitive verses and a classic-rock building bridge/chorus that's still remarkably good fun, and features some great free-form guitar work from Day, and hooky Hammond organ.

'Loose Fit' (Shaun Ryder, Paul Ryder, Mark Day, Paul Davis, Gary Whelan) [Single]

This uses a *very* Happy Mondays groove to underpin a guitar motif that's so highly reminiscent of Pink Floyd's 'Wish You Were Here', it's amazing there wasn't a lawsuit. Essentially, the song is built from little else, with the verses consisting of little more than drums and vocals, which betray its roots as a studio-written track. Even though the chorus elevates matters – being wonderfully upbeat and featuring some soulful backing by Rowetta – it still feels like it's merely a breathing space before returning to the guitar. Released as a single in March 1991 – some months after the album – it reached number 17.

'Dennis And Lois' (Shaun Ryder, Paul Ryder, Mark Day, Paul Davis, Gary Whelan [Deep Cut]
Kicking off with a very funky sample straight out of Wild Cherry's 'Play That Funky Music', it was probably the piano similarity to 'Step On' that ultimately prevented 'Dennis And Lois' from being a single contender. It's a joyous romp named after (but not about) a New York couple who were regulars on the Madchester scene and supported bands on their US tours. To top matters off on the fun, this is the only song in this book that incorporates a catchphrase from British all-round entertainer Bruce Forsyth.

'Bob's Yer Uncle' (Happy Mondays, Paul Oakenfold, Steve Osborne)
Without wanting to get too personal, what do you want to hear when you're making love? Serge Gainsbourg? Barry White? Or Shaun Ryder? If it's the latter, then boy are you in for a treat because here's the Happy Mondays going full-on sexy. Or seedy. The band take to their remit with such gusto, that the song even includes a husky lead flute solo and Rowetta's soulful panting. It should probably be the stuff nightmares are made of, but it's tremendous fun. As Ryder himself stated: 'I'm not capable of writing something sexy, but I can write something dirty that sounds sexy'.

'Step On' (John Kongos, Christos Demetriou) [Single]
The album's longest song – 5:17 seconds – this was also the band's joint-biggest chart success, the single version reaching number 5, although 'Step On' outsold 'Kinky Afro', and is perhaps their most well-known song in the US. A cover of John Kongos' 1971 single 'He's Gonna Step On You Again', this is a dramatic reinterpretation that manages to sound true to its source, yet so completely Happy Mondays that it's hard to believe they didn't write it. The recording was originally intended for a compilation for US label Elektra, but the results were so strong, they decided to keep it to release as a single. And what a single it is – superbly embellished by Ryder's 'Your twisting my melon, man!' addition that became so ubiquitous with his persona that it even formed the title of his autobiography.

'Holiday' (Shaun Ryder, Paul Ryder, Mark Day, Paul Davis, Gary Whelan)
From the longest to the shortest, 'Holiday' is a pipsqueak in comparison, and is even stretched out by field recordings of a plane at the beginning and end. The collection's funkiest song, with a really laid-back groove that never really goes anywhere, the piece is elevated by some really cool keyboard strikes, the sound of seagulls, and probably the funniest line on the entire album: 'I smell dope, I smell dope, I smell dope, I am smelling dope'. Ultimately, the effect is a bit like when a classic sitcom makes a movie and transplants the action to a

holiday resort. But this is the Mondays, so instead of mistaken identity, there's a mammoth amount of drugs and a run in with airport security instead. 'Holiday' also has a neat segue into the record's final song.

'Harmony' (Shaun Ryder, Paul Ryder, Mark Day, Paul Davis, Gary Whelan) [Deep Cut]
Amusingly, 'Harmony' is sung by a man for whom harmony can be an abstract concept at the best of times. The first of two mentions in this book of the song from the Coca-Cola jingle: 'I'd Like to Teach The World To Sing (In Perfect Harmony)' by The Hillside Singers, here Ryder simply steals the lyrics, declaring that once he's taught the world to sing, he'd then like to 'Cut it up in little tiny bits and give it all away for free'. (To find out what Noel Gallagher did with the accompanying tune, skip ahead to 1994.) This has a woozy, enjoyable, laid-back guitar groove but comes across a bit like a hidden track: which it might've been better placed as. It also has a remarkably-abrupt ending.

Optional Extras
Partly due to the era and partly to the music itself, Happy Mondays' extras include many remixes of existing tracks. Do these work? Are they better? Are they worse? Ultimately, it's all up to the listener to decide, although most of the ones currently available seem to be remixed to increase length rather than to create something radically different. The only other bonus track currently available is 'Tokoloshe Man': another single written by Kongos, recorded for the compilation album 'Step On' was originally intended for. The song is reasonably faithful to its origin, and retains the cowboy/country feel, although it now includes a jaunty selection of mid-1990s keyboard sounds to back it up: could there be anything else? In 2019, all four Factory Records albums were planned for a vinyl reissue which would include a download code giving exclusive access to rarities and remixes. By the time of their release in early 2020, the download code no longer contained additional songs, meaning that, for the moment, the joys (or otherwise) of additional material must remain a mystery.

1991 – A trial run?

With the UK stuck in what seemed like a downward spiral of never-ending recession and unemployment, 1991 was the year that saw widespread rioting break out across the country's urban estates. Partly inspired by the earlier Poll Tax riots and usually ignited by local events, these uprisings were seemingly without wider ideological intentions, although their protagonists were noticeably disenfranchised white youth that increasingly felt they had no place or voice in society.

As international developments – such as the end of apartheid in South Africa, and the dissolution of the Soviet Union – pointed toward something like a new world, the best the UK seemed to be able to offer was being able to get groceries on a Sunday and even then it was because the stores took it upon themselves to defy the arcane trading laws, rather than any feeling that the government was pushing the country forward. The short Gulf War in January (when the UK joined a coalition of 35 countries in response to Iraq's invasion of Kuwait), may have helped introduce a more modern style of on-the-spot news reporting to the British audience, but this wasn't reflected in the coverage of domestic urban unrest which was largely referred to as base criminality rather than a cry for help.

While it's unfair to the incredible musicians who created their greatest work in this period to simply refer to it as a trial run for Britpop, it's certainly useful shorthand. British guitar groups and the largely independent industry around them, were getting tastes of success that had probably been unthinkable dreams when they started out. As musical shifts witnessed the last days of baggy and the increasing dominance of *grebo* (essentially a dirtier, punkier take on indie), rave culture was becoming increasingly urbanised and commercialised. This led to some truly incredible music, as this chapter will attest to. However, it never really felt like the soundtrack to your glory days, even if new late-night TV shows such as *The Word* did have an uncanny ability to celebrate youth culture in all its grubby glory.

Britain's youth needed a music that expressed the way it felt, and – for now, at least – that voice was found in America, following the release of Nirvana's *Nevermind* album. Its lead single 'Smells Like Teen Spirit' seemingly encapsulated a lost generation on both sides of the Atlantic, with the lines 'I found it hard, was hard to find/Oh well, whatever, never mind', while actively laying the issue on the line: 'Here we are now, entertain us'. The British musical response would not be immediate.

To represent 1991, the albums we have chosen, sum up what was an exceptionally-vibrant time for alternative UK music. There's the baggy after-party (featuring the emergence of Blur with *Leisure*), the grebo movement (Carter USM) and Primal Scream's epic genre-melding *Screamadelica,* all with pride-of-place, along with a host of other records that broke through to some degree of acceptance within the mainstream, influencing musicians who had long dreamt of success but didn't necessarily believe it was possible.

Key Album: Carter USM – 30 Something (1991)

Personnel:
Jim 'Jim Bob' Morrison: performer
Les 'Fruitbat' Carter: performer
Recording sessions: November 1990, Important Notice Studios, Mitcham, South London
Producers: Sex Machine, Simon Painter
Record label: Rough Trade
Chart position: UK: 8
Release date: 18 February 1991

Pete: I know folks just a couple of years older than me (people's whose musical judgement I really rate) that say seeing Carter USM for the first time was like a light-bulb moment for them. For a massive number of folks, they were The Clash of their generation, tying together political messages with razor-sharp tunes. For that alone, they should be applauded, or at the very least, added to the school syllabus.

Matt: I'm not sure I was aware of them – apart from maybe sniggering at the name – until the Schofield incident. Even then, I don't think I knew anybody who had any music by them, so it was a long time before I actually heard anything other than the odd single. It's unfortunate, as they're really not what you expect; probably my favourite grebo band, even if that banner title does them no justice or favours.

The Band

Morrison and Carter had been in various bands together throughout the early-1980s, before finding some limited success in Jamie Wednesday. When that band split in August 1987, Morrison and Carter were left to play a scheduled gig as a duo backed only with a drum machine. Thus, Carter The Unstoppable Sex Machine (Carter USM) was born. Although their first single was released in 1988, it was their second – 'Sheriff Fatman': released in 1989 – that became their signature song, and the debut album *101 Damnations* followed soon after. The band toured constantly, and their live shows became famous for the wild experiences of the audiences. 1991 saw the band have further chart success but also make headlines with a song banned by the BBC, and Fruitbat infamously rugby-tackling presenter Phillip Schofield live at the *Smash Hits Poll Winners Party* in front of millions of television viewers. The headlines continued into 1992, with the band banned from Glastonbury for insulting organiser Michael Eavis (for cutting their set short), and a continuing struggle with the intense media scrutiny. Over the following years, the band's fame waned despite musical development and the introduction of additional members, eventually amicably calling it a day as a six-piece band in 1998. Since then, there have been a number of live reunions featuring only

Carter and Morrison. The last, in 2014, was billed as the final ever live Carter USM show.

The Album

What are Carter exactly? Indie? Alternative? Alternative dance? Straight out punk rock through a late-1980s filter? At the time, they were considered grebo, and the band were lumped in with Pop Will Eat Itself, The Wonder Stuff and Ned's Atomic Dustbin. Perhaps that's fair – they do fit the mould, and grebo itself was an interesting, press-invented forerunner to Britpop itself; almost a trial run for how far a perceived movement can push a group of bands. However, ultimately, Carter USM were their very own beast. Lyrically smart – even more than The Clash to whom they were always heavily indebted – and tying their message to exceptionally catchy buzz-saw masterpieces, *30 Something* was the album in which they melded the two with perfection. Not afraid of using a pun or several, or of occasionally wearing their influences on their sleeves, this record offers an interesting counterpoint to Primal Scream's *Screamadelica*, in that it hits many of the same genre-defying markers yet brings a completely different result. At the end of the year, *NME* placed *30 Something* at number 8 in its albums-of-the-year list. To be fair, it deserved to be higher, but for Carter USM, it opened the door to pop stardom and the 101 damnations that came with it.

'Surfin' U.S.M.' (Morrison, Carter) [Deep Cut]

Kicking off with a sound clip from the BBC sitcom *Red Dwarf* – of Chris Barrie as Rimmer, giving his bunkmate Lister a lecture on ageing – *30 Something* leaps into action with a fantastic football-style chant of 'You fat bastard!', an absolutely pulsating backing track and a David Bowie 'Wham, bam! Thank you, mam!' steal. Unusually for this book so far, this track is (almost) an instrumental. But is it – as the title suggests – a surf track? No, it's not. But it's not exactly an indie track or a dance track either. It's just exhilarating.

'My Second To Last Will And Testament' (Morrison, Carter)

Starting with a sample of Michael Caine from the movie *Alfie*, this continues in a similar vein to 'Surfin' USM', but is more of a thrashy, trashy punk song, with Morrison settling his worldly affairs, including what should happen to his organs (Lucky Daphne gets his heart).

'Anytime Anyplace Anywhere' (Morrison, Carter) [Single]

Perhaps a surprising choice for a single, given its darker edge in contrast to so much else on this record, this does feel weighty (despite a chorus from a Martini advertising slogan), and is a definite step up from their debut *101 Damnations* and – in terms of *30 Something* itself – the preceding tracks. Its final third includes some brooding building keyboard lines and amazing guitar work from Carter. The single reached number 83 in October 1990: just over four months before the album's release.

'A Prince In A Pauper's Grave' (Morrison, Carter) [Deep Cut]

This is the point on *30 Something* where you realise Carter USM have the ability to be so much more than what you expect. Beginning with Morrison singing over a simple organ line that feels like it's been transplanted from not only another album but a different era altogether, it's the story of Johnny, who is drinking 'to the memory of a prince in a pauper's grave'. The song takes flight at around 1:30 with a marching style drum rhythm, while the final minute and a half are utterly transcendent and something quite special indeed.

'Shopper's Paradise' (Morrison, Carter)

With The Clash being a clear influence on Carter USM, in terms of both style and message, it's no surprise that at some point, Uncle Joe should make an overt appearance. But it's still a surprise that – following a hooky keyboard line – there should still be a direct Strummer steal from The Clash's *London Calling* track 'Koka Kola'. It's an inspired piece of larceny – the rest of the song feels like an updated version, including 'Grace & Favour'-style product lists wonderfully including 'Top floor, Shoppers' Paradise/We've got a drunk Father Christmas and the antichrist'. On balance, this does feel a little like a leftover from *101 Damnations*, but that's no bad thing, and the ironic take on consumerism – 'The big shop is open and the world is wonderful!' – is actually quite joyous.

'Billy's Smart Circus' (Morrison, Carter)

What pop song in its right mind starts with the line 'To die for his mother country/Isn't every father's wish'? Well, this pop song for a start, but this shows the lengths Carter USM would go to to get a message across, linking probably the record's greatest chorus with lyrics that state 'And if I put this gun against my head/And pull the trigger, I'll be dead'. It's on songs like this that you can't help but feel that – partly thanks to Britpop – Carter USM have been given a raw deal in terms of the respect they should have in British music.

'Bloodsport For All' (Morrison, Carter) [Single]

Released one month before the album and reaching 48 in the singles chart, this song ties a glam riff straight out of the early-1970s to lyrics regarding racism and bullying in the British army. In a spectacularly unfortunate piece of timing (or wonderful piece of planning), it also coincided with the start of the Gulf War and managed to get banned by the BBC. Built around a thrilling kick-drum-led central section and Carter singing 'And the coldest stream guards of them all/Sang 'God Save The Queen and bloodsports for all', it's so damn fist-pumpingly perfect that you don't even notice they're rhyming 'all' with 'all'.

This is a textbook example of how to get the kids pogoing to a message, and it's infectious stuff.

'Sealed With A Glasgow Kiss' (Morrison, Carter)

Racing in at 100 miles an hour, this is both the album's shortest song and its punkiest by far. Despite this, it still finds time for a great little keyboard and guitar solo, and a euphoric chorus.

'Say It With Flowers' (Morrison, Carter)

It'll all be over by Christmas. But what if it isn't? Starting off with a simple guitar and vocal from Morrison, the Edwin-Starr-like pump of 'War!' kicks the song up several gears as the lyrics discuss the juxtaposition between Christmas at home and on the battlefield: a message only made stronger due to the proximity of the first Gulf War. Although never promoted as such, this is very much a Carter Christmas song, in the mould of Jona Lewie, but far bleaker.

'Falling On A Bruise' (Morrison, Carter)

This is the beautiful and powerful conclusion (almost) to *30 Something*, and at almost six minutes in length, it's an absolute epic in Carter USM terms, with a total change of pace. Featuring a lush layering of piano and guitar that occasionally threatens to become a 1980s pop cliché, Morrison delivers a genuinely moving reflection on everything that is modern life. Less world-weary and more earth-exhausted, it all boils down to one question: If you had the chance, would you do it all again? 'I'd change everything' is the response, which says it all really. The second half is a gorgeous swell of guitars, keyboard horns, descending piano and powerful drums before a minute-long fade out, which feels earned, before giving way to another snatch of dialogue from *Alfie*.

'The Final Comedown' (Morrison, Carter)

The album's second-shortest song (2:05), is actually more a sketch than a song, but it's a beautiful and deserved final kiss-off for the album, and, in many ways, for modern life as well. The fact that it still sounds relevant some 30 years on, is both a testament to the writing and possibly a bleak comment on progress. A keyboard swell, a gentle piano line and some fine synth-strings later, we've reached the end of Carter USM's masterpiece. The final words go to Morrison: 'We should celebrate I think/With the bloodiest of Marys/But I'm too fucked to drink'.

Optional Extras

Carter USM were a band that, by their own admission, didn't demo or jam on songs. Everything recorded was used, which, unfortunately, means bonus and unreleased material is non-existent. Despite this, a deluxe version of the album was released in 2012, including the five B-sides from the two singles, a festively-altered song from a limited edition 7" promo, and a concert recorded for BBC radio. Of the B-sides, two are covers and exactly what you'd expect from the band; Monkees and Soft Cell songs. The remaining band-written tunes include 'Re-educating Rita': a punky number making nice use of a nursery rhyme, and '2001: A Clockwork Orange', which is similar in sound to 'Surfin' USM', but with a slightly unsettling vocal consisting of samples of children describing their ambitions. The most unusual song is 'Randy Sarf Git' – a rock instrumental clearly inspired by The Monkees, but different from and far heavier than anything else on the album. Finally, 'Christmas Shopper's Paradise' was a gift from the band, handed out at the Town and Country Club on 14 December 1990, and features a 'Yuletised' or sleigh bell version of 'Shopper's Paradise'. Unnecessary maybe, but a fun version nonetheless, and indicative of the extras available: nice to have, fun to listen to, but nothing more than that.

The Farm – Spartacus (1991)
Recording sessions: 1990
Producers: Stan Cullimore, Paul Heaton, Suggs
Record label: Sire, Produce
Chart position: UK: 1
Release date: 4 March 1991

Pete: The Farm are a band you'd think I'd just naturally know more about, given that I grew up on a farm. However, my relationship with them has always been a victim of the overpowering presence of 'All Together Now', which is one of those songs that conjures up memories of New Labour for me, even more than D:Ream's 'Things Can Only Get Better'.

Matt: Out of all the bands reviewed in this book, I think The Farm are the one that have made the absolute most of one of their songs. With multiple remixes being released over the years, through its use by various football clubs, a political party, and even as a slight Atomic Kitten rewrite, it's been everywhere. Sadly though, it never seemed to encourage listeners to explore the parent album.

The Album
The Farm's debut may be perfectly of its era with baggy grooves prevailing, yet its brief time at the number-1 spot in 1991 proved something of a vindication for the Liverpool band. They had definitely put in the work, and it was time now to reap some of the rewards. With a production team that reads like stunt casting (the band were more than happy to use their contact book of people they'd met along the way), elements of gospel ('Higher And Higher'), pop-punk ('Groovy Train') and even folk ('Tell The Story') make for a much greater listening experience than the packaging suggests – which was a fake soap box: a trick that many Britpop bands would repeat throughout the 1990s.

This is also The Farm album which included the lightning-in-a-bottle single 'All Together Now' – a song that has seemingly transcended the pop and now exists in its own right as a ubiquitous modern classic used in adverts, by football teams and even the Labour Party.

Standout track: 'All Together Now'

The Wonder Stuff – Never Loved Elvis (1991)

Recording Sessions: 1990-1991
Producer: Mick Glossop
Record label: Polydor
Chart position: UK: 3
Release date: 27 May 1991

Pete: Being a secret folky at heart, I loved The Wonder Stuff. I remember always being so happy when they got played on the school bus radio. It was just an awesome mixture of genres and sounded like nothing else going that I was aware of. In fact, they're probably responsible for making me a secret folky in the first place, although that probably means I missed the point. Most of all, the singles were just so brilliantly catchy.

Matt: This album was the band's most successful, partly due to the quality of catchy songs and their most popular/famous single, 'The Size Of A Cow'. I do wonder how many people were caught-out, though: buying the album after hearing 'Dizzy', and finding out it wasn't actually on the album or written by the band.

The Album

1991 was a heck of a year for The Wonder Stuff. The most interesting of the Black Country three (which also included Ned's Atomic Dustbin and Pop Will Eat Itself), the band had developed from their indie origins into a more folk-influenced style, and with their third long-player *Never Loved Elvis*, they reached the peak of their powers. A run of amazing high-charting singles that would stand the test of time, paved the way for an album of exceptional breadth and clarity, showing off an exceptional mastery of their genre, and the wonderful lyricism of bandleader Miles Hunt. 'Welcome To The Cheap Seats' is especially noticeable for its bridge line 'In another world, he could wear a dress'. Within five years, Britpop's laddish aspects were to make any such sentiment seemingly impossible. Their year would be seen out by joining forces with comedian Vic Reeves, for the (slightly novel) mega-party-banger that was their cover of 'Dizzy'. It would be the only time the band reached number 1, but they'd remain number-1 forever in their fans' hearts.

Standout track: 'Welcome To The Cheap Seats'

Key Album: Blur – Leisure (1991)

Personnel:
Damon Albarn: lead vocals, keyboards
Graham Coxon: guitars, backing vocals
Alex James: bass
Dave Rowntree: drums, percussion.
Recording sessions: 'She's So High': Summer 1990, Battery Studios, Willesdon (Producers: Steve Lovell, Steve Power)
'Sing': Late-1990, Roundhouse, Chalk Farm (Producer: Blur)
'There's No Other Way': January 1991, Maison Rouge studios (Producer: Stephen Street)
'Fool', 'Birthday', 'Wear Me Down': Early 1991, unknown, but likely Maison Rouge (Producer: Mike Thorne)
The rest of the album: Spring 1991, Maison Rouge studios (Producer: Stephen Street)
Producers: Stephen Street, Steve Lovell, Steve Power, Mike Thorn, Blur
Record label: Food
Chart position: UK: 7
Release date: 26 August 1991

Pete: Blur were my entry point into Britpop. Not with *Leisure* though: I had to backtrack to that from *Modern Life Is Rubbish*. Although, if I met Damon Albarn, I expect we'd have nothing in common whatsoever. It was the first time I remember a band that felt like they'd been created just for me. An experience I'm sure I wasn't alone in feeling.

Matt: I'd heard the singles 'She's So High' and 'There's No Other Way'. I even saw them on *Top of The Pops*, but there wasn't enough there for me to want to get or even listen to the album at the time. I think that's the view of many people when it comes to *Leisure*: there are some really good bits, but you have to work hard to find them. Although, with the benefit of hindsight, you can see where the band were going.

The Band

Albarn and Coxon originally met at secondary school in Essex, and became good friends, whilst Coxon and Rowntree came to know each other from being part of the Colchester band scene. By 1987, Albarn had moved into London and was under contract with the owners of the Beat Factory recording studio, where he became part of a number of short-lived projects experimenting with styles and ideas. Coxon followed, attending Goldsmith's College, where he met fellow student Alex James. By December 1988, Coxon, Rowntree and James had all joined Albarn in the new band Seymour – the name originating from a 1959 J. D. Salinger short story that covered such weighty topics as religion, philosophy, family and suicide. Things moved swiftly: a demo was recorded, gigs played, and the Food record label were interested. By the end of 1989, Albarn was out of contract, and the band had a record deal on the table. But before that could be signed, the label wanted a name change. They'd correctly realised that the origins of the band name were likely to be lost on the majority of the music-buying public, and that it was just too *studenty*. The band were supplied with a list of suitable new names, and Blur was born. 1990 saw them touring and recording before releasing their debut single 'She's So High' in October. Although fashions quickly changed and the band looked likely to be dropped, the release of their sophomore album *Modern Life Is Rubbish* made Blur one of the leaders of the Britpop genre, and they gained huge popularity from subsequent releases. By their fifth album – released in 1997 – Blur had moved away from the classic Britpop sound, to a more lo-fi underground style, with subsequent albums exploring further experimentation and new styles, culminating in the brooding electronic *Think Tank* in 2003 (which also witnessed the departure of Coxon due to personal reasons brought on by alcoholism and increasingly erratic behaviour). Although effectively being on hiatus – with Albarn and Coxon concentrating on solo music careers, James focussing on cheese production and Rowntree on local politics – Blur still occasionally emerge (with a returned Coxon) for either a series of gigs or to release new music, including the 2015 album *The Magic Whip*.

The Album

After the initial single 'She's So High' almost hit the top 40, and subsequent singles nailed it, the pressure was on for Blur to follow up with an album that would place them as artists of standing. *Leisure*, to be fair, doesn't achieve this, but it does lay down much of the groundwork that their later albums would build upon to massive success. So, what is wrong with *Leisure*? Considered within the context of its time, nothing much really. It's a product of its time, largely aping the popular baggy and Madchester sounds that were shifting units and which got them noticed in the first place. However, despite hit singles and the odd flourish of greatness, it does have the feel of a group finding their feet. Little did anyone know that within a few short years, Blur would no longer be following but *leading* the pack, with *their* sound being that aped by the numerous bands being hurriedly signed to follow in the band's wake.

'She's So High' (Damon Albarn, Graham Coxon, Alex James, Dave Rowntree [Single]

A chiming guitar chord from Coxon, and Blur are here. Originally Blur's first steps into the wider world, this single was released in October 1990: some ten months before *Leisure*. It was a fair success for an unknown band, reaching 48 in the charts, being awarded single of the week in *NME*, and giving the band and label confidence to press forward. Originally a double A-side with 'I Know' (which was lost by the time the album was put together), this was a decidedly baggy song: on-trend with the time, though hardly groundbreaking. Repetitive, loose feeling, featuring great bass and a reverse guitar solo, the track almost feels almost like it's pushing boundaries. 'She's So High' remains joyous, and has been a crowd-pleaser throughout the band's career.

'Bang' (Damon Albarn, Graham Coxon, Alex James, Dave Rowntree) [Single]

'Bang' is not a good song. Even the band have essentially disowned *Leisure*'s third single, claiming it was rush-written under record company pressure for a single to follow-up the indisputable success of 'There's No Other Way'. It did okay on that front, reaching 24 in July 1991, but, sadly, includes some of the record's worst lyrics. 'Bang goes another year/In and out of one ear' has always stood out for some personal derision, although there is a hint of the future – 'Sitting in an SDT/Waiting for an underground train/To rumble underneath my feet' going some way toward the feeling later conjured on the subsequent album *Modern Life Is Rubbish*.

'Slow Down' (Damon Albarn, Graham Coxon, Alex James, Dave Rowntree)

For a song called 'Slow Down', this actually packs quite a wallop and highlights Coxon's interest in the noisy style of My Bloody Valentine, among others. The record's shortest song (3:11), and an enjoyable outing for Alex James' distorted bass (which would be put to great effect years later on the hit single 'Song 2'), this sounds monstrous and grungy before its time, until it inevitably sounds a bit baggy, but it soon gets monstrous and grungy again. Special mention should be made of its preposterous, noisy instrumental section, which segues very satisfyingly into the song's final verse.

'Repetition' (Damon Albarn, Graham Coxon, Alex James, Dave Rowntree) [Deep Cut]

'Repetition' includes some great work from Coxon, with a lead-like stuttered Townshend guitar riff making the whole thing sound like it's slowing down. Given that the song also includes the line 'Slow down, don't be so eager to let me go', it feels like the song titles of tracks three and four could be easily interchangeable. Though the song may not be a belter, the woozy melody at the end of the chorus offers a glimpse of what the band were capable of.

'Bad Day' (Damon Albarn, Graham Coxon, Alex James, Dave Rowntree)

Beginning with a hooky, wheezy melodica riff from Albarn, this feels like it's going to be a game-changer. That's before you hit the eight-second mark and the band kick in with the typically baggy rhythm that can be found repeatedly on *Leisure*. 'Bad Day' is essentially a simple groove that includes some cool instrumental breaks from Coxon's guitar, combined with *Rubber Soul/Revolver*-era Beatles influences that, in the end, don't really pay off.

'Sing' (Damon Albarn, Graham Coxon, Alex James, Dave Rowntree) [Deep Cut]

The album's longest song at over six minutes, and fully deserving of every second, this lost treasure is actually a demo that couldn't be improved upon. The song later reached true prominence, given a new lease of life when used to enormous effect in Danny Boyle's 1996 movie *Trainspotting*. But that was a good few years down the line yet, and on *Leisure*, it comes across as something of an oddity with its simple stuttered piano strikes, atmospheric guitar, pounding drums, and a bass line that mirrors the melancholy vocal melody: slowly building, as if a mantra. 'I can't feel, 'cause I am numb', sings Albarn, neatly summing up the track's overall feeling. Considering vinyl was still a valid format in 1991, this was quite a magnificent way to round off side one and is the album's undisputed highlight.

'There's No Other Way' (Damon Albarn, Graham Coxon, Alex James, Dave Rowntree) [Single]

This is *Leisure*'s banger. Released in April 1991 as the second single and smashing its way into the top 10, settling at number 8, it's another typically baggy groove, with Happy-Mondays-style tambourine omnipresent, yet upbeat, joyous and with pandemic levels of catchy. A hit on the indie dance floors of the nation as well as on the radio, it melds vague, trippy psychedelia with pure pop sensibilities and a fist-pumping chorus. It opened doors for the band, placing them squarely into *Smash Hits* territory with a single of the week, and was also a hit in the music press.

'Fool' (Damon Albarn, Graham Coxon, Alex James, Dave Rowntree)

Although not much to look at, really, 'Fool' plods away in a sunny, upbeat manner and is a lot of fun, with some classic 1960s-style chorus harmonies and a rather brilliant breakdown section halfway through. Again, this is indebted to My Bloody Valentine, but it's still fun, as it makes the song feel temporarily as if it's gone into reverse.

'Come Together' (Damon Albarn, Graham Coxon, Alex James, Dave Rowntree)

By far the punkiest song on the record – and the first in the 1991 batch to have 'Come Together' as a title – this doesn't have a lot to offer in terms of nuance: lyrically hitting the nail on the head with the line 'So why, why/Can't we come together? Why?'. It certainly seems unlikely that Albarn is singing about the ultimate futility of mankind's unity. It all but stops at the halfway point, and there's a brief pause where you feel the song may make a break for greatness, but instead, it settles into more or less the same one and a half minutes being played again. The outro is particularly enjoyable, though, giving Coxon an opportunity to let his fingers do the talking.

'High Cool' (Damon Albarn, Graham Coxon, Alex James, Dave Rowntree)

It's that baggy backbeat again! 'High Cool' is a bit light, really, and although we'd like to presume that the band thought the laid-back feel (propelled by James' bass) was pretty hip, the song is actually named after a setting on the air-conditioning unit at their rehearsal space. This perhaps says all you need to know about the band's feelings towards the song. The middle-eight is heightened by a vocal section much in the same mould as 'Repetition', which is repeated toward the end. This could – and probably should – have been a B-side, as it would not have been massively missed from the album as a whole.

'Birthday' (Damon Albarn, Graham Coxon, Alex James, Dave Rowntree)

Often overlooked as a lesser or even quite annoying song, 'Birthday' is actually quite a beautiful piece, in the mould of 'Sing', which it almost mirrors in its placing on the record. Slightly let down by Albarn's insistence on repeating the word 'day' in every verse-one line, it's still atmospheric stuff. Presumably, its placement as the album's last grand emotional statement was secured by the fact it all kicks off with a minute to go, which would've appealed to the band at this early stage in the game. We all know this is where 'Sing' deserved to sit on the album though, right?

'Wear Me Down' (Damon Albarn, Graham Coxon, Alex James, Dave Rowntree)

'Wear Me Down' as the album's last song is a curious choice. Never feeling quite like it deserves to follow 'Birthday' – especially with Albarn's dreary and depressing verse vocal style – the chorus does at least hold a feel and style that would be used to far greater effect when *Modern Life Is Rubbish* followed in 1993. It also employs possibly the album's grungiest Coxon riff, which is made special use of in the central instrumental section.

Optional Extras

There is an incredible amount of extra material available from this Blur period. Not only are there a dozen additional Blur and Seymour songs released as A and B-sides and compiled over deluxe editions and an EP, there are also a number of demo and alternate versions of these songs. There should be little to distinguish between Blur and Seymour songs, but on listening to the Seymour material, there is quite a difference in the sound, with scratchier, abrasive, overly-busy songs and performances that sound amateurish in comparison to the polished Blur recordings. They are demos, of course, and they do have their own charm, but as Seymour songs, they could never have fit with the style of *Leisure*. The songs written and/or recorded over the same period as the rest of the album continue with the Madchester sound the label pushed for ('I Know', 'Inertia'), but also provide further proof of Coxon's love of noise with 'Down', 'Won't Do It' and 'Explain'. There are also hints to the styles and influences that would be explored on later albums, including the Bowie/Barrett-inspired character songs of 'Mr Briggs' and 'Uncle Love', plus a couple of psychedelic numbers in 'Luminous' and 'Berserk'. Swapping a few of these songs for those that made it onto *Leisure* might've actually made it a more-rounded experience, and perhaps even an album more fondly remembered by the band and critics alike.

Key Album: Primal Scream – Screamadelica (1991)

Personnel:
Bobby Gillespie: lead vocals
Andrew Innes: guitar
Robert Young: guitar; lead vocals on 'Slip Inside This House'
Martin Duffy: keyboards, piano
Henry Olsen: bass; guitar solo on 'Damaged'
Phillip 'Toby' Tomanov: drums, percussion
Denise Jackson: guest vocals on 'Don't Fight It, Feel It'
Jah Wobble: bass on 'Higher Than The Sun (A Dub Symphony In Two Parts)'
Recording Sessions: 1990-1991: Initial demo sessions were held at the band's studio in Hackney, except for 'Come Together', which was one of the last songs demoed at Innes' House. The bulk of the material was recorded in summer 1991 at Jam Studios, Finsbury Park, London. Various other recording, production, mixing and remixing sessions took place, at Townhouse Studios, Bark Studios, Eden Studios, Chiswick, and Olympic Studios, London.
Producers: Andrew Weatherall and Hugo Nicolson. Except 'Movin' On Up' and 'Damaged' (Jimmy Miller), 'Higher Than The Sun (The Orb) and 'Slip Inside This House' (Hypnotone and Andrew Innes with additional production from Weatherall)
Record label: Creation
Chart position: UK: 8, USA: 31 (Heatseeker's chart)
Release date: 23 September 1991

Pete: My brother-in-law tells this fantastic story about how he booked Primal Scream for a show at Exeter Uni and ended up crewing for them on the night. Apparently, during the soundcheck, they played 'Come Together' by the Beatles, which already confused matters, but not as much as the gig would for those who'd heard the band's single 'Come Together'. Apparently, loads of punters had come for a rock and roll concert and ended up wondering what the hell was going on when they got hit by the band's fusion of acid house and guitars. It was a hugely successful show, though.

Matt: You get everything on this album – sounds from the past, sounds that were ahead of their time when released, and sounds that are still forward-looking and fresh today. I'm not even sure this album should be included in the book! It's more than Britpop! But as it's such a melting-pot of styles, you can hear the same Britpop influences running through it.

The Band

Gillespie had been part of a number of short-lived Glasgow based punk rock bands during and since school, including one with Innes and future record label boss Alan McGee. In 1982, Gillespie formed Primal Scream as a duo with school friend Jim Beattie. Limited success led to Gillespie also joining The Jesus and Mary Chain as their drummer, where he remained for two years until he was issued with an ultimatum to decide between the now-signed Primal Scream or continue on the drum stool. Gillespie chose Primal Scream, and focussed on difficult recording sessions for the debut album, between touring commitments and the band seemingly coming and going on a whim. In 1987, their debut album was released, but was poorly received, leading to still further lineup changes and a switch in musical direction. They released their second album a year later, which met with further confusion and even worse reviews. Deciding to go all in, Primal Scream then switched things up again, combining a melting-pot of styles and influences with an array of up-and-coming, musically sympathetic producers, including acid house DJ Andrew Weatherall and The Orb. The result was the incredibly successful *Screamadelica*, which was preceded by two singles that turned the band's fortunes around. But the follow-up album proved to be difficult, with further scrapped sessions and another sound change that almost led to the band splitting in 1995. By 1996, the lineup changed again, with the arrival of Gary 'Mani' Mounfield from the recently-split Stone Roses, and a new drummer. This team released the successful *Vanishing Point* the following year, with a return to the *Screamdelica* sound, but less upbeat and far darker. This direction continued on subsequent albums, with occasional detours to an older Primal Scream sound, while the band dealt with issues and controversies, including drugs, drink and vague accusations of Nazism. The last album of new material was released in 2015. Primal Scream continue to tour, and are natural festival headliners.

The Album

Screamadelica is an album for the people. Although modern music is made up of so many subgenres that it seems unlikely that consensus could ever be found again, in 1991, Primal Scream made their play to create something for everyone. By marrying their own brand of trippy, Stonesy indie rock to Andrew

Weatherall's destroy-and-rebuild production skills, *Screamadelica* had it all. Completely impossible to define by style, this was something that the indie kids, the club kids, the soul kids and the rock kids could all chill out and listen to together, each finding something to love in its hour-long running time. Sure, not everything in its eleven tracks appeals across the board, but there is enough for everyone and then some to spare. Following the album's 1992 Mercury Music Prize win, the record proved to be not so much a stepping stone as a bridge into the mainstream for Creation, which along with Food, was to become the home of Britpop in the years to come. *Screamadelica* retains its place as one of the most enduring and popular records of the 1990s.

'Movin' On Up' (Bobby Gillespie, Andrew Innes, Robert Young) [Deep Cut]

Kicking off with chunking indie chords and a soulful Gillespie vocal, this is Primal Scream doing The Rolling Stones, and who better to get the sound right than the producer of arguably the best era of Mick and the boys: Jimmy Miller. Within 30 seconds, there's a gospel choir and a joyous 'Love shines on' motif creating a bold, exhilarating opening that feels bigger than its relatively short (for this album at least) running time. 'Movin' On Up' instantly transgresses anything previously achieved by the band or the genre (if Primal Scream even nestle within a genre), and the song also contains an interpolation of 'Yoo Doo Right' by Can, who've come up before in these pages, as an influence on the Madchester scene.

'Slip Inside This House' (Roky Erickson, Tommy Hall)

A cover of the song by the 13th Floor Elevators, but through a Primal Scream filter, and containing samples from Sly and the Family Stone, this track has a trippy Indian sitar line over a fresh-feeling rhythm, pulled into life by some striking piano work. In many ways, it feels like a cut from the Happy Mondays' *Pills 'N' Thrills and Bellyaches* album, partly due to guitarist Robert Young's on-point vocals, which made the cut when pretty much every other band member had taken a run at them but not made the grade.

'Don't Fight It, Feel It' (Bobby Gillespie, Andrew Innes, Robert Young) [Single]

Very much in the feel of a-million-and-one other early-1990s club songs, but placing Primal Scream at the heart of a scene that previously couldn't have been further away, the track's whistle-style samples and stripped-back groove are once again pulled into shape by some excellent piano. Like 'Slip Inside This House', the vocal is again taken not by Gillespie (the band's actual singer), but instead by guest Denise Jackson. Her input does wonders and helped propel the single to number 41 in the charts when released in August 1991, shortly before the album's release.

'Higher Than The Sun' (Bobby Gillespie, Andrew Innes, Robert Young) [Single]

When this was released as single in June 1991, we can only presume what the indie kids made of it. But it's also fair to assume that Primal Scream didn't care because they knew by this point just how big the sandbox they were playing in, was. The album's shortest song (and utilising samples from Young-Holt Unlimited and Take 6), it's essentially classic Primal Scream psychedelia through the filter of producers The Orb. As singles go, it acted as a gateway drug for what was coming on *Screamadelica,* and reached 40 in the charts. However, it's fair to say that it isn't the most exciting or interesting song on the record.

'Inner Flight' (Bobby Gillespie, Andrew Innes, Robert Young)

Kicking off with a sci-fi soundscape that promises much, yet never really goes anywhere, this is a series of sonic experiments, creating a trippy, unsettling feeling which at points is almost nightmarish: not surprising given that it utilises samples from Brian Eno, among others. 'Inner Flight' never feels essential, but it is also the album's most beautiful song, especially in the flute-synth-led central section.

'Come Together' (Bobby Gillespie, Andrew Innes, Robert Young) [Single – original version]

Released in August 1990 as the album's second single, this did spectacularly well, reaching number 26. However, that was in a radically different form to the album version. We can only assume that – amongst all those that praised *Screamadelica* as a work of art – there must've also been the odd indie kid who took the album back to the record shop to complain that track six wasn't just broken but devastated. Now taking up an absolutely mammoth 10:21, Weatherall completely repurposed the album version as a house track, complete with Jesse Jackson speech samples giving the track its central hook. It builds and builds but never really achieves catharsis...

'Loaded' (Bobby Gillespie, Andrew Innes, Robert Young) [Single]

...unlike 'Loaded', which is 100% pure catharsis! Originally released in a version three minutes shorter than that on the album eighteen months later, this is a bold, uncompromising single: created by producer Andrew Weatherall after being asked to do a remix of 'I'm Losing More Than I'll Ever Have' from the band's second album. With the instruction to 'Just f*cking destroy it', he took them at their word, leaving little more than a seven-second sample from the original. Referred to by *Muzik* magazine as 'Sympathy For The Devil' for the E-generation' – but actually far closer to a pilled-up track from The Beach Boys' *Pet Sounds* – 'Loaded' contains numerous samples, but none more iconic than the introductory dialogue from the 1966 movie *The Wild Angels.* This is joyous stuff: a perfect counterpoint to 'Movin' On Up'. The single reached 16, giving Primal Scream their first top 40 hit, and bagging them a spot on *Top Of The Pops.*

'Damaged' (Bobby Gillespie, Andrew Innes, Robert Young) [Deep Cut]

More of a classic Primal Scream song – with actual lyrics and a song structure no less – perhaps we're just showing our indie-kid roots by labelling this as a deep cut. However, amidst the album's spectacular ambition, it's quite reassuring to see a glimpse of the actual band still peeking out through the samples and remixes. Built around guitar and a low-key piano line, this is *Screamadelica*'s most Rolling Stones-like track, with Duffy sounding like their 1960s/1970s session pianist Nicky Hopkins, setting Primal Scream up for their 1994 album *Give Out But Don't Give Up*. Again, this is produced by Jimmy Miller, and while it (sort of) doesn't fit on the album, it's perfectly placed to remind the listener that they are listing to an actual band.

'I'm Comin' Down' (Bobby Gillespie, Andrew Innes, Robert Young)

A really chilled-out track, with the repeated refrain of 'Drifting, drifting, drifting, drifting' backed by an alternating gentle/busy saxophone part, this doesn't necessarily go anywhere or add anything to the album experience other than to further its genre-breaking manifesto.

'Higher Than The Sun' (A Dub Symphony In Two Parts) (Bobby Gillespie, Andrew Innes, Robert Young)

Featuring Public Image Ltd bassist Jah Wobble, this begins with a wordless refrain from Gillespie, then builds and builds until – at the three-and-a-half-minute mark – it turns on a sixpence into something far more house-music orientated. With an excellent rising-and-descending organ line and a tack piano that again feels as if it were pulled straight out of The Beach Boys' *Pet Sounds*, the song may claim to be in two parts but has actually got four distinct and separate movements: in true symphony style.

'Shine Like Stars' (Bobby Gillespie, Andrew Innes, Robert Young)

The albums second-shortest song, with what sounds like a 56k internet modem connecting (remember them?) before the introduction of a childlike melody, 'Shine Like Stars' feels like a lullaby from a children's nighttime toy (although there's a strong possibility something illicit may have been added to the bedtime milk: something you should never do). As its pipe organ wheezes the album's last, this is a beautiful way to round off the album: an incredible piece of work.

Optional Extras

A 20th-anniversary boxset has been released that includes various mixes of songs, a recording of a gig at The Hollywood Palladium and a bonus EP originally released in 1992. The mixes include the original single A-sides (which were remixed for the album) and other remixes that were used as B-sides. As mentioned earlier, if you were a fan of the single but later disappointed with the album versions, you can at least now obtain both, as they are very different. 'I'm Losing More Than I'll Ever Have' – originally on Primal Scream's second album, and completely rewritten as 'Loaded' – is also included for completeness. The live gig includes two covers as part of the encore: The Stooges' 'No Fun' and John Lennon's 'Cold Turkey'. Combined with the other live cover of MC5's 'Ramblin' Rose' – released as a B-side – there's an opportunity to hear the band's dirty rock-and-roll influences, which they absolutely make the most of. A further cover is on the *Dixie-Narco* EP: part of a two-song session recorded in October 1991 at Memphis' legendary Ardent Studios. 'Carry Me Home' – a Beach Boys song by Dennis Wilson – is performed sympathetically, though it misses the original's rich texture. 'Stone My Soul' is a piano-led number, more reminiscent of early solo John Lennon material. The final song is the album outtake (and namesake) 'Screamadelica' – a funky, laid-back tune where the song title is repeated, backed with spacey keyboards and trumpet loops. It could've easily fit halfway through the album. There were a number of releases throughout 2021 to celebrate the album's 30th anniversary, culminating in the double album *Demodelica*, which contains early demos and work-in-progress mixes of all the songs. These versions really give the listener the opportunity to hear the building blocks of these songs, from their initial simple demos to the finished article. They also show that the band already had a lot of the ideas for the songs worked out before they were handed over to various producers. Most interestingly, they display the initial starting points for various songs, including the blues-based rock of the 'Hey Bulldog' piano riff ('Don't Fight It, Feel It') to the country guitar intro of 'Suspicious Minds' ('Come Together') that become unrecognisable as the songs take shape. It's a fascinating alternative version of the album.

Teenage Fanclub – Bandwagonesque (1991)
Recording Sessions: 9 April-12 May 1991
Producers: Don Fleming, Paul Chisolm, Teenage Fanclub
Record label: Creation
Chart position: UK: 22
Release date: 19 November 1991

Pete: What an awesome band Teenage Fanclub are! Even though I get all the elements that make up their sound, they just don't sound like anyone else, do they? Everything on *Bandwagonesque* just sounds exceptionally fresh and original, even now. No wonder they were so influential.

Matt: I came to Teenage Fanclub via Nirvana and was expecting raw punk rock! *Bandwagonesque* though is melodic, poppy, guitar rock that can trace its roots to The Byrds, The Beatles, The Beach Boys and Big Star. This is one of those bands and albums that quite rightly make the end-of-year and end-of-decade lists.

The Album

The third album by Glasgow's Teenage Fanclub caused ripples that no one could've expected, and gave the Creation label an unexpected overseas hike into the bargain. Equal-parts noisy and jangly, with big hooks and perfectly sweet 1960s pop harmonies, its stand-alone moments were criminally overlooked by the UK top 40: only 'What You Do To Me' made it. However, they fared much better on the American *Billboard* chart – 'Star Sign' reaching the lofty height of number 4 – *Bandwagonesque* showing it was possible for British alternative music to make genuine waves across the pond. When the year's final lists were compiled, the record managed to critically outrank far-more-famous offerings (Nirvana's *Nevermind* being the most surprising in hindsight), the band becoming an unlikely influence on the American grunge and alternative rock scene for years to come, not to mention on later Britpop bands such as Silver Sun.

Standout track: 'What You Do To Me'

1992 – American rock

By 1992, the grunge revolution was looking more like a soap opera. The undisputed leader of the scene – Kurt Cobain – had married the outspoken Courtney Love of the band Hole, and, as drug and split rumours abounded, Nirvana ended their summer festival tour at Reading, with Cobain being gently pushed onstage in a wheelchair, before leaping to his feet and tearing through an energetic set in the hope of dispelling concerns once and for all. It worked for now, but with the other Seattle bands struggling with their own demons, the movement was teetering on the abyss and looking like it was over before it really began.

Meanwhile, if you wanted to talk about the UK's ascending pop music, there was only one band worth talking about. Hailing from Manchester, and seemingly trouncing all others, were five young men with their eyes clearly set on the prize: the era of (No, no, not *them* yet!) Take That had begun.

Elsewhere, there was further hope that 1992 would be a year of change, yet it was not to be. April's general election had promised at worst a hung parliament, and at best, a new government under Neil Kinnock's Labour Party. The result was a low-key victory (in terms of seats) for John Major's Conservatives, meaning the party would stumble on until 1997 as *the* government of Britpop's glory days. It's often airbrushed from the popular narrative, but Tony Blair, if anything, only ever presided over Cool Britannia, which may have seemed similar, but was fundamentally different.

Reflecting this expectation/reality juxtaposition, it was a year of contradictions. As the Maastricht Treaty was signed, effectively founding the EU and the freedom of economic movement that would define the next 30 years, unemployment in Britain hit a five-year high and seemingly proved there had been some point to 1991's unrest. Meanwhile, just as the world seemed to be opening up, staying home had never felt so unsettling, with the IRA stepping up their mainland bombing: including a near miss at number 10 Downing Street itself.

This was, however, a big year for women (And to fantastically illustrate this in the year's contradictory manner, all the year's album choices are exclusively by men) with Betty Boothroyd – the first female Speaker of House of Commons – elected, while the Church of England finally allowed women to be priests. Meanwhile, the biography of Diana, Princess of Wales, threatened to blow the bloody doors off the whole royal establishment (but didn't, obviously) just in time for Her Majesty to celebrate the Ruby Jubilee.

Against this backdrop, what would go on to become the world of Britpop, was beginning to find its feet. Channel 4 began *The Big Breakfast* – a daily early-morning show tailored for a younger audience, giving many their first sight of broadcaster Chris Evans. Meanwhile, on the alternative underground, new bands were forming, bolstered by an ethos that reacted to the dominance of grunge. Perhaps they weren't all making records yet (except for Suede), but a number of shoots could already be seen.

But it's fair to say that Take That were not exactly quaking in their boots.

As 1992 was a year where the zeitgeist could've turned in various directions, the albums chosen to represent the year are a mixed bag. From the proto-Britpop of Denim's debut to Morrissey's resurgence (and unhelpful political undertones), what's clear, is that bands increasingly had something to say, even if it wasn't all in the sloganeering style of the Manics' 'Generation Terrorists'.

Key Album: Manic Street Preachers – Generation Terrorists (1992)

Personnel:
James Dean Bradfield: lead vocals, guitars
Richey Edwards: rhythm guitar
Sean Moore: drums, drum programming, percussion, backing vocals
Nicky Wire: bass
Recording sessions: July-December 1991: Black Barn Studios, London (Produced by Steve Brown, with The Bomb Squad on 'Repeat (Stars And Stripes)') Note: While some sources state the band were recording continuously for 23 weeks, conflicting information indicates the bulk of the album was recorded in a 12-week block beginning in August/September 1991, with other songs (including initial singles) recorded at different sessions. This suggestion also fits with a UK tour the band completed at the beginning of August.
Producers: Steve Brown; The Bomb Squad ('Repeat (Stars And Stripes)')
Record label: Columbia
Chart position: UK: 13
Release date: 10 February 1992

Pete: I'll be the first to admit it – I only came to the Manics with *Everything Must Go* in 1996, and I was totally unaware of the huge following they had. However, when I moved to Wales the following year, I discovered they were essentially gods in their home nation, and I had a lot of catching up to do! Friends were keener that I had an exhaustive knowledge of the back catalogue than they were about me learning the language.

Matt: '4REAL' was my first experience of the Manics. I didn't know what they sounded like, but they certainly looked the part with their dark glam look, and when Edwards did that to his arm, what were you supposed to think? The album did disappoint me slightly, as I felt it suffered from quantity over quality, but the message was certainly powerful.

The Band

Formed at school in South Wales in 1986, the band included cousins Bradfield and Moore, with Wire initially on guitar before switching to bass in 1988, just in time for the release of debut single 'Suicide Alley'. Richey Edwards joined shortly afterwards, and the band began to build a following due to their punk ethic, strong political views, immense self-belief and controversial behaviour:

including the infamous 4REAL incident in May 1991, when Richey cut the words into his arm in front of journalist Steve Lamacq. After a series of short-lived deals for single and EP releases, the band signed with Columbia to record their debut album. The second album *Gold Against The Soul* had a harder rock edge and was released in 1993, while *The Holy Bible* (1994) changed musical direction again, was critically acclaimed but sold poorly. Sadly, Edwards – who had a history of severe depression, self-harm and other mental health issues – disappeared in February 1995, his car found near the Severn Bridge between England and Wales. This devastating blow almost saw the Manics disband. But with the blessing of James' family, they continued and released the commercial and critical Britpop hit *Everything Must Go* in 1996. The band have continued to build upon this success worldwide, touring and releasing albums to this day.

The Album

Consider an alternate universe: a world where Britpop – if it could still be called that – had an altogether different flavour; a world in which the music scene would've been more aggressive, more political, more learned and perhaps even a little more clichéd musically (if such a thing is possible when it comes to Britpop). Landing with their major-label debut – like their heroes The Clash before them – Wales' Manic Street Preachers predicted big things. With their own signature blend of glam/rock/trash (but played by an exceptionally competent and literate quartet of free-thinkers), the intention was quite simple: create the greatest rock album ever made and sell 16,000,000 copies worldwide. The result was, sadly, somewhat different. The album missed the mark by being a bit flabby, overproduced and outlandish, and clearly in hock to their (then unfashionable) American glam-metal idols and The Clash (*London Calling* is clearly the model). This was a double album where a single album would probably have more than sufficed. All the same, though, the Manics were on the musical map and supported by an exceptionally passionate fan base that propelled them repeatedly into the charts, making them one of the great cult acts of the early-1990s. *Generation Terrorists* is a record that practically screams its desire to be found controversial – but ultimately never was, and the fact the band would see out the 1990s as national icons and hometown heroes, seemed, at this point, as preposterous as much of the album's contents. Yet it still begs the question: What if they had been right? If they had pulled off the unthinkable with their debut, it would've undoubtedly changed the history of the decade – its six singles mapping out an altogether different path that would've still had indie at its heart but would never have become so wrapped up in the patriotically-pedestrian.

'Slash 'N' Burn' (Lyrics: Richey Edwards, Nicky Wire; Music: James Dean Bradfield, Sean Moore) [Single]
Opening with a bang and a clear desire to lay waste to those that would pretend to the crown they so desired to make their own, 'Slash 'N' Burn' is all

Guns N' Roses guitar chopping and maximum sloganeering that would be the chief weapons in the Manics' armoury. With a title stolen from the US army's Vietnam policy, this is exhilarating stuff, even if the verses never do measure up to the chorus chant. Released as a single one month after the album release, it reached number 20 and was remarkably already the fourth single taken from the record.

'Nat West-Barclays-Midlands-Lloyds' (Lyrics: Richey Edwards, Nicky Wire; Music: James Dean Bradfield, Sean Moore) [Deep Cut]

Definitely the album's silliest song, with the most ridiculous title and chorus line going, it still proves to be a surprising (and irritating) earworm. A decent-sized slab of chugging rock with a surprising bit of piano at the end that hints at something grander, this may not feel necessary, but it'll gnaw away in your head for days if you're not careful – especially when passing any bank, which probably meant the band's desire to get an anti-consumerist message across, worked.

'Born To End' (Lyrics: Richey Edwards, Nicky Wire; Music: James Dean Bradfield, Sean Moore)

A song ultimately made by its verses' catchy callbacks (delivered by drummer Sean Moore), this turns down the dial somewhat into a more-pedestrian rock style, with a message that rather impenetrably ties together the twin evils of American brands and nuclear Armageddon: which is a pretty Manics thing to do really.

'Motorcycle Emptiness' (Lyrics: Richey Edwards, Nicky Wire; Music: James Dean Bradfield, Sean Moore) [Single]

The album's greatest single and longest song – clocking in at over six minutes – is also its standout moment. A mini-masterpiece of a sort, it proved the band didn't have to have everything turned up to eleven in order to push the agenda forward. Displaying a subtle melody and relaxed tempo, this has a genuinely melancholy air that allows it to stand taller than its peers. Perhaps it is a little long, and perhaps it does have some unnecessary instrumental moments, but it's still glorious stuff, and shows the band have the ability to handle their guitars in a completely different manner to a ram-it-down-your-throat Guns N' Roses pastiche. This was the band's most successful single to date, hitting number 17 and remaining in the charts for eight weeks: a record they wouldn't surpass until their Britpop high-water mark.

'You Love Us' (Lyrics: Richey Edwards, Nicky Wire; Music: James Dean Bradfield, Sean Moore) [Single]

Wonderfully raw in that slightly grating manner that only exceptional musicians can achieve when they attempt to do something as basic as punk, this is still

51

magnificently snotty stuff. It's almost impossible not to like a song with a chorus that states – no, *demands* – 'You! Love! Us! You! Love! Us! You love us! You love us!'. Released just a handful of weeks before the album hit the shelves, this incredibly wonderful piece of arrogance was already the record's third single and hit number 16. As if it weren't already brilliant enough, it also gives over a quarter of its running time to a false ending/double-time outro, which caused outbreaks of pogo rioting on indie dance floors across the country for years to come.

'Love's Sweet Exile' (Lyrics: Richey Edwards, Nicky Wire; Music: James Dean Bradfield, Sean Moore) [Single]

With five months to go before the album's release (when it reached number 26), this does have a slight feeling of being somewhat standard fare and is notably disliked by the band. Often referred to as the album's most metal-sounding song due to its underlying chugging guitar, it's actually more like soaring pop with a vague disco rhythm lurking in its midst. Again, this showed just what the band could achieve if they took the space to breathe, even if it does have a staggeringly unnecessary guitar solo lurking at its heart.

'Little Baby Nothing' (Lyrics: Richey Edwards, Nicky Wire; Music: James Dean Bradfield, Sean Moore) [Single]

A piece of epic piano-pop trapped inside a Manics song, this is the album's only duet, including the vocals of guest and former pornographic actress Traci Lords in order to underline its message of female sexual exploitation. Amazingly, the band claimed they'd wanted Kylie Minogue on it (at this point, a bubblegum pop star), but that *that* was never going to happen. However, such are the winds of fate that the post-Britpop Manics *did* end up writing for Minogue in 1997 on what was considered to be her *indie* album *Impossible Princess*, *and she performed* this song live with them. The version here is perfect, though, even without the sample from *A Streetcar Named Desire* originally tacked on the beginning, and the single reached number 29: the final cut taken from the *Generation Terrorists* campaign.

'Repeat (Stars And Stripes)' (Lyrics: Richey Edwards, Nicky Wire; Music: James Dean Bradfield, Sean Moore)

The first of two outings for 'Repeat' on *Generation Terrorists* is essentially a remix of the later track by The Bomb Squad: Public Enemy's production crew. It's an interesting diversion, but ultimately leaves the listener wondering why it's on the album and why it exists in the first place. Industrial in tone, and coming across like a factory in grinding overdrive, its sampled drums, added space and lurking US anthem give the lyric room to breath, even if The Bomb Squad did initially mistake the phrase 'dumb flag scum' for something far more homophobic in nature (and absolutely out-of-kilter with the Manics' image and intent).

'Tennessee' (Lyrics: Richey Edwards, Nicky Wire; Music: James Dean Bradfield, Sean Moore)

A piece of epic American-style rock, the best that can be said about this former B-side is that it doesn't feel out of place. But that doesn't mean it feels necessary, its messages being vaguely impenetrable and definitely delivered better elsewhere.

'Another Invented Disease' (Lyrics: Richey Edwards, Nicky Wire; Music: James Dean Bradfield, Sean Moore) [Deep Cut]

Now *this* is the most metal song on *Generation Terrorists*. With screaming lead, chugging verses, double-time bridge drums and still enough time for a soaring pop chorus, it may ultimately be just another anti-consumerist song with possibly (according to some fans) something about AIDS being invented in a lab (Although that does seem a bit unlikely despite the title's acronym), and may be the album's high point when it comes to filler.

'Stay Beautiful' (Lyrics: Richey Edwards, Nicky Wire; Music: James Dean Bradfield, Sean Moore) [Single]

Clearly, a single from its opening power-chord slices, 'Stay Beautiful', has a wonderful 'Why don't you just... [Guitar line]' chorus that fans would fill in for them live. Go on, see if you can guess what it is they'd sing back at the band. The album's first single, and released a remarkable nine months before it, this clearly showed that Columbia were keen to start capitalising on their new signing, given the band were still busy recording the album. Punky in nature, the song scraped the top 40 by hitting 40 itself yet feels oddly dated given what the rest of the album sessions would produce.

'So Dead' (Lyrics: Richey Edwards, Nicky Wire; Music: James Dean Bradfield, Sean Moore)

By the time 'So Dead' rolls in, there's a feeling that the album has probably done what it came to do and is treading water. This is fun stuff, perhaps, but it feels somewhat exhausted given all that's come before, no matter how many solos are thrown at the wall or chorus slogans chanted. It does end on a great guitar and drum-roll outro, though.

'Repeat (UK)' (Lyrics: Richey Edwards, Nicky Wire; Music: James Dean Bradfield, Sean Moore)

Air-raid warnings, police sirens, machine guns, screaming! The second outing for 'Repeat' (now in its original UK trappings) is a much punkier Clash-style song and is genuinely enjoyable, even if we have (sort of) heard it all before, five songs earlier. 'Repeat after me/F*ck Queen and country' yells Bradfield, and it's hard not to get caught up in the enormous fun the band appear to be having. Both indulgent and altogether exhilarating, it's genuinely hard to know which is the better version of the song, which is probably what led to the double inclusion.

'Spectators Of Suicide' (Lyrics: Richey Edwards, Nicky Wire; Music: James Dean Bradfield, Sean Moore)

This is the record's slowest song and does feel somewhat out of place. Somewhat meandering, somewhat woozy, sadly, it never reaches the height it feels destined for, possibly because the lyric never quite seems to match the melody. In 2020, the song would have a second lease of life, released as a charity single featuring former Pipette (and fellow Welsh singer) Gwenno.

'Damn Dog' (Jacob Brackman, Billy Mernit)

Amazingly, this is the only song on all of *Generation Terrorists* where the lyrics feel truly wedded to their melody, which is perhaps unsurprising given that the song is a cover: originally featured in the movie *Times Square*. The record's shortest song – and perhaps one of the most unnecessary, given the band really didn't need to cover anyone on their albums (and never would again) – it's an enjoyable enough piece of bluesy rock.

'Crucifix Kiss' (Lyrics: Richey Edwards, Nicky Wire; Music: James Dean Bradfield, Sean Moore)

Just check this out for an opening lyric!: 'So mighty so hegemonic so hating so desecrating so there so nowhere so hurting'. The Manics do their best here to spear religion on the wall, even going so far as to make a vague comparison between Jesus and the Nazis. Perhaps this is in poor taste, but this *is* the Manic Street Preachers, and they know what they're doing – combining some furious rock with a wonderfully aggressive lyric to power its message home.

'Methadone Pretty' (Lyrics: Richey Edwards, Nicky Wire; Music: James Dean Bradfield, Sean Moore)

Here to help push the record to double-album proportions, this is another anti-consumerist piece that certainly does nothing to glamourise drug use, despite what its detractors may level at it. Perhaps this song would've had more impact if placed earlier in proceedings, but here it just feels a bit knackered, really.

'Condemned To Rock 'N' Roll' (Lyrics: Richey Edwards, Nicky Wire; Music: James Dean Bradfield, Sean Moore)

Closing proceedings with a wonderfully-resigned title and some maximum guitar workouts, this is the album's second-longest song: just a few seconds shy of 'Motorcycle Emptiness'. Two elements stand out. The first is the Axl-Rose-style squeal at 2:40: poor James Dean Bradfield had been waiting for a staggering eighteen songs to give that a go! The second is the descending vocal at the climax of each chorus, which would be put to maximum use on the 'From Despair To Where' single a year later. So closes *Generation Terrorists*: bloated, preposterous, yet still an essential what-if moment.

Optional Extras

The album's 20th-anniversary edition includes earlier demos of the majority of the songs, plus some singles. Unsurprisingly, the demos offer punkier and less-polished versions, and in some cases, removing the glam metal sheen delivers a far more enjoyable version than those that made the final cut. In addition – and not included in the 20th-anniversary release – is an additional album's worth of B-sides, some of which are brand new songs recorded during the album sessions or before, while others are earlier versions of tracks from older releases. There are also a couple of live covers that are more punky and aggressive than the originals, but still show a lot of joy for the source material of Alice Cooper and Guns N' Roses. 'Sorrow 16' is a fun punky number that sits well as a 'Motown Junk' B-side, but has some dubious lyrics and ends bizarrely, shouting out the letters of 'beautiful'. 'We Her Majesty's Prisoners' is the second 'Motown Junk' B-side, and suffers from similar lyrical problems, though the music has some interesting moments, including a rare use of piano in the chorus. 'Starlover' is a straightforward rock number with a shouty chorus – it doesn't try any harder than that, and doesn't outstay its welcome, while 'R. P. McMurphy' – named after the protagonist in *One Flew Over The Cuckoo's Nest* – is a real change of pace; the song centred around acoustic guitar and piano, with a 'Na na na' chorus. Despite its rough edges, it's worth seeking out. With 'Soul Contamination', it's straight back to rock and dodgy lyrics, although there are some nice musical touches to maintain interest, and again it's not very long. 'Democracy Coma' is definitely a cut above the other B-sides, being a more modern and up-tempo rock effort that meant it was chosen to replace some of the more concerning songs on the album's American release. 'A Vision Of Dead Desire' was a rerecording of the early track 'UK Channel Boredom': given away for free with fanzines in 1990. Although it's more polished, it's a lacklustre effort. 'Ain't Going Down' features only Bradfield in a call-and-response verse, with chorus harmonies to an acoustic guitar (although there are occasional electric guitar flourishes that seem to preview the music they'd later create). 'Bored Out Of My Mind' is another acoustic number that never really gets going but does offer some nice moments and, with a bit of work, might've been a nice respite on the album. As if that isn't enough, there may even be more material to come. In a 2010 interview with *REPEAT* fanzine, Steve Brown suggested that multiple alternate versions of songs exist, as well as musical experiments and possibly other outtakes. However, based on what's already been released, this is likely to only interest the most hardcore of fans.

Ocean Colour Scene – Ocean Colour Scene (1992)

Recording sessions: 1990-1992
Producers: Hugo Nicolson (Tracks 3, 7); Jimmy Miller (1, 2, 4, 6, 8, 10); Steve Osborne (11, 12); Tim Palmer (5, 9)
Record label: Fontana
Chart position: UK: 54 (Following the release of *Moseley Shoals* in 1996)
Release date: 1 March 1992

Pete: I came to Ocean Colour Scene with 1996's *Moseley Shoals,* but I don't think that was unusual, given the band had been hunkered down for years creating an album they actually wanted to make after this debut. What's interesting is you can see glimpses of what they'd become here, as if they were right all along but were just biding their time.

Matt: I first heard of the band after 'The Riverboat Song' was used on *TFI Friday* to introduce the guests; both the show and album were launched at the same time. I always gave this album a miss, though, until much later, as I'd read the band weren't pleased with it. It wasn't the same as *Moseley Shoals,* and wasn't even considered very good by anyone: band included. But it's not as bad as it's made out to be – you can definitely hear some ideas that would be expanded on for their next album.

The Album

As with Blur's *Leisure*, Ocean Colour Scene's first album is a slightly curious beast. Although all the band's trappings are in evidence (Great vocal sweeps and some cracking retro guitar work),they're obscured by a vaguely-baggy sound delivered largely at the behest of their record company. Indeed, the standout moments are where they cast off these unnecessary trappings for a more natural 1960s bent: standout track 'Justine' being pure Rolling Stones with a defter touch and beauty. It would be four years before the band followed it up with the all-conquering *Moseley Shoals* – a Britpop beast if ever there was one – a period of soul searching within the group and with an ultimate desire to create the music they wanted to, rather than play the industry game. Although the band largely discount their debut record, and its critical reception was lacklustre, it's still promising stuff, and shows that even if they were being forced to play in the same ball pit as their peers, they were still a cut above in terms of talent.

Standout track: 'Justine'

The Charlatans – Between 10th and 11th (1992)

Recording Sessions: 1991
Producer: Flood
Record label: Situation Two

Chart position: UK: 21
Release date: 23 March 1992

Pete: To me, there always seems to be a touch of 'always-the-Britpop-bridesmaid' about The Charlatans, which is manifestly unfair given the incredible chart success and longevity they've had. They really trounce a lot of the bands you think of more often as Britpop. I suppose, essentially, they just rose above the whole thing.

Matt: Are The Charlatans Britpop, Madchester or something else entirely? They never quite seem to fit into the right style at the right time, which means they often get overlooked or just miss the boat altogether. Their contribution shouldn't be ignored, though.

The Album

Despite *Between 10th and 11th* registering a sharp fall in favour from their 1990 debut (which hit number 1), The Charlatans' second album is still something of a lost moment of greatness. Named after the address of New York's Marquee club (A world away from their Birmingham and Cheshire origins), and far more American and soulful in its overall sound, the weakest moments are when they slip back into their original baggy style, on tunes like 'Tremelo Song'. The album's undoubted high point is 'Weirdo', which might've only lightly troubled the UK top 20, but slammed home at number 1 on the US *Billboard* chart; its wheezing organ intro alone being absolutely undeniable hit material, while elements of its melody would go on to inform the Super Furry Animals 'The Man Don't Give A F*ck' single. Although this isn't so much a difficult second album, it is a record somewhat out of balance due to the weight of 'Weirdo'. However, its mixture of signature sound and expanded horizons, proved The Charlatans weren't playing the same game as those around them. The whole record is a lost gem.

Standout track: 'Weirdo'

The Lightning Seeds – Sense (1992)

Recording sessions: 1991
Producers: Ian Broudie, Simon Rogers
Record label: Virgin
Chart position: UK: 53
Release date: 6 April 1992

Pete: Ian Broudie really is like some sort of evil Britpop mastermind, isn't he? I can't think of anyone else who had their fingers in so many of the pies that defined the 1990s and beyond. The fact that he kept his own rather brilliant band going on top of all the production work he was doing, is just phenomenal.

Matt: 'Life Of Riley' slipped me by when it was released. But later – when it appeared on *Match of the Day* for Goal of the Month – I became aware of it, just as *Jollification* and 'Lucky You' were released.

The Album

Ian Broudie – a man who cuts through this book like a stick of rock – is certainly someone who could be held responsible for putting the 'pop' into Britpop. The Lightning Seeds – largely his solo production project – are a band of pure pop sensibilities, and their sophomore offering *Sense* showed just how far Broudie could push this particular envelope. Pure shimmering production values mixed with just enough indie guts, make the songs here as natural in a sweaty room as they are in the pages of *Smash Hits*. Although many tricks of the alternative trade are in evidence – elements of baggy and the chiming keyboards of the dance scene – this is ultimately an album which showed that guitars delivering pop music was valid: standout single 'Life Of Riley' hitting number 28 in the charts. Also of note is the line in 'A Small Slice Of Heaven' – 'She says it's time to make decisions/But turns on breakfast television': as if the thematic lyrical template for Britpop had been set out in one single line.

Standout track: 'Life Of Riley'

Key Album: Morrissey – Your Arsenal (1992)

Personnel:
Morrissey: vocals
Alain Whyte: guitars
Boz Boorer: guitars
Gary Day: bass
Spencer Cobrin: drums
Recording sessions: February 1992, Utopia Studios, Primrose Hill: 'The National Front Disco', 'We Hate It When Our Friends Become Successful' and a number of B-sides.
March 1992, Wool Hall, Bath: The rest of the album, and possibly further work on songs from February sessions.
Producer: Mick Ronson
Record label: HMV
Chart position: UK: 4, USA: 21
Release date: 27 July 1992

Pete: Oh no. Morrissey. He's a tricky one. I freaking love The Smiths – I suppose most indie types do – and I think this is a brilliant record. But I can't help but wish that maybe on just 30 or 40 occasions, he'd chosen to keep is mouth shut rather than let journalists know what was on his mind.

Matt: Morrissey is a controversial figure, and I've never quite decided on whether he's sincere or sarcastic with some of his views and statements. If you can put that to one side, this album is a great collection of songs but may also surprise many with its inclusion, given how he's currently viewed.

The Band

The first mononymous artist of the book, Morrissey was raised in Manchester, where, upon leaving school, he took a series of jobs that helped fund his interest in music and attending gigs. As the short-lived singer in at least one local punk band during the late-1970s and early-1980s, his stature was high within the local music community, and to supplement his income, he also wrote and released several books on bands and film stars during this time. One of these books led to Johnny Marr asking Morrissey to join a band he was putting together in 1982. Within a few months, they had a name – The Smiths – and were preparing to record their first demo. The following year saw a number of singles released, culminating in the 1984 debut album that reached number 2 in the charts – kick-starting a level of fan worship that made them the unparalleled stars of the 1980s indie scene. Subsequent albums built on this success both in the UK and US, but the relationship between Marr and Morrissey, deteriorated. The Smiths split in 1987, shortly before the release of their fourth album; Morrissey immediately returning to the studio to work on his debut solo album. He's continued to release albums and tour regularly ever since, and remains a successful, incredibly popular and influential figure, despite his outspoken and often controversial opinions on a number of topics, which has seen him criticised in the media and occasionally even disowned by fans. But hey, you don't have to like the man to love the music, *right?*

The Album

Oh, Morrissey. Was this where it all began to go so wrong? Without getting too embroiled in the politics, there are at least two songs on *Your Arsenal* that raised eyebrows at the time, and feel almost unacceptable by 2020s standards. Don't worry; you'll spot them when you get to them. Matters were not helped when, in August 1992 (a couple of months after the album's release), Morrissey hit the Madstock stage, draping himself in the Union Flag in front of an audience of skinheads. There is a counter-argument, of course – it was Madness' audience that day, and he was even booed offstage by the very skinheads he was allegedly supporting. Yet the article was published in *NME,* and sh*t, sticks. Remarkably, Madness went on to become national darlings and play on the roof of Buckingham Palace, while the Union Flag was soon to be appropriated by everyone across British popular music (Geri Halliwell, Noel Gallagher, we're looking at you), becoming positively *de rigueur* by 1996. However, from this point, Morrissey was forever tainted by the question 'Is he a racist?' – something that hasn't been helped due to an ever-increasing string of inflammatory sound bites over the years. So now that's over with (for now), let's concentrate on *Your Arsenal* as an album. Perhaps scuppered by its own punning title, this is actually a heavyweight piece of work, possibly his greatest solo effort, and flits between styles with enviable ease, while being constantly anchored by Morrissey's unique voice and lyrical themes. Produced by rock legend and oft-forgotten power-behind-the-throne of David Bowie – Mick Ronson – it rightly received much critical acclaim and even scored a Grammy nomination. *Your Arsenal* is the sound of an icon coming out swinging after a critically-mauled previous outing, just at the point when a legion of younger British artists were getting ready to stamp their own names into musical history. If it had been released two years later, perhaps its legacy would've been very different.

'You're Gonna Need Someone On Your Side' (Lyrics: Morrissey; Music: Mark E. Nevin)

Firing out of the gates with Morrissey's most muscular rock song to date, this is dark, surfy, powerful, and perhaps just a little bit like the theme from 'The Munsters' turned up to eleven. We're into full-Morrissey action pretty quick, as he declares disappointingly, 'You're gonna need someone on your side and here I am/You don't need to look so pleased', although you can practically feel the joy bursting from him as he gets the chance to let his quiff down for the first time in ages. This music was written by Mark E. Nevin (who also wrote the majority of Morrissey's previous album *Kill Uncle*), and he also provided 'I Know It's Gonna Happen Someday' toward the end of the record: a song that couldn't feel further away. Depending on your source, this song was either written for a rumoured and ultimately-scrapped rockabilly mini-album or was part of a larger collection of instrumentals provided to Morrissey for lyrical consideration.

'Glamorous Glue' (Lyrics: Morrissey; Music: Alain Whyte) [Deep Cut]

Chugging along enjoyably with massive guitar thrashes (that surely influenced Black Rebel Motorcycle Club's 'Spread Your Love') and a lyrical anti-work/anti-people theme that feels somewhat phoned in for the 1980s fan base, this is still an absolutely perfect follow-up to the album opener, keeping things ticking over in a powerful style. By the time Morrissey is repeating the 'London is dead' refrain, you're completely hooked. A popular song with fans, it was finally released as a single in 2011. Interestingly, this also sounds very much like a template for later Britpop group Echobelly (who, unsurprisingly, Morrissey loved), like some great indie snake, gorging on its own tail.

'We'll Let You Know' (Lyrics: Morrissey; Music: Alain Whyte)

The longest song on *Your Arsenal* (5:17), and by far the most Smiths-sounding cut here, this is essentially an acoustic song, supposedly about football fans/hooligans, augmented by picked electric in the vein of Smiths B-side 'Jeane'.

During the central section, the song slowly evolves into a wall of discordant noise, much like that feeling when you're waiting to hear back from someone and start to realise the call isn't going to come. Then suddenly, without warning, a whistle welcomes Morrissey back to the fray with the line 'We are the last truly British people you will ever know': which, to ears of the 2020s, may sound a little difficult, but maybe not as much as...

'The National Front Disco' (Lyrics: Morrissey; Music: Alain Whyte)

Sidestepping the whole 'Is Morrissey a racist?' question, let's consider this song on its merits. For a song often remembered as being a difficult single, it's actually nothing of the sort. It's just an album track that – while muscular, upbeat and quite fun – never really lives up to expectations, doesn't really have a chorus, and definitely, shockingly even, doesn't even employ a disco rhythm. Arguments have been made that, to understand the lyric, you must also accept there's a level of irony at work, which isn't unlikely, given Morrissey has form in this area. However, he also has form for saying things that really fuel the fire of his detractors. Let's just move on.

'Certain People I Know' (Lyrics: Morrissey; Music: Alain Whyte) [Single]

Released as a single in December 1992, this peaked at 35, which perhaps isn't surprising, as it actually isn't massively strong. Given the media furore that had taken place around Morrissey throughout the year, perhaps this was a decision to play it safe with a largely inoffensive song which – despite featuring a T. Rex-style guitar line played by Ronson – actually comes across more like an early British proto-rocker from the 1950s Larry Parnes stable of pop/rock acts. This is the album's shortest song at 3:11, and even then, it probably goes on a bit too long.

'We Hate It When Our Friends Become Successful' (Lyrics: Morrissey; Music: Alain Whyte) [Single]

Yeah, okay, maybe lyrically it's a bit on the nose, even for Morrissey, but as a single, it does have a big fan-pleasing laugh-along chorus and a very enjoyable 'It should've been me' section. Preceding the album by two months and reaching number 17 – much to the disgust of some reviewers, who believed it was his weakest single to date – the worst you can actually say about this, is it's just a bit by-the-numbers.

'You're The One For Me, Fatty' (Lyrics: Morrissey; Music: Alain Whyte) [Single]

What can you say? It's downright rude, probably isn't really on, has the ability to shock and surprise, and is still downright hilarious. The song – actually an ode to Madness singer Chas Smash, and a play on the Marvelettes song 'You're The One For Me Bobby' – stays on theme with an excellent girl-group style outro and an impressive almost-rhyme of 'Battersea' with 'Fatty'. All in all, it shouldn't be brilliant, but it is, and reached number 19 when released as a single in July to support the album's release.

'Seasick, Yet Still Docked' (Lyrics: Morrissey; Music: Alain Whyte) [Deep Cut]

Another acoustic song in the style of 'We'll Let You Know' – but this time lushly woozy rather than simply unsettling – there's a surprising familiarity with The La's album, though at a much steadier tempo, and the overall effect with background synths and guitar is ultimately quite beautiful. At just over five minutes, this beautiful, doomed love song is best summed up by its opening line: 'I am a poor freezingly cold soul, so far from where I intended to go'.

'I Know It's Gonna Happen Someday' (Lyrics: Morrissey; Music: Mark E. Nevin)

Played by Morrissey with a completely straight bat, despite essentially being the equivalent of some great lost Shirley Bassey standard, this is a truly grand piece of work, from the pen of Mark E. Nevin, who wrote the album opener. However, this is the absolute flipside – almost as if Nevin wanted to demonstrate the full range of Morrissey's ability in two hits. Beginning and ending with radio static as if the listener is discovering the song on a radio late one lonely night, it's lyrically tight, unusually sincere and ultimately wonderful.

'Tomorrow' (Lyrics: Morrissey; Music: Alain Whyte)

Although 'Tomorrow' does begin with an epic quality, this is no overblown final statement. With a prominent bouncy bass line, it quickly leaps into a pulsating pop song so catchy and reminiscent of U2 in the 1980s that it was even released as a US single in September 1992. 'Put your arms around me, I won't tell anyone', Morrissey sings, suggesting there's an intimacy between him and his listening public that cannot be broken, no matter how often he might strain that relationship in the years to come.

Optional Extras

The album's first single included songs from an October 1991 live show in London, while the remaining singles all had new songs as B-sides that have already been gathered on various compilations. These were either recorded during the album sessions or at later B-side sessions in 1992. With such strong album material, they struggle to make an impression, and the songs often sound more like ideas than fully-developed pieces. 'Pashernate Love' is one of the more interesting songs of the group, and was obviously well-thought-of, as it was bizarrely used to bulk out the expanded version of *Kill Uncle*.

'There Speaks A True Friend' has a Beatles feel to it, especially with the 'Good Morning, Good Morning' guitar line, and ends with a confusing and abrupt 'I Want You (She's So Heavy)' stop. A jangly Byrds introduction leads into the chugging rock of 'Let The Right One Slip In', whilst 'Jack The Ripper' starts with a dripping guitar effect and acoustics before turning into something that wouldn't sound out of place coming from Seattle in the same period. 'You've Had Her' continues the darker sound with an almost sitar-like guitar backing a heavily-processed Morrissey vocal. As a footnote, a 2014 remastered *Your Arsenal* reissue was released with a lost live US show from October 1991. Shortly afterwards, fan websites started discussing previously unknown alternate versions of the B-sides 'Pashernate Love', 'There Speaks A True Friend' and a solo acoustic version of 'Seasick, Yet Still Docked'. It's suggested that these were also planned for the 2014 reissue but were ultimately scrapped and left in the vaults.

Key Album: Denim – Back In Denim (1992)

Personnel:
Lawrence: Vocals
Bill Phillips: Bass
Jerry Conway, Pete Phipps: Drums
Adrian Amsterdam, Nick Lawrence, Neil Scott: Guitar
Pete Smith, Pete Z., Brian O'Shaughnessy, Brian Pugsley, Siobhan Brooks: Synthesizer/Piano
Recording sessions: May 1990-July 1992: Bark Studios, RAK Studios, Abbey Road Studios, London (Initial sessions began at Bark with Brian O'Shaughnessy producing. John Leckie then took over and added to existing recordings at both RAK and Abbey Road. Increasing costs and the breakdown of the relationship between Lawrence and Leckie saw the sessions return to Bark, with O'Shaughnessy completing and mixing the album, apart from some additional mixing on the title track after the album was completed).
Producers: John Leckie, Brian O'Shaughnessy
Record label: Boy's Own Recordings
Chart position: N/A
Release date: 11 November 1992

Pete: *Back In Denim* is one of the great lost records of the period, I reckon. Everyone that I knew seemed to have bought it on CD, although my copy was taped, obviously. It's massively surprising to discover it wasn't bigger at the time, as I just thought it had been massive and a key moment in the creation of Britpop. Perhaps it was just a thing local to Worcestershire.

Matt: I'm going to be completely honest and admit this album passed me by. I'm not sure how or why, but it did. I came across it much later, as a lot of people had it and it always made the Britpop lists.

The Band

Denim is effectively the solo project of the mononymous Lawrence, which he began in 1990. Previously he was the founder, guitarist/vocalist and principal songwriter of the indie pop band Felt, which had split in 1989 after a productive and influential (but ultimately unsuccessful) decade of music. Lawrence looked backwards for a new musical direction and soon signed to Boy's Own Recordings. Unfortunately, the album sessions proved lengthy and costly, meaning that by the time the debut album was released, the label was rather unhappy. No band existed to tour the album, and only critics were listening to it. By 1996, a new label was in place, a second album released and a live band created to support Pulp on their arena tour. Lawrence's dream move to EMI in 1997 – with a potential hit song, airplay and a third album – was unfortunately scuppered by timing and title. 'Summer Smash' coincided with the death of Princess Diana, and the single was immediately stopped. Everything was now on hold, and a compilation of B-sides, covers and a few new songs were hastily released as Lawrence called time on the band, moving on to form Go-Kart Mozart, who released their first album in 2000. Sadly, the stress of recent years took their toll on Lawrence, and he suffered a breakdown, leading to a dark decade of money and housing problems, plus further issues with mental health and drugs: all of which were eventually documented in the film *Lawrence of Belgravia*. A rushed album was released in 2005, comprised of some songs planned for the unreleased third Denim album, with the remaining songs included on Go-Kart Mozart's 2012 follow-up. A fourth album was released in 2018, and supporting interviews suggested further albums, reissues and live gigs were planned, although nothing has materialised so far.

The Album

Denim is the brainchild of a man with a dream. The no-need-for-a-surname Lawrence had spent a decade being disappointed, yet – like Lee Mavers of The La's before him – he wanted to achieve his vision. In a move that somewhat pre-empted an important part of the Britpop story – that of iconic figures enjoying second-wave success – a new decade for Lawrence meant a new band. But Denim were not to be just any band. Having been lumbered with a string of independent contracts and small budgets throughout his career, Lawrence was now dead set on making a bid for mainstream success. He secured the budget and hung out in New York, working on what he considered would be his masterpiece: *Back In Denim*. An album essentially dedicated to its writer's 1970s upbringing and so deadly serious in intent that it comes right out the other side, it deals with its subject matter through a wry smile. Incorporating glam, MOR, indie, punk, cheesy synth, splashes of flamenco and lashings of (ironically) American rock, Lawrence places himself heart-and-soul at the centre of proceedings. With a voice part-Lou-Reed/part-Brummie-drawl and eight-parts tongue-too-stuffed-in-cheek-to-speak, *Back in Denim* is like an awkward one-man British invasion on a feedback loop – mocking his influences while making enormous use of them (even including drummer Pete Phipps from the Glitter Band, for his distinctive sound), setting out a stall in subject and style, for a Britpop that would amazingly soon become the mainstream.

'Back In Denim' (Lawrence) [Deep Cut]

Stadium beats! Chanted choruses! Rock guitars! Quasi-rap verses! 'Twist And Shout'-style vocal rises! For an artist with such independent credentials, when it comes to *Back In Denim*, Lawrence makes it clear from the off that he's now playing in a much bigger playpen, and wasn't ashamed who knew it. He even kicks off with the lyric 'Here I am back again with a bang'. Built around Queen's 'We Will Rock You' rhythm and some hyper-fast electronic keys, this also takes the time to (almost) borrow from Jimmy Cliff with a middle-eight of 'You Can Get It If You Really Try', and incorporates a truly dirt-filled keyboard riff, plus a general feeling of glam pomposity. As statements of intent go, this is pretty clear.

'Fish And Chips' (Lawrence) [Deep Cut]

For an album that's so spiritually in love with the 1970s, there's also a remarkable amount of 1980s-influenced material. This song is a case in point, feeling at times like a direct lift from The Vapours' 1980 hit 'Turning Japanese'. This is the record's shortest song (3:17)and its punkiest offering by far.

'Bubblehead' (Lawrence)

Chugging away like a lost song by The Cars, 'Bubblehead''s chorus is notable for being the record's one moment where we see Lawrence return to a more Felt-like whimsy. Though the 'Woah oh oh oh' backing vocals sound odd at the onset, they soon prove to be the song's irresistible hook, and it closes with a minute-long outro somewhat reminiscent of The Velvet Underground, albeit with added squelchy keyboard.

'Middle Of The Road' (Lawrence) [Single]

Like many of the album's songs, this does just what it says on the tin. Lawrence takes the most MOR backing he can (listen out for the Springsteen-esque guitar stabs), over which he chooses to list everything he hates about music, before declaring, 'You will find me in the middle… of the road'. Is it honest? Is it tongue-in-cheek? Does it matter? It's certainly fun, even taking the trouble of doing that trick of playing an instrument *loud,* shortly after mentioning that instrument (Skip to 0:50 to see what we mean). At the three-minute mark, a fantastic female backing vocal particularly bolsters the rather stunning outro. Released as a single in January 1993, this was perhaps a little too knowing to make much impact on the charts, so it didn't. But it's a huge amount of fun.

'The Osmonds' (Lawrence)

As the album centrepiece, this is either a masterpiece or a song desperately in need of a chorus. Whichever of these you plump for may well depend on your listening mood, given that this song lasts in excess of eight minutes and never seems to really get going. However, there is certainly some joy in listening to Lawrence essentially listing everything he remembers about the 1970s, returning time and again to the amusing lament, 'There were Osmonds, lots of Osmonds/There were lots of little Osmonds everywhere'. Featuring a variety of different ways of attacking what is essentially the same material, there are moments of Spanish guitar, piano ballad, and even one moment when it seems like it might leap into some form of *Screamadelica*-inspired monster. But ultimately, it settles into its lush orchestral instrumentation for an outro that remarkably takes over a minute and a half to push through.

'I Saw The Glitter On Your Face' (Lawrence)

Synth strings, flamenco guitar: this must surely be the album's most romantic song, right? Well, yes, but it's also a breakup song, probably best summed up in the lines 'I don't love you anymore/This isn't news, so I'll use this old tune'. Possibly the album's weakest moment – due to Lawrence not quite having the vocal chops to tip this over the line into glorious pastiche – it does feature the payoff line 'What it is to be free!', which feels less redemptive and more like a final stab in the heart.

'American Rock' (Lawrence)

Another let's-do-what-it-says-on-the-tin tune. 'American Rock' even begins with the on-the-nail line 'American rock! Ooh yeah!/Don't you ever wonder why the whole world is falling in love?', that has a tongue pushed so firmly into a cheek that its remarkable it hasn't made a bid for freedom. Featuring verses that lean heavily on The Velvet Underground's 'Sweet Jane', Lawrence attempts to outdo Lou Reed by fitting in more syllables than should ever naturally fit into a verse phrasing. It's all a bit of an MOR chug, really, and even the soaring moments never get as big as perhaps they could. Yet it still embeds itself in the mind, filling its four and a half minutes with American sounding phrases, on-point guitar licks and another cracking string-led outro.

'Livin' On The Streets' (Lawrence)

Starting with a sample of a street fight and sirens, this actually comes across somewhat like The Clash during their oft-derided *Cut The Crap* period. A punky chorus and lyrics that would be cool if they weren't presumably set in Birmingham ('Take a ride in any car and claim this is mine'), Lawrence's outro powers are missing somewhat here, and the full effect feels a little elusive.

'Here is My Song For Europe' (Lawrence)

Starting off slow and somewhat angelic, before kicking off in earnest after 30 seconds of what can only be described as the sonic equivalent of a Bucks-Fizz-like skirt moment, Lawrence makes his bid for the Eurovision song contest. But he does it in his own inimitable style, with a truly off-kilter synth solo around the halfway point, and a bit of punk guitar thrown in for good measure. In an unusual move – with Lawrence looking uncomfortable throughout – he performed the song in December 1992 on Vic and Bob's TV music show *Popadoodledandy*. Typical of Denim's luck, though, the show never got past the pilot stage and remained locked in the archives for decades.

'I'm Against The Eighties' (Lawrence)

If the 1980s were the decade that made Lawrence as a musician, this song hits the nail on the head, rejecting his past in favour of, well, the only-slightly-more-distant past. 'I took a look around, there was nothing going down, in the eighties', he sings. But this is no downbeat album closer – it's an epic seven minutes and twenty seconds of purely joyous, upbeat rock and roll. Of course, technically, it's probably all over as a song after three minutes, but that's when Lawrence unleashes his most explosive outro yet, sneering 'That's the 80s, boy' and breaking into a glorious string section that sounds like the template for McAlmont & Butler's later Britpop mini-masterpiece 'Yes'. A final flute hook and a shout of 'bye bye' from the Lou Reed handbook, and *Back In Denim* is done – Lawrence having achieved the illogically impossible: an English album of Kinksian *Village Green Preservation Society* proportions that uses American trappings to make its mark.

Optional Extras

This is probably the only release in this book where little material beyond the album is available. Interviews mention many demo sessions taking place, but we've found no reference to any unreleased songs or even any alternative/early versions of those released. Furthermore, due to Lawrence's view of the band as a studio animal, live shows were a rarity, and there's no evidence that any live shows from the time were recorded. All that *is* available – and adds little – are songs that focus more on the synth-pop sound rather than the album's glam rock: the 1992 Kraftwerk-inspired electronic single 'Supermarket', and the B-sides of the 'Middle Of The Road' single. These include a fun cover of the theme from the late-1970s sitcom *Robin's Nest*, and two songs (one an instrumental) about ape-hangers: the handlebars on chopper bikes.

Part Two. 1993-1996 – The Britpop Boom

1993 – Yanks go home!

On 19 March 1993, *Select* magazine fired the starting pistol. Though it would take another year for the term 'Britpop' to find its way into common parlance, this was it: where it all began in earnest.

Against a Union-flag backdrop that had been used to condemn Morrissey eight months earlier – now being used to represent a rejection of cultural imperialism (even if it did leave some with a sour taste) – Suede's Brett Anderson found himself as the face of a new movement. Even though the media were perhaps premature in their chosen key-players, there was certainly more than enough bands coming out of London club nights (such as Smashing, Blow Up and Syndrome) to lump together in an attempt to create a scene from a spirit, and sell a few magazines along the way. 'St Etienne, Denim, Pulp, The Auteurs and the Battle for Britain', said the over-excitable tagline – but could even *their* mighty combined forces be enough to fight the American influence? In short, no, of course not. Nothing is ever as simple as that. Nirvana still hit number 1 in September with their album *In Utero*, followed in October by Pearl Jam with *Vs:* which was also a worldwide success. Meanwhile, British pop reasserted itself, with Take That's second album *Everything Changes* being so well-received, it even got nominated for the Mercury. While Suede were rightly feted, frankly, others were just more famous.

In wider news, the *Select* cover was lost amongst unnecessary and heartbreaking tragedies. The murders of James Bulger and Stephen Lawrence allowed the government to whip up a supposed moral panic regarding single mothers, in a backfiring attempt to find support for Major's tired 'Back to Basics' campaign (which was later ruined by various amusing MP scandals), while also reminding many of the latent racism inherent in British society. Something new was needed, and internationally there was a feeling it might actually exist. 'The Third Way' – as espoused by new US President Bill Clinton – focussed attention on the ideas of growth, entrepreneurship, enterprise and wealth creation (in line with increased social justice and state support) as a new way forward. It seemed bright; it seemed new, and, although his hour was yet to come, it was close enough for the Shadow Home Secretary Tony Blair, to be taking notes on.

Meanwhile, at Radio 1, new controller Matthew Bannister made sweeping changes, removing the old-guard DJs in order to attract a new and younger audience. One of its flagship shows – *The Evening Session* hosted by Jo Whiley and Steve Lamacq – would be pioneering in its drive to champion the new sounds of the underground.

Something was definitely stirring: it just needed a name.

The albums chosen to represent 1993 are very much in tune with the *Select* cover, and it might amaze some to find that three of them were released on the very same day. For Suede, Blur and The Auteurs, this is the first flush of British pop as an art form before the media grabbed hold of it and made it a consumable; while, in The Boo Radleys' *Giant Steps*, we witness the heights bands were already achieving before being pulled inside the Britpop bubble.

Radiohead – Pablo Honey (1993)

Recording sessions: September-November 1992
Producers: Sean Slade, Paul Q. Kolderie, Chris Hufford
Record label: Parlophone
Chart position: UK: 22
Release date: 22 February 1993

Pete: Funny thing, but when I first became aware of Radiohead, I thought they were an American band. It actually took me far longer than it should've to realise they weren't... years in fact... I probably first realised I'd made a boo-boo around the time of the War Child *Help* album. Perhaps it was because of how Radiohead had been marketed at America and how the 'Creep' single achieved massive success over there, which then got reflected back onto the UK rather than building here first.

Matt: I don't think Pete was alone in considering Radiohead as an American band. This album, and particularly 'Creep', was often (unsurprisingly) compared to American alternative rock such as Nirvana and ultimately got overlooked. The years have mellowed this view, and though the album does share a lot of the same DNA, more is now being made of the moments where Radiohead's distinctive style shines through.

The Album

Not an American band in the slightest, but actually hailing from Oxford, Radiohead made an instant impression with their debut album, picking up mostly positive reviews and peaking at number 22. However, the album had a long hangover in the shape of the 'Creep' single – the never-ending popularity of which has seemingly cast a shadow upon all their subsequent 1990s triumphs (of which there were many). *Pablo Honey* does have the feel of an American alternative rock album and shows many of its influences on its sleeve – especially the loud/quiet template set out by Pixies and an abundance of moody grunge. However, if you want to have a genuinely good time, then this is the Radiohead album for you: most notably in the exhilarating end-of-days rush of the single 'Anyone Can Play Guitar', which easily stands up to its more famous counterpart.

Standout track: 'Creep'

Saint Etienne – So Tough (1993)

Recording Sessions: Summer-Autumn 1992
Producer: Saint Etienne
Record label: RMS, London

Chart position: UK: 7
Release date: 22 February 1993

Pete: Saint Etienne felt like a London band: as in, if you weren't from London, then you wouldn't really get them. Which is kind of fair, I suppose. They're also the first band I remember that affected me with what would become known as the 'sleeper-bloke' phenomenon: the men in the band being thrown into the shade by singer Sarah Cracknell, even though she was a relative latecomer to the band.

Matt: Describing Saint Etienne purely as a Britpop band is just unfair, as they explored and used various musical styles across songs and albums. But at the same time, the Britpop themes featured especially high on this album.

The Album

Plugging ambient dance into 1960s pop, with a huge amount of sampled films and found sounds, may not, on the face of it, give the impression of a great album. However, Saint Etienne's second long-player does just this. Stylistically out of kilter with many of the other records covered in this book, the album balances some genuinely sweet pop moments with a dark and nightmarish final quarter. With singer Sarah Cracknell now fronting the three-piece full-time – though she doesn't appear on nearly as many of the songs as you might think – *So Tough* was the band's commercial peak in the UK, and also an artistic triumph in that it managed to conjure up a miniature sound-painting of London. Given this, the album title seems odd – it's a pretty straight (though partial) name-steal from a middle-period Beach Boys album, although the California sound has little impact on this St. Etienne album at all.

Standout track: 'You're In A Bad Way'

The Auteurs – New Wave (1993)

Recording sessions: August-September 1992
Producers: Phil Vinall, Luke Haines
Record label: Hut
Chart position: UK: 22
Release date: 22 February 1993

Pete: Everyone used to talk about The Auteurs in revered tones, almost like they were somehow holy. There was a sense that if you were into Britpop, you were absolutely allowed to be into The Auteurs, but you had to accept that your judgement was wrong about everything else ever and apologise profusely for owning anything by Oasis.

Matt: The Auteurs' debut album was, and still is, critically acclaimed. But it's also one of those albums you seemed to have to be in the know about. For many, it was probably discovered via some kind of best-album list, which is a good thing for Luke Haines, just as long as Britpop isn't mentioned in the same breath.

The Album

Still sounding fresh after 30 years, the debut album from The Auteurs stands the test of time largely due to it not sounding like any of its immediate peers. Eschewing all the trends of 1993 and preceding years, this is a record more in debt to The Beatles, or more specifically, John Lennon's solo work. Songwriter Luke Haines may not have enjoyed being added to the Britpop gang in the years to come (in fact, he was rather grumpy and adamant that he wanted nothing to do with it), but it can't be denied that he certainly played a part in its development, making it okay to take inspiration from classic 1960s/1970s sources.

Understated yet catchy alternative rock at its best, *New Wave* may share both feel and theme with Denim's debut, but The Auteurs are very much their own group. Also, narrowly missing out on the Mercury Music Prize (won by Suede), certainly makes for some tantalising *what-if* postulations.

Standout track: 'Show Girl'

Key Album: Suede – Suede (1993)

Personnel:
Brett Anderson: vocals
Bernard Butler: guitar, piano
Mat Osman: bass
Simon Gilbert: drums
Recording Sessions: January or March 1992: 'The Drowners' single sessions at (first) Protocol studios, London.
Mid-1992: 'Metal Mickey' single sessions, initially at Protocol Studios and then either re-recorded or remixed at Maison Rouge Studios, London.
Late-1992/Early-1993: The rest of the album recorded and mixed at Master Rock Studios, Kilburn, London (with some initial sessions at Angel Studios, Islington, London)
Producer: Ed Buller
Record label: Nude
Chart position: UK: 1, USA: 14 (Heatseeker's chart)
Release date: 29 March 1993

Pete: For anyone not raised on Bowie – and to be honest, he wasn't that big in rural Worcestershire in 1993 – Suede on *Top Of The Pops* provided a real generation splitting 'what-the-hell-was-that?!' moment. I was instantly sucked in, even if I had no real ability to relate to the subject matter!

Matt: Anderson's voice has always been polarising, but for me, this album contains some of the worst offenders. Sometimes it meshes with a song and adds another level, while at other times, it's almost fighting against the other instruments. Weirdly, it's only on *this* album, and I've never understood why, as the live versions of these songs don't have the same effect.

The Band

Suede were formed in London in late-1989 when guitarist Bernard Butler answered an *NME* ad to join a band consisting of childhood friends Brett Anderson, Mat Osman and Justine Frischmann (who was in a relationship with Anderson) while at University College London. The band began with a drum machine, but due to its unreliability, a human replacement was sought, with Simon Gilbert finally joining in June 1990. A number of demo recordings were made, one of which was voted the winner on a London radio demo show several times in a row. In early-1991, Frischmann split with Anderson to start dating Blur frontman Damon Albarn (creating the great love triangle of Britpop), later ultimately forming Elastica. Suede's popularity with the music press grew, but it wasn't until early-1992 that they finally signed to a record label – Nude Records – their first singles and album following shortly afterwards. Successful festival and award-ceremony appearances helped build upon their renown, yet Anderson also became notorious for various attention-grabbing comments, while Butler's relationship with the band members disintegrated. During sessions for the 1994 follow-up album *Dog Man Star*, these differences – both personal and creative – proved to be too much, and Butler left the band. Despite the positivity of UK critics, the album struggled to maintain the band's initial success, and the singles performed badly. Undaunted, Suede regrouped with Richard Oakes replacing Butler; keyboardist Neil Codling joining a year later. In 1996, their third album was released to mainstream success, although the next two albums could not maintain momentum. Dogged with stories of drug abuse, alcoholism and exhaustion, Suede disbanded in 2003. In 2010, they reformed for live shows, and in 2013, released a new album. Two further well-received albums have since been released, with a new album expected soon.

The Album

Suede: the hype, the hysteria, the hostility! Offering a stark contrast to the dirt, sweat and grubbiness of Madchester, grebo and shoegaze – while positively flipping two fingers to all that grunge had to offer – Suede truly stuck out when they first struck out in 1992. Like all peacocks, they were built to be seen as well as heard, and Brett Anderson's Bowie-esque glamour – mixed with an often-turbulent Morrissey/Marr relationship with guitarist Bernard Butler – provided the music press with all it needed to throw in their lot with the boys from London's satellite towns. Soon, Suede were everywhere.

'The best new band in Britain' may have been sexy and hedonistic, yet they were also smart and headstrong enough to know that what would truly set them apart would be their debut album being an artistic triumph rather than simply a collection of hit singles. And so we have *Suede* – a record that looked at what it was truly like to be young and living in London in the early-1990s and making no apologies for what it reported. Lying in the gutter but staring at the stars, there's glitter, unapologetic drug use, filth, fury, dancing and death – all wrapped up in songs that were either stompingly good fun or strikingly tender and chilling. Quickly pulled from the indie circuit to find themselves performing on *Top Of The Pops* and the *Brit Awards* (when they weren't even nominated), the album even went on to win the Mercury Music Prize. The time of indie as it was previously understood to be, was over. Success (and ridicule) was nothing to be ashamed of. Although the band's initial impact may have been comparatively short-lived, it was enough to kick-start the Britpop movement as we know it, with *Suede* often cited as the first true Britpop record. As for *their* feelings on the matter, perhaps that should come from Anderson directly: 'I felt partly responsible for it; like I'd given birth to some awful child'.

'So Young' (Brett Anderson, Bernard Butler) [Single]

Charting at number 22 when released as a single almost two months after the album (which is quite an achievement given that the majority of the fan base would've played this lead track into the ground by then), 'So Young' begins the album in remarkable style. A song about being dispossessed and young, seeking the illicit thrills and crashing lows of narcotics, the song almost acts as an overture for all that's to follow. Let's face it; if you don't like this, you probably won't like the next ten songs. Hooky, and with a hint of Marr to Butler's guitar, the song features some wonderful virtuoso piano in its central section, and lush, romantic sweeps into the choruses, which just goes to prove that just because you're dirty, doesn't mean you can't be beautiful. A great start to a great album, of course, but maybe a more daring choice would have been.

'Animal Nitrate' (Brett Anderson, Bernard Butler) [Single]

Keeping up the pace with probably *the* killer pop single of Suede's early career, 'Animal Nitrate' has it all – a hilarious on-the-nose drug-referencing title that *still* managed to get past pretty much every radio executive in the land when it was released one month before the album (charting at number 7, where it stayed for a fortnight), soaring vocals and a try-not-to-pogo chorus of 'What does it take to turn you on?' For a lyric so bleak ('In your broken home he broke all your bones/Now you're taking it time after time'), it's amusing to discover the song originally had the working title 'Dixon', due to Butler's weaving chorus guitar sounding similar to the theme from *Dixon of Dock Green*.

'She's Not Dead' (Brett Anderson, Bernard Butler)

From the exhilarating to the beautifully bleak, 'She's Not Dead' highlights a lighter musical touch but an even darker lyrical side. Detailing the suicide of a woman 'locked in a car somewhere with exhaust in her hair', it's sobering stuff, elevated by its falsetto chorus and superb guitar gymnastics. With drums that sound more like the woozy wash of the sea, this song has an ability to really haunt you if you're not careful.

'Moving' (Brett Anderson, Bernard Butler) [Deep Cut]

Possibly the record's punkiest moment – and certainly its fastest – 'Moving' shows Anderson playing in the androgynous playground that led him to declare he was 'a bisexual man who's never had a homosexual experience' (something he's attempted to clarify ever since). With lyrics that skirt the lines of innuendo ('So we are a boy, so we are a girl', 'If you can take it, I can take it'), and a quiet flanged-vocal chorus, it's blistering stuff that plays to the mosh pit: not least in Butler's classic-rock solo moment.

'Pantomime Horse' (Brett Anderson, Bernard Butler) [Deep Cut]

One of the album's most affecting songs – albeit one in which Anderson again dips his toe into ambiguous sexuality – 'Pantomime Horse' deals with confusion and sexual awakening, with enough delicacy that it was possible for your parents to hear it and comment, 'That's a nice song, dear'. With some exceptional imagery ('I was cut from a pantomime horse'), it's a brooding yet tumultuously histrionic ballad ('Well did you ever, did you ever go round the bend?'). Ultimately, the listener can take whatever they desire from it. Although, for the dedicated and dispossessed, it was a call to arms and is still a favourite of the band and their fans to this day.

'The Drowners' (Brett Anderson, Bernard Butler) [Single]

Suede's debut single (which reached number 49 in May '1992) begins with rolling drums that really make an impact, before Butler's stabbing guitars punctuate a lilting Beatles-like verse and an anthemic chorus. As an introduction to the band, this perhaps now feels somewhat subdued, and the production difference is evident given it doesn't have quite the same sheen as the rest of the album. However, in 1992, it was more than enough for *Melody Maker* to dub Suede 'The best new band in Britain' and set them up for a roller-coaster year. 'You're taking me over', sings Anderson to his audience: Little did he know it was the other way around.

'Sleeping Pills' (Brett Anderson, Bernard Butler)

Turn the histrionics up to maximum: we're going in! 'Oh, Angel, don't take those sleeping pills/You don't need them', cries Anderson. Though this lyric may cover some of the same ground as The Rolling Stones' 'Mother's Little Helper', sonically, it's about as far-removed from the blues as orange. Originally considered for single release before someone realised what a belter 'Animal Nitrate' was, you can't help but wonder what 'Sleeping Pills' as a single might've done for the band's fortunes – although it's a safe bet it wouldn't have been positive. Occasionally bordering on plain silly ('You're a water sign, I'm an air sign, gone, gone to Valium'/'Sweet F.A. to do today') – but holding it's own by keeping its nerve, even when you think Butler is about to fly off into a different song – this is hauntingly striking.

'Breakdown' (Brett Anderson, Bernard Butler)

'Breakdown' can be a hard listen. It's a truly heartbreaking song dealing with the emotional and true-life impact of a close friend's depression and untimely death. For anyone so affected, it's difficult to not get a lump in your throat with lines like 'Try not to go too far inside your mind' and 'If you were the one, would I even notice?'. Acoustically-led and one of the album's most straightforward songs, its power comes from pure simplicity and rawness. There's no need for theatrics here.

'Metal Mickey' (Brett Anderson, Bernard Butler) [Single]

Speaking of theatrics, and bringing the mood up by a considerable margin, here's the giant glam-stomp of 'Metal Mickey'! Another single with an unexpected origin story, it was originally based on 'The Shoop Shoop Song' and there *are* definite similarities, though not enough to result in any form of legal action. The second single released (reaching 17: Suede's first time in the top 20), this is the band letting loose and having some genuine fun. Yes, of course, it's about a stripper, and yes, of course, there's a heart of darkness lurking within it ('She sells meat'), but when Anderson yelps, 'Oh dad, she's driving me mad!', it's hard to not smile as well as shimmy, while Butler's short solo has echoes of The Kinks' guitarist Dave Davies in its wilful abandon.

'Animal Lover' (Brett Anderson, Bernard Butler)

Remaining upbeat and exceptionally danceable, this song that could've easily been a single had it been written by any other band in the early-1990s or earlier. Admittedly, it's all somewhat silly (What's not to enjoy about a song that includes the line 'I see you're moving like wildlife from the waist'?), but it's also heart-racing stuff, with guitars switching between stabbing chord shapes and exceptional weaving lead. Its finest moment is the elongated outro that really allows Butler to stretch his musical legs in some muscular, soaring guitar workouts that could've easily been enough to call time on the album in bombastic style. It just soars!

'The Next Life' (Brett Anderson, Bernard Butler)

To end on such spirit-lifting glee just wouldn't be Suede, though. Instead, the album's final word goes to this piano ballad. Written in tribute to Anderson's mother, who passed away while he was a student, this is wrenching yet hopeful stuff, made only more striking by its mixing of the spiritual and the mundane. Given the song's power, it seems cheap to mention, but there must've been more than one future Britpop star taking note. Standing in stark contrast to the rest of the album, with no guitars on show and the histrionics replaced with simple emotion, 'The Next Life' is one of the great album closers of the 1990s.

Optional Extras

The *Suede* album has had two deluxe editions released: the first in 2011 and a further expanded version in 2018. There are some content differences, with the 2011 version having an early demo of 'Just A Girl' featuring Justine Frischmann (an interesting, folkier, harmonised version of a later B-side), and both having different live performances included on CD and DVD. Overall, they contain all the B-sides and demos of songs from sessions throughout 1991 and 1992, with some additional rarities thrown in. Anderson has often been critical of the songs that made up *Suede* compared to the B-sides, and it's easy to see why. 'My Insatiable One' and 'To The Birds' are far stronger songs than some on the album. Other B-sides are less strong but still worth seeking out – 'He's Dead' and 'Where The Pigs Don't Fly' both having epic endings and being slightly uncomfortable listening, while 'Painted People' is a guitar-fuzz punk-rock song compared to the gentle confessional of 'The Big Time'. 'High Rising' and 'Dolly' explore similar themes, and the rarities include a nice instrumental ('Diesel') and two covers. The demos really only show the songs progressing and offer little further. Not included – and existing only on bootlegs – are the demos 'C'mon, C'mon, C'mon' – which sounds like Suede doing U2 – and 'Wonderful Sometimes', which is a cross between The Cure and The Smiths. In 1991, the single 'Be My God'/'Art' was pulled just before release (allegedly due to being unhappy with the recording), but the low-quality version available on the internet does hint at the Suede sound and the direction the band were moving in. Regarding further album-session material, Ed Buller has mentioned unfinished and unreleased instrumentals in interviews, but unfortunately, these are unlikely to ever see the light of day.

Key Album: Blur – Modern Life Is Rubbish (1993)

Personnel:
Damon Albarn: vocals, piano, keyboards, sleigh bells ('Chemical World')
Graham Coxon: guitar, backing vocals, percussion ('Turn It Up', 'Miss America')
Alex James: bass
Dave Rowntree: drums
Recording Sessions: October 1991-January 1992: Matrix Studios, Little Russell Street. John Smith and Blur producing 'Oily Water', 'Intermission', 'Commercial Break', 'Miss America', 'Resigned' and multiple B-sides.
October 1992: Matrix Studios, Little Russell Street. Steve Lovell producing 'Sunday Sunday', 'Villa Rosie'.
November-December 1992: Maison Rouge. Stephen Street producing 'Coping', 'Colin Zeal', 'Blue Jeans', 'Advert', 'Turn It Up', 'Pressure On Julian', 'Starshaped'.
January- February 1993: Maison Rouge. Stephen Street producing the 'For

Tomorrow' and 'Chemical World' singles.
Note: The 'Popscene' single was recorded with Steve Lovell in February 1992.
Initial September 1992 album sessions at RAK Studios with Andy Partridge
producing, were abandoned.
Producers: Blur, John Smith, Steve Lovell, Stephen Street
Record label: Food
Release date: 10 May 1993
Chart position: UK: 15

Pete: What a great album. Even though it has its faults, I find it difficult to pick
them out, as the whole thing just delivers such a massive rush of memories.

Matt: I have always felt this album is unfairly overlooked. Despite being a
massive progression, it had to deal with the fallout from critics over the first
album. Then it got overwhelmed again due to the massive success of *Parklife*.
Such a shame, as it's a really great album.

The Album

Hang on… what happened to Blur? Weren't they that baggy band from 1991?
The ones who sounded a bit like all your favourite bands in a blender but
served in some really nice-looking glasses? Following the ascension of Suede
(which Blur saw as a blow to them personally), coupled with a disastrous
American tour (which saw the band deliver just as many blows to each other),
Damon Albarn looked at the world around him, raised an eyebrow, and began
to write about what he saw: often quite literally. Blur were already yesterday's
news, and seemed destined to become tomorrow's chip paper – not helped
by the March 1992 'Popscene' single, which had no home on either *Leisure*
or *Modern Life Is Rubbish,* despite being a fantastic listen and a wonderful
expose of what the press had dubbed 'The Scene That Celebrates Itself'.
Hitting only number 32, 'Popscene' was a long drop from the glory days of
the previous album. With the band looking like it was going to get dropped,
Albarn threw the dice with a more-thematic collection, overhauling the band's
image into suits and bovver boots and writing songs that echoed the tradition
of The Kinks rather than whatever was happening in Manchester at the time.
The end result is a magnificent album that achieves its objectives, even if it is
perhaps one song too long and occasionally hasn't quite found its feet. Drifting
through various styles, themes and recording techniques/sessions, it's an album
that takes you on a journey. One of the first truly great Britpop releases, its
Anglocentricities would be hailed in the music press, even if the sales figures
didn't set the world on fire. The jury might've still been out about whether this
direction had legs or whether it was simply a project album from a last-chance
group wanting to do something special, but by inspiring devotion to the Blur
cause, the follow-up album *Parklife* would cement the band forever in musical
history.

'For Tomorrow' (Music: Blur; Lyrics: Albarn) [Single]

And then the sun came up, and all the world was refreshed. Just for clarity, this is no longer the sound of *Leisure*. It isn't even the sound of the (sadly) failed experiment of single 'Popscene'. This is a different Blur and instantly marked by the introductory stabs of an acoustic guitar. The band are taking their time, giving the music real space to breathe and do its thing. But what is its thing? Well, this is uncharted territory for Blur; a song propelled by a great bass line, jangling guitars and a rhythm that accentuates all the hooks. Although it has a 'la la la' chorus that could've so easily been ridiculed, the true strength of 'For Tomorrow' is its lyric. Gone is the vaguely-trippy, baggy, just-sing-the-words-that-rhyme model of previous outings – in their place, a Ray-Davies-like observation crossed with a David-Bowie delivery (even more prominent on the demo). A tale of everyday London girls and boys (No, not yet) around Primrose Hill, 'Trying not to be sick again' as they meander through their lives, its true killer moment is the outro, where Albarn breaks into monologue mode – something he rarely ever did again – giving the slightly melancholy air a real boost. Written and recorded after the bulk of the album – on the orders of a record company concerned the album had no hits – it was released as a single in April 1993, and with only weeks to go before the album release, it hit number 28. Perhaps not seen as a success in terms of sales, it still signalled a real step change for the band, and is in many ways the high-water mark of its parent record.

'Advert' (Music: Blur; Lyrics: Albarn)

'Food processors are great!' snarks a sample before something that sounds like a computerised factory-line, only to quickly be supplemented by some really punky guitar from Coxon. Albarn is in first-person mode here, heading home from work and seeking refuge in the adverts he sees on the underground. Given that the Manics were tackling the anti-consumerism agenda at roughly the same time, this is a much more fun and lighthearted way of spearing the same target: simply observing and wishing that they'd 'Say something! Say something else!'.

'Colin Zeal' (Music: Blur; Lyrics: Albarn)

This is possibly the first true outing for an Albarn character song (which would take centre stage on subsequent albums). But it doesn't feel like it's been pulled straight from The Kinks' 1960s handbook: being more like an agitated new wave song. Admittedly, it doesn't really go anywhere after the opening one-two punch, and even has an 'ah ah aaaahh' element that could be taken from *Leisure*, but it's still a great album track.

'Pressure On Julian' (Music: Blur; Lyrics: Albarn)

With an oozy-woozy guitar line and a drum kit that feels like it's playing in reverse, this is like someone having a bit of a breakdown through the medium of pop song. A character song about a trolley attendant called Julian – in keeping with Albarn's new way of tackling his material – the 'magical transit children' line was taken from graffiti seen in King's Cross.

'Star Shaped' (Music: Blur; Lyrics: Albarn) [Deep Cut]

Graham Coxon gets his moment to shine here, delivering not just chiming, hooky guitars, but partially singing the lead vocal, supplying the chorus responses and the key 'We don't think so/You seem star shaped' moment. Its high point is a lush instrumental breakdown in the Kinks mould at 1:38, before Coxon pulls out an absolutely storming guitar solo, finishing on a synth note which increases in pitch and earned Graham the credit of 'anti-cat and dog Moog tone'. Initially planned as a single; frankly, it should've been.

'Blue Jeans' (Music: Blur; Lyrics: Albarn)

On first listen, 'Blue Jeans' may have a slight air of *Leisure* about it, and although it's easy to overlook, it is, in fact, a real gem. Despite its baggy nature and stripped-back feel, this simple tale of buying clothes on the Portobello Road Market is actually an early outing for some real Blur-style romance: the sort that often comes with both a resigned yet heartfelt quality. 'I want to stay this way forever', sings Albarn with no irony or subtext. It's hard to not have a lump in your throat, especially when he adds, 'Don't give up on me yet/Don't think I'm walking out of this'.

'Chemical World' (including 'Intermission') (Music: Blur; Lyrics: Albarn) [Single]

Released two months after the album, its second single was written and recorded following the US label's demand for something they felt they could push. Would 'Chemical World' appeal to the American market? Perhaps; it did peak at 27 on the US Alternative Airplay chart. But in the UK it simply reached 28: the spot that 'For Tomorrow' previously held. Another character song with hints of the psychedelic (The 'holes' its chorus refers to can't help but evoke The Beatles' 'Four thousand holes in Blackburn, Lancashire' from 'A Day In The Life'), it still seems like a slightly odd choice for a single. But then, *Modern Life Is Rubbish* works best as an album – proven here by the song's coupling with 'Intermission' (a knockabout pub piano tune that builds and builds into a frenzy of misfiring drums and guitars, originally used to open Seymour gigs). Coupled together, the two songs become more than the sum of their parts.

'Sunday Sunday' (Music: Blur; Lyrics: Albarn) [Single]

There's something of the music hall and *Sgt Pepper's...* in 'Sunday Sunday': a song about – you guessed it – Sunday. So, while it's all roast lunch with the family, naps and walks in the park, what really shocks you, is that the song hasn't been around for decades. Driven by Rowntree's positively huge, bouncing and pounding rhythm, the song is augmented with wonderful horns and is a real joy to listen to. It's also a big fan favourite, best deployed to snap the audience back to attention after more indulgent moments. Released as a single in October 1993 – six months after the album – it still managed to be its most successful single, getting to number 26. Still low perhaps, but the groundwork had been laid.

'Oily Water' (Music: Blur; Lyrics: Albarn) [Deep Cut]

In all honesty, this has always been a slightly difficult listen, due to the fact that it actually does feel like gloopy fluid being poured directly into your earhole. Blasts of sonic clarity interrupt tremolo and wah-wah/reverb guitar, distorted megaphone vocals and a bass that goes for a blobby wander, despite the overall nauseating effect. It's a return to the My Bloody Valentine *Leisure* moments: this description should not put you off.

'Miss America' (Music: Blur; Lyrics: Albarn)

This continues very neatly from 'Oily Water', with what is best described as the album's darker, unsettling segment. The album's most laid-back moment – led chiefly by an acoustic guitar and echoing percussion (Graham Coxon *playing* a chair apparently, though it sounds like dripping taps), the song has a mildly-psychedelic Lennon-worthy lyric, about the loneliness of Miss America. Hollowly hypnotic in nature and almost beautiful, this song weirdly begins with a drunken shout of 'Michael!', which sticks with you down the years, and means you can rarely hear the name shouted without starting to hum the song. 'Miss America' is also notable for being the album's most overt anti-American statement.

'Villa Rosie' (Music: Blur; Lyrics: Albarn)

Slightly lifting the unsettling segment with a crashing rock intro and calls of 'Whoa oh!' (which megahit 'Song 2' would return to some years later), this catchy song is about office workers getting drunk each night at the Villa Rosie pub. Staccato verses are thrown into relief through a real sing-along chorus and the repeated phrase 'So tasty' (which still leaves a slightly sour taste in the mouth), while 'Coming home, that nagging doubt there in your belly' is a particularly on-point description of anyone who has actually lived this life.

'Coping' (Music: Blur; Lyrics: Albarn)

Lurking so close to the end, 'Coping' is a relentless highlight, with punky stabs, robotic, punchy verses and a great keyboard solo that makes the whole thing delirious mosh-pit-friendly fun. As the closest the album gets to the 'Popscene' single that was considered such a failed experiment, it helps lift the mood of the so-far-so-unsettling second side. 'The emphasis is on coping', sings Albarn, which helps to tie it all in.

'Turn It Up' (Music: Blur; Lyrics: Albarn)

'Kazoo, kazoo you are mine/Kazoo kazoo every time', begins 'Turn It Up', and you already know you're in for the album's weakest track: supported only by a belter of a punch-along chorus. At this stage, however, it feels like one song too many, and the nonsense lyric is far better suited to *Leisure*, even if it's still a great piece of pop with some real guitar-hero Coxon moments.

'Resigned' (includes 'Commercial Break') (Music: Blur; Lyrics: Albarn)

Stripped back, led by flanged guitar and with a truly world-weary edge, 'Resigned' is the perfect ending for an album that has relaxed and mellow resignation at its heart. After all, modern life may be rubbish, but what can you *do* about it? An epic in length only, this eschews bombast or beauty, instead delivering a gentle hypnotic wash – its high point being the repetitive, seemingly never-ending outro that fully draws you in, washes you out, and gets you ready for one more spin. Although this is the album's final statement, the song is coupled with 'Commercial Break': a counterpoint to 'Intermission', and the Seymour set-closer. Similar in style but punkier in attitude, it brings the curtain down with some fast stabs and amazingly does feel necessary to the album as a whole. In an age of Americanism in British music, Blur had achieved the unthinkable: a British-sounding album dealing with British themes for a British audience.

Optional Extras

For an album that had such a difficult creative path, it's not surprising that there are multiple versions of songs, with some that made it to the final album being the original demos, some promoted from – and demoted to – B-sides, and others that never left the demo stage. The *Blur 21* box set includes a bonus disc of such rarities, with demos and some alternate versions of album songs, but it seems likely there could be more in the archives. The alternate versions vary between minor differences and quite drastic alternatives, such as the aborted Andy Partridge versions (It's interesting to hear what Blur sound like through the filter of The Beatles or XTC). Early demos that never went any further don't really include any hidden gems, although 'Seven Days' and 'Beached Whale' could've been reasonable B-sides.

The deluxe album (and *Blur 21*) includes all the album-single B-sides plus the orphan 'Popscene' single. This is the sound of a band searching for inspiration and trying something new -heavy on brass; it's a direction the band never really explored again. Many of the B-sides of this and later singles were originally planned for the second album, and are a mix of woozy numbers and guitar workouts ('Mace', 'Badgeman Brown', 'Into Another', 'Bone Bag', 'Beachcoma', 'My Ark'), and, ultimately, it was for the best they were left off. 'I'm Fine' is heavily indebted to mid-period Beatles, complete with a backwards middle section, and is actually from the 1990 'Sing' sessions. 'Garden Central' is a drone-like instrumental with Albarn wordlessly joining in at various points – a really different and interesting track which is probably the best song on the 'Popscene' single, and perhaps should've been on the album as an alternative to 'Intermission'. 'Peach' is a much gentler tune, featuring a harmonium and sounding like the Velvet Underground & Nico, complete with stuck-record ending. 'When The Cows Come Home' is a psychedelic-1960s tune with oompah band, very much in the vein of 'Magical Mystery Tour': more specifically 'Your Mother Should Know'. 'Es Schmecht' – with staccato guitar, trippy bridge and dissonant saxophone – is quite a departure from previous B-sides, probably due to being recorded after the album's release. 'Young And Lovely' is a great pop song that should've made it to the album, with hints of Nick Drake and Scott Walker, also echoing 'A Day In The Life' at certain points. Unfortunately, Blur attempted a few covers in this period too – 'Maggie May' is a pretty lacklustre effort, despite a dirty guitar solo; 'Substitute' is a very sloppy live version, and there's also a further perfunctory version of 'Oliver's Army'. They even tried out some old standards and traditional tunes: 'Daisy Bell', 'The Wassailing Song' and 'Let's All Go Down The Strand'. While more effort was put into these – and a good time clearly had by all – though, they hint at some of the themes/sounds explored on the next album. They're a confusing addition to the catalogue.

Key Album: The Boo Radleys – Giant Steps (1993)

Personnel:
Sice: vocals
Rob Cieka: drums, percussion
Tim Brown: bass, keyboards
Martin Carr: guitar, keyboards, vocals
Recording Sessions: February-March 1993: First Protocol Studios, London
Producers: Martin Carr, Tim Brown, Andy Wilkinson
Record label: Creation
Chart position: UK: 17
Release date: 31 August 1993

> Pete: I just cannot for the life of me understand why people don't shout about this record from the rooftops. It was critically acclaimed at the time, certainly, but anyone I mention it to these days just shrugs back. It should be held up as a textbook example of a masterpiece.

> Matt: Most of the singles from this album don't do it justice. It's a melting pot of styles, genres and dynamics, leaving the listener wondering what has just happened. I don't think I've experienced an album where there is so much going on in every song and that constantly catches you off-guard.

The Band

The Boo Radleys were formed in 1988 by childhood friends Martin Carr, Simon 'Sice' Rowbottom and Tim Brown, in Wallasey, Wirral, Merseyside. Initially using a drum machine, the band went through a succession of drummers before settling on Rob Cieka in 1990. By this point, they'd already released their debut album, through Preston-based indie label Action Records, followed by an EP on Rough Trade (shortly before it collapsed). In 1991, the band signed with Creation Records and released their second album *Everything's Alright Forever*. *Giant Steps* followed in 1993, receiving massive critical acclaim. But it wasn't until the 1995 single 'Wake Up Boo' that the band became widely known. The accompanying album *Wake Up!* was a commercial success, but the response to the following two albums was mixed. No longer wishing to continue, the band disbanded in 1999. Principle songwriter Carr continued as a solo musician, releasing a number of albums as Bravecaptain, and under his own name. In 2021, the remaining band members released a new EP and look set to continue.

The Album

This is a public service announcement: *Giant Steps* is not an album to listen to if you have a hangover. In fact, it's not an album to listen to if you're feeling delicate in any way, shape or form. However, it *is* an album to listen to if you're clear of mind and body and want to hear something truly outstanding. Before Britpop had even fully tested the ground, The Boo Radleys created something special and managed to lyrically embrace the fear, long before 1998 when it became fashionable to do so (We're looking at you, Pulp). Already on their third album, and having survived just as many media-generated musical movements, the Liverpool band were now tagged as shoegaze.

Tired of industry pigeonholing and keen to push the band to its limits, bandleader Martin Carr took a great leap into the unknown with *Giant Steps*. Making a direct title-steal from John Coltrane's iconic 1960 jazz album – and featuring a fair bit of jazz influence itself – this is a 64-minute monster of an album containing seventeen songs: none of which outstay their welcome (the longest being a very acceptable 5:17). The winner of various industry plaudits – including Album of the Year in both *NME* and *Select* – the fact that sales (especially of its singles) never matched the acclaim should perhaps not be a great surprise. This is an album of massive ambition, fusing everything that should be impossible to fuse. Shoegaze, pop, reggae, noise rock, prog, orchestral, psychedelia, 1960s guitar pop, dub and dance all have their moments, on a record so dense that using a form as basic as the written word, feels insulting to the sonic experience. The band would, of course, go on to greater chart success and even became household names thanks to the hit single 'Wake Up Boo!'. But in terms of their albums, this was a defining moment.

'I Hang Suspended' (Martin Carr) [Deep Cut]

Initially, a minute-long sound collage of distorted backwards vocals and instruction-manual audio, the striking drums and guitar solo must've surely been marked in a certain Gallagher brother's notepad at some point. Even more striking is it then giving way to a rather fuzzy, descending-chord melodic pop, with catchy stop-starts and a sugar-sweet chorus, as Sice sings 'I hang suspended on your words'. As album openers go, it pretty much defines *Giant Steps* in four minutes. Although it's exceptionally listenable, it's anything but a straightforward indie pop trip.

'Upon 9th And Fairchild' (Martin Carr)

Somewhat repeating the opener's trick book (and giving the listener an air of understanding before the record gets seriously freaky), this begins with an extended introduction of drums and scrawling feedback, as Sice finds space for an unexpectedly melodic, distorted vocal. What you don't expect is it then becoming a dub reggae song or a punky thrash, yet it manages to fit all of these elements into five minutes, including a false ending that resumes with snatches of dark cello. Lyrically, it's desolate and abandoned – 'Vultures circle and the bills and demands fill the floor' – providing a genuinely haunted feel.

'Wish I Was Skinny' (Martin Carr) [Single]

Essentially a shopping list of self-improvement, neuroses, insecurity and self-doubt, this is surprisingly one of the album's most upbeat songs, and that's not just comparatively speaking. With jangle pop, summer-fun guitars driving the song forward, and a 1950s rock 'n' roll lead guitar catching the ear, the single reached 75 when released in October 1993. Its true highlight is found in the outro, where a repetitive organ instrumental builds up and up: starting in an almost lo-fi manner before reaching a siren-like crescendo. By the time it crashes disconcertingly (which allows it to fit seamlessly into the album), you don't realise quite how big and beautiful the song has gotten.

'Leaves And Sand' (Martin Carr)

Sometimes musicians like to have a little fun with the listener, lowering the volume to such an extent that you're tempted to reach for the dial or put an ear next to the speaker. *Do not do this with 'Leaves And Sand'!* Playing the quiet/loud trick for all it's worth, The Boo Radleys flip between psychedelic verses and massive noise-pop instrumentals, while fear-infused lyrics give sonic form to the consideration that just because you're paranoid, it doesn't mean they're not after you. It's pretty stunning stuff.

'Butterfly McQueen' (Martin Carr)

A song of many parts – boasting at least two sections that could be the intro – it's hard to keep up with 'Butterfly McQueen'. Jangling guitars, folk-rock picking, screeching jazz trumpet, double-time fuzz indie and psychedelic wig-outs all have their part to play in this song named after American *Gone With The Wind* actress Butterfly McQueen (What she made of it is not on record). Like many moments on *Giant Steps*, it's notable how much Sice's ability to deliver a melodic vocal line can anchor a song, especially given how the accompanying instrumentation should by no rights allow such a thing to exist.

'Rodney King (Song For Lenny Bruce)' (Martin Carr)

Following an instrumental segue from 'Butterfly McQueen', this incredibly short sketch of a song is built around the repetition and build of an electronica-style organ. The closest to dance music the album gets, the entire vocal consists of 'Do you know my name before you tear me apart?/Do you care who I am?', which fits with the title – Rodney King being a victim of US police brutality in 1991; comedian Lenny Bruce being subjected to repeated overzealous law enforcement, dying in 1966 while fighting obscenity charges.

'Thinking Of Ways' (Martin Carr)

Like a lost song from The Beach Boys' *Pet Sounds* (if Brian Wilson had ever attempted to write a song about the paranoia-inducing effects of day drinking), this showcases exactly how great Sice is a vocalist. With beautiful vocal stacks held in almost perfect isolation, the woozy beer-filled lyric (and encroaching fear) is brought to the fore by some surprising trad-jazz moments that deliver a massively unsettling effect. 'I'll just have one more/It can't do any harm', goes the second voice. This is a lie.

'Barney (...And Me)' (Martin Carr) [Single]

The album's biggest chart success – hitting 48 when released as a single in February 1994 – is at face value a more straight-ahead slice of indie pop. But listen past the jangling acoustics, and you'll find a lot more than you expect. Jazz flute, noisy psychedelic fry-ups, and even a blink-and-you'll-miss-it Beach Boys vocal stack at the three-minute mark combine to explain why this didn't make a bigger impact on the record-buying public. The outro is a glorious template for what 2000s bands like Los Campesinos! would go on to achieve with the pop format.

'Spun Around' (Martin Carr)

A two-and-a-half-minute sketch of sorts, beginning with an organ and acoustic guitar, which create a massively calming effect – you should probably know the score by now: things are going to get nasty. 'My God is nowhere to be found', sings Sice, and with the demonic backwards vocals, you don't half believe him, as 'Spun Around' suddenly takes an abrupt 180-degree turn into massively-distorted vocals about taking too many pills and reeling at the sink.

'If You Want It, Take It' (Martin Carr)

As one of the album's most straight-down-the-line songs, it may come as some relief to find yourself in territory marked by heavy drums and clear riffs. Featuring a great descending vocal line and pitch gymnastics, there's an air here of what The Boos would bring later when they felt greater pressure to deliver in the charts. On *Giant Steps,* however, it makes for the weakest track due to obvious retro organ and rock guitars.

'Best Lose The Fear' (Martin Carr)
A grown-up song about the relationship difficulties faced by the touring musician ('It's not your fault that she has changed/It's not her fault you're still the same'), this is a remarkably sweet ballad full of repetitive vocal hooks that burrow their way into your mind for a long stay. You could almost be lulled into feeling that the album really has lost the fear, but there's more going on underneath, with some pretty freaky jazz elements lurking in the mix.

'Take The Time Around' (Martin Carr)
Although this features some melodic verse moments, don't be lulled into a false sense of security: they're just there to throw some wonderfully noisy Neil Young-esque thrash pop into relief. Featuring a massive rock solo with at least three guitars all playing separate lead parts (yet remarkably not becoming awful in the process), there's a real sweet-and-sour mixture at work here, not least in the double-tracked vocals over the outro's gorgeous backing vocal. As the lyrics suggest, it's best to 'Feel the power surging through/Let it wash all over you'.

'Lazarus' (Martin Carr) [Single]
If you should decide to only listen to one song from *Giant Steps* (and you shouldn't) but still want to get a feel for the album, then it should be 'Lazarus'. Pulling off the unachievable by managing to combine every strand of *Giant Steps* into one song, we are treated to dub reggae, shoegaze, noise pop, bombastic horn sections and a sweetly-distorted lead vocal in the background while the 'ba ba ba' backings take centre stage. Peaking at 54 when released as a single, it may not be a popular comment, but there were better choices to be had if chart success was truly the goal. Despite this, it's an incredible, masterful piece of work given all it crams into its four and a half minutes. Special note should be made of how the loud sections kick in: even if you know they're coming, they seem to catch the song off guard and jolt the listener back into focus.

'One Is For' (Martin Carr)
The countdown to the album's finale is actually marked with two songs that are essentially sketches. The first – 'One Is For' – is a pastoral piece of folk that channels something of The Rolling Stones' 'Ruby Tuesday' into something that feels ultimately redemptive, while…

'Run My Way Runway' (Martin Carr)
…is downright spooky. With jazz trumpets, strobing helicopter synths and whooshing sounds that are definitely designed to not please the ear, there's

still a beautiful vocal lurking underneath: remarkably extolling the virtues of going on a happy holiday. It's probably not the best song to get you in the mood for a fortnight in Benidorm, though.

'I've Lost The Reason' (Martin Carr)

Although it never states the song title, this is a song about searching for an answer to the great mystery of life, simultaneously setting out to destroy the individual. With choruses full of noisy pop bombast, there's a quite-stunning trumpet-led orchestral section before the second verse, which shows the true care and attention the band were putting into every second of this record. Laid-back and dreamy with 'sha la la la' verse harmonies, there's something ultimately hopeful about 'I've Lost The Reason'. Plus, it's got some really great jazz flute.

'The White Noise Revisited' (Martin Carr) [Deep Cut]

Closing the album with a joyous piece of 1960s-influenced jangle pop is this song of two distinct parts. With verses referencing The Beatles as if through a fear filter (imagine John Lennon's 'boat on a river' heading into the heart of darkness), by the end, we're into a big sing-along (featuring Denim's Lawrence, no less!) supported by a proud solo trumpet. Being the incredible closing moments to an incredible album, it's easy to imagine this song as an alternative closer to *The Rolling Stones Rock and Roll Circus* concert. In fact, if The Stones had ended with this, it would've made for a much better show.

Optional Extras

In 2010, an expanded album edition was released containing the preceding EPs and all the single B-sides, including an off-putting number of 'Lazarus' remixes. Both EPs feel in some ways more structured than the album but still hint at psychedelia, jangly pop and dirty fuzz, throughout. The album-single B-sides are more in keeping with the album, but they take a step further into experimental noise and nightmare soundscapes, and also switch to acoustic/electric pop. There are also some different ideas, such as the ethereal backing on 'Tortoiseshell', the rocking-out of 'Sound Of Speed', and the shimmering 'Let Me Be Your Faith'. The band's Kinks influences are also more to the fore in 'Peachy Keen' and The Byrds' 'Eight Miles High' with 'Further' – definitely both worth seeking out. On the other hand, a demo tape of nearly all the album songs (plus some B-sides) which has been uploaded to the internet, is for hard-core fans only – badly recorded and probably only intended for reference purposes, it's unlikely to see a proper release, yet it's worth seeking out for the song sketch 'You're Not To Blame': which has some similarity to 'I Hang Suspended'.

1994 – The field is thrown open title?

1994 was the year that everything changed for Britpop. On Tuesday, 5 April, a single gunshot fired in Seattle, Washington, marking not only the tragic early end of the grunge movement's one great voice, but it also sounded the death knell for the American influence on British alternative music. Nirvana's Kurt Cobain was gone, and the field was wide open. Though various post-grunge bands would emerge, and the dark and strange *Vitalogy* by grunge's other big player – Pearl Jam – proved to be a massive hit, the writing was on the wall. The music press had already thrown itself behind *Select* magazine's new world (well, 'new British') order, and now – as a surprise last-minute addition to all the arty bands they'd been championing – five lads from Manchester arrived on Creation Records: full of optimism, massive choruses, and the desire to become the biggest band on the planet. The era of Oasis had begun.

The UK had experienced a depressing start to the year. In late February, the gruesome discovery of murders committed by Fred and Rosemary West at their Gloucester 'House of Horrors' meant the media would be full of little else for months to come. The sudden 12 May death of John Smith – leader of the opposition Labour Party – only added to the feeling that things could only get worse, and Wet Wet Wet's well-produced cover of The Troggs' 'Love Is All Around' (which hit number 1 on 29 May and stayed there for a staggering three months) only seemed to confirm it.

But change was in the air. The Labour Party election of 21 July placed onetime singer of the (thankfully) short-lived Ugly Rumours into a position of leadership. Tony Blair was now a single – albeit huge – step away from real power, and his New Labour party would soon go on to pull everything that was exciting, innovative and forward-thinking about domestic culture under its umbrella of Cool Britannia.

But that was a way down the road yet. John Major's Conservative government still had some distance left to run, and their sights were firmly set on the British alternative to the alternative – rave culture – which in November found itself stymied with the passing of the Criminal Justice and Public Order Act 1994. One month later – and despite The Prodigy's earlier attempts through *Music for the Jilted Generation* to keep the scene alive – the nail was driven firmly into rave's coffin, with the release of the second and final Stone Roses album: the perhaps underrated but still limp and knackered *Second Coming*.

Grunge was dead, and rave culture was in terminal decline. But did the new wave of the new wave really have what it took to take their place? Yes. Yes, it did.

The albums chosen to represent 1994 really are some of the best of the Britpop genre. With key albums by Blur, Oasis and Pulp each delivering a flush of real success for the bands, this was the last year when Britpop could really be considered as alternative or indie. You could practically hear the champagne corks popping.

Key Album: Pulp – His 'N' Hers (1994)

Personnel:
Jarvis Cocker: vocals, school piano, Vox Marauder guitar, EMS Synthi A
Russell Senior: Fender Stratocaster guitar, violin, bowed bass
Candida Doyle: Farfisa Compact Professional II organ, Stylophone 350S, Korg
Trident II, Fender Rhodes, Wurlitzer piano, Hohner clavinet, Steinway grand piano
Nick Banks: drums, percussion, treated cymbals, timpani, fire extinguisher
Steve Mackey: Fender Jazz Bass
Recording Sessions
July 1992: 'Babies' at Island Records Fallout Shelter, London
July 1993: 'Lipgloss' at Britannia Row Studios, London
October 1993-February 1994: The rest of the album (plus overdubs/remixes) at
Britannia Row Studios, London
Producer: Ed Buller
Record label: Island
Chart position: UK: 9
Release date: 18 April 1994

Pete: Not yet the household-name heroes they would become; this is the
record that does all the groundwork for Pulp. It's the opening shot of three
records that pretty much sum up the entire Britpop experience.

Matt: Unless you were really in the know, you probably hadn't heard much
Pulp by 1994, but all that was about to change. Having Jarvis Cocker as a
frontman – who seemed happy to turn up anywhere and had a view on pretty
much everything – didn't hurt. Plus, the band also had a collection of great
songs and a sound that was now in fashion. As a result, they quickly became a
staple feature in the music press.

The Band

Jarvis Cocker initially formed Pulp in Sheffield in 1978, and after some initial
interest from John Peel, many of the original members left for university,
leaving Cocker to find new players and record an unsuccessful debut mini-
album in 1983. Another incarnation of the band was formed shortly afterwards
that included Russell Senior. Further lineup changes followed, as well as
limited musical releases, including a not-well-received follow-up album.
Despite this, by 1989, the band – now including Doyle, Banks and Mackey –
had stabilised, and they were ready to record their third album: which, once
completed, sat on the shelf until 1992.
    In the meantime, the mainstream press started to notice the band, which
increased in line with the rise of Britpop. In 1995, tour manager Mark Webber
joined on guitar, the single 'Common People' was released (reaching number
2), and Pulp burst into the popular imagination by filling in for The Stone
Roses as Glastonbury headliners, pushing their fifth album *A Different Class* to

huge success. In 1996, Cocker achieved worldwide notoriety by invading the stage during Michael Jackson's *BRIT Awards* performance, and the following year, Senior left the band. There was a long delay in producing a new album (eventually released in 2008) due to Cocker struggling with drug addiction and a relationship breakup. Despite some limited touring and being well-received, the band withdrew from public life for the next two years. They released a new album in 2001, but the audience had moved on, and after limited touring, Pulp again went on hiatus, with Cocker becoming a solo artist.

In 2010, Pulp announced their reformation for a series of gigs – including festivals – throughout 2011. This reformation continued into 2012, culminating in the release of previously-unreleased tracks at the beginning of 2013 before the band once again went on hiatus, and Cocker returned to his solo work.

The Album

His 'N' Hers was Pulp's fourth album in what had already been a remarkably long – albeit not particularly successful – sixteen-year career (Think about it, that's longer than Blur and Oasis put together). With an almost-definitive lineup now locked in place, and a style that had moved away from the uni-serious or funky style of the previous decade, Pulp were now firing on all cylinders, and both they and their label, knew it: recruiting producer Ed Buller (who appears to have worked on this in the midst of Suede's masterpiece *Dog Man Star*). Released one week before Blur's *Parklife* (and, sadly, overshadowed by that record's phenomenal success), *His 'N' Hers* is still an absolute masterpiece of a different type of Britpop – an earthier, more kitchen-sink approach, additionally drawing on 1970s/1980s sounds, which might've been seedy and voyeuristic, but were also startling in their ability to transcend the mundane, and *stun*. Although this album wouldn't be the one to make Pulp and their unique frontman Jarvis Cocker into household names, it brought them a giant's-step closer.

'Joyriders' (Lyrics: Jarvis Cocker; Music: Pulp)

Straight in without even drawing breath, 'Joyriders' is an aggressive album introduction, arching an eyebrow at those kids who hang outside your house, causing a ruckus on a Saturday night. It also has a genuinely disturbing edge in its tale of a girl being taken to a reservoir. Despite a great instrumental break from keyboardist Candida Doyle and guitarist Russell Senior, this is still the album's shortest song and lays the ground for the album as a whole.

'Lipgloss' (Lyrics: Jarvis Cocker; Music: Pulp) [Single]

This is Pulp at their funkiest, throwing out awesome guitar licks over a disco verse before kicking into a more by-the-numbers chorus. When released as a single in November 1993, it narrowly caught the top 50: a sterling achievement for the band at the time, with greater yet to come.

'Acrylic Afternoons' (Lyrics: Jarvis Cocker; Music: Pulp)

Offering a genuinely spooky introduction (special note should be made of Doyle's keyboards) followed by a semi-disco rhythm, we are delivered an unsettling backdrop against which Cocker switches between a breathless pant and an excited whinny, singing about lying under the kitchen table in the afternoon, as kids 'play outside, and wait for their mothers to finish with lovers'. Should such subject matter be *this* disturbing? Perhaps it should.

'Have You Seen Her Lately?' (Lyrics: Jarvis Cocker; Music: Pulp)

Unusually, Cocker appears to struggle a bit with the vocal in the early stages of this song. It's a tale of a destructive relationship that should've probably been a B-side. But it does include the excellent lines:

> You're not his mother
> And you're not sister and brother
> He's not even your lover
> He's just a piece of luggage that you should throw away

'Babies' (Lyrics: Jarvis Cocker; Music: Pulp) [Single]

Although this is the band at their most pop, it's still Pulp. So, rather than a tale of boy-meets-girl, this is a tale of boy-spies-on-girl-from-a-wardrobe. It is, of course, brilliant. Originally released as a single back in 1992, the song still found its way onto the record, and a remixed version hit number 19 when released as part of the *Sisters* EP a month after the album's release. Pulp in the top 20? Unthinkable. It might've gestated for three years, but 'Babies' gave Pulp the blueprint that would propel them into the mainstream with the following album *Different Class*.

'She's a Lady' (Lyrics: Jarvis Cocker; Music: Pulp)

Unapologetically borrowing heavily from Gloria Gaynor's 'I Will Survive', this gothic slab of Eurodisco is a tale of lost love and its aftermath. Verse two has an interesting excursion into what could possibly be termed, rap. Thankfully, this section is short but, surprisingly, necessary.

'Happy Endings' (Lyrics: Jarvis Cocker; Music: Pulp)

Kicking off with lush (or perhaps sickly) synths and guitar swells, this feels in a peculiar way like it's been pulled straight out of the great American songbook. A well-worn tale of love-lost and hope for the future, if stripped of its Pulp instrumentation, The Carpenters could've easily delivered it to dazzling effect.

'Do You Remember The First Time?' (Lyrics: Jarvis Cocker; Music: Pulp) [Single]

The album's second single (released on 21 March) hit number 33, which seems inexplicably low for such a standout song, but it was Pulp's first foray into the top 40. There were plenty more to come. Weaving a tale loosely based on Cocker losing his virginity – and all the mental anguish that comes with such a seminal moment in a young man's life – it's widely regarded as one of Pulp's greatest songs. Notable mention should be made of Mark Webber, who helped write elements of the song – not yet a full-time band member, he soon would be: completing what is now considered the classic, definitive Pulp lineup.

'Pink Glove' (Lyrics: Jarvis Cocker; Music: Pulp)

This is essentially what it sounds like when Cocker gets put in the friend zone. It could've been kind of spiteful, but it's actually quite a heartbreaking and heartfelt understanding of what people will do to make a significant other happy. A driving track with a scatting and ranting vocal, unfortunately, the song kind of runs out of puff two-thirds of the way through.

'Someone Like The Moon' (Lyrics: Jarvis Cocker; Music: Pulp)

Built around a childlike, attention-all-passengers keyboard line and intricate instrument layering, this song is a beautifully put-together piece, but is also the album's weakest song. But it does allow a moment to breathe before the record's closing statement.

'David's Last Summer' (Lyrics: Jarvis Cocker; Music: Pulp) [Deep Cut]

The odd thing is, if this had been released in 1997, it would've essentially been the perfect kiss-off to the Britpop glory days. Perfectly summing up long-lost youthful summers where tents were pitched in gardens and the future felt like a foreign land, there's a certain film-like quality at play: 'And as we came out of the water, we sensed a certain movement in the air, and we both shivered slightly and ran to collect our clothes' (If you didn't experience that in your late-teens, you probably studied and did well in life). One of Pulp's most narrative and Bowie-like songs (something that would find its more natural home on their next album), it's remarkably up-tempo for an album closer , and has a crooning chorus, funk break and an epic ending. Hazy, lazy and slightly disturbing, at just over seven minutes, it doesn't outstay its welcome but does take the opportunity to stretch its legs as the autumn chill descends.

Optional Extras

The deluxe version of *His 'N' Hers* was released in 2012, containing B-sides, demos, radio sessions and an EP from the period. The demos have the classic Pulp sound, with 'The Boss' standing out as one of the fastest, punkiest numbers they ever attempted and offers something a bit different to what you'd expect. 'Your Sister's Clothes' (from *The Sisters EP*) features a great chorus, and a descending violin line coupled with repetitive cycling organ and piano phrases. The remaining EP and single B-sides all have their own charm,

Above: Inspiral Carpets were linked to the growing Madchester scene. Formed in 1983, they split at the height of Britpop.

Below: Blur - leaders of the Britpop genre and one of the first bands to move away from the classic Britpop 'sound'.

Left: *Life* is usually considered as Inspiral Carpets' debut and is indebted to post-punk and 1960s garage, with the strong backing of Farfisa/Hammond Organ. (*Mute*)

Right: The La's eponymous and only studio album is a mixture of Merseyside mysticism and trademark 'rattle and roll'. (*Go!*)

Left: Happy Mondays' part-indie/part house music third album is by far their most successful record and defining statement. (*Factory*)

Right: *30 Something* is lyrically smart and ties Carter USM's message to some exceptionally catchy buzz-saw masterpieces. (*Rough Trade*)

CARTER
■ THE UNSTOPPABLE SEX MACHINE ■
30 SOMETHING

leisure.
blur

Left: *Leisure* is a product of its time, largely aping the popular baggy and Madchester sounds. It's a group finding its feet. (*Food*)

Right: *Screamadelica* is an album for the people - completely impossible to define stylistically, it has something for everyone. (*Creation*)

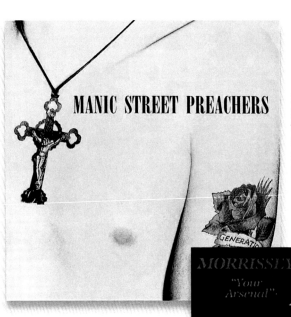

MANIC STREET PREACHERS

Left: With The Manics' own signature blend of glam/rock/ trash, *Generation Terrorists* was intended by the band to be the greatest rock album ever made. (*Columbia*)

Right: *Your Arsenal* is a heavyweight piece of work, possibly Morrissey's greatest solo effort, flitting between styles with enviable ease. (*HMV*)

Left: *Back in Denim* is the brainchild of one man. It incorporates glam, MOR, cheesy synths, flamenco and lashings of American rock. (Boy's Own Recordings)

Right: *Suede* describes living in London in the early 1990s. There's glitter, unapologetic drug use, filth, fury, dancing and death. (*Nude*)

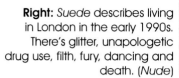

Left: *Modern Life Is Rubbish* is one of the first genuinely great Britpop releases, with songs that followed the tradition of The Kinks. (*Food*)

Right: *Giant Steps* is massively ambitious, fusing styles to produce an album to avoid if you have a hangover. (*Creation*)

Above: The Manic Street Preachers built a following due to their punk ethic, strong political views, immense self-belief and controversial behaviour.

Above: Through the 1990s, Radiohead gradually moved away from alternative rock/ Britpop to a radical new sound built on diverse instrumentation.

Above: Ocean Colour Scene plugged themselves into Britpop with such force that they leapt straight into the mainstream without passing go.

Above: Suede offered Bowie-esque glamour and a stark contrast to the dirt, sweat and grubbiness of Madchester, Grebo and Shoegaze.

PULP. HIS 'N' HERS.

Left: *His 'n' Hers* is a different type of Britpop – a kitchen-sink approach, drawing on 1970s/1980s sounds, which transcend the mundane. (*Island*)

Right: Blur's lengthy third album is quite rightly one of the defining and best-selling albums of the entire Britpop movement. (*Food*)

oasis *Definitely Maybe*

blur
PARKLIFE

Left: *Definitely Maybe* is an early high point for both Oasis and Britpop, becoming the fastest-selling album in UK history. (*Creation*)

Right: *Elastica* was a post-punk blast with songs of sex and suggestion, simultaneously jagged, smooth, angular and melodic. (*Deceptive*)

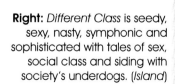

Left: *(What's The Story) Morning Glory?* was mostly written on acoustic guitar, leading to it being a much more artistic and crafted affair than its predecessor. (*Creation*)

Right: *Different Class* is seedy, sexy, nasty, symphonic and sophisticated with tales of sex, social class and siding with society's underdogs. (*Island*)

Left: *The It Girl* features vignettes on the doldrums of suburbia and movie references backed by an indie-rock racket. (*Indolent*)

Right: *Everything Must Go* brought The Manics the success that they had previously dreamt of, but it came at a heart-breakingly high price. (*Epic*)

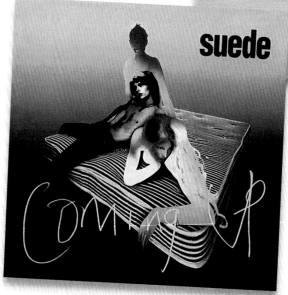

Left: With Butler gone, Suede aimed their sights firmly at the public's pop jugular and the band set out to make their own version of a Britpop record in *Coming Up*. (*Nude*)

Right: With *Blur*, out went the oompah and the oi's and in came noisy guitar aggression plus emotional sensitivity and fragility. (*Food*)

Left: *OK Computer* delivered a mighty wake-up call to Britpop using a template that continues to dominate music. (*Parlophone, Capitol*)

Right: *Urban Hymns* is widely accepted as the zenith of The Verve's artistic abilities. Not bad, considering it shouldn't really exist. (*Hut*)

Above: Pulp formed in 1978 and, with the rise of Britpop, the band found mainstream success with their disco-influenced pop-rock.

Above: Oasis's sound matured from the Madchester stereotype into something with greater rock and roll sensibilities that led to superstardom.

Above: Elastica's debut album was released to instant critical and commercial success on both sides of the Atlantic, despite accusations of plagiarism.

Above: Sleeper paid their dues as a Britpop opening act and, following a couple of incredibly successful years, became Britpop's first casualty.

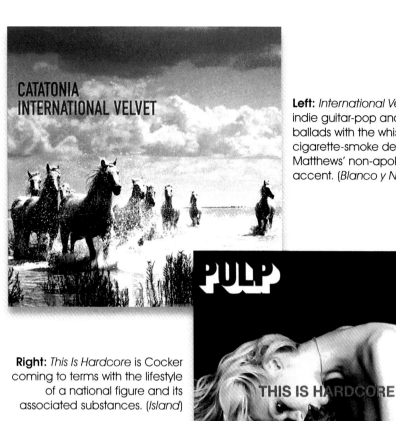

Left: *International Velvet* mixes indie guitar-pop and tearjerker ballads with the whiskey-and-cigarette-smoke delivery of Matthews' non-apologetic Welsh accent. (*Blanco y Negro*)

Right: *This Is Hardcore* is Cocker coming to terms with the lifestyle of a national figure and its associated substances. (*Island*)

Left: *The Good Will Out* - a huge slab of orchestral rock and roll balladeering about breaking up and moving forward. (*Hut*)

Right: *Performance And Cocktails* is an album of world-weary wisdom, acoustic ballads and up-tempo rock about the mundane. (*V2*)

Left: *13* is another musical reinvention with ambient noise-filled experimental soundscapes of electronica, Americana, noise and pop. (*Food, Parlophone*)

Right: *The Man Who* saw Travis change tack from glam-infused rock to classic songwriting, ballads, introspection and heartbreak. (*Independiete*)

Above: The Bluetones brought 'a little charm and a lot of style' while exploring a lighter side of Britpop and introducing a West Coast influence to their music.

Below: Despite the Britpop party winding down, Catatonia had a classic Britpop album on their hands and wanted in to the movement.

and perhaps the 'Love Is In The Air' horror synth of 'His 'N' Hers' or the hypnotising 'Deep Fried In Kelvin' could've suited the album well. 'Razzmatazz' (included on the album's American versions) was also included on the *Intro – The Gift Recordings* compilation album of singles released on the Gift Records label throughout 1992, which also features an earlier mix of 'Babies'. These songs offer an insight into the band's direction and the songs that would end up on *His 'N' Hers*. It's definitely worth tracking down.

Key Album: Blur – Parklife (1994)

Personnel:

Damon Albarn: lead and backing vocals, keyboards, Hammond organ, Moog synthesizer, melodica, vibraphone, recorder, programming

Graham Coxon: guitar, backing vocals, clarinet, saxophone, percussion

Alex James: bass; vocals on 'Far Out'

Dave Rowntree: drums, percussion, programming

Recording Sessions: Maison Rouge Studios; August-September 1993: 'Parklife', 'Jubilee', 'Badhead', 'Clover Over Dover', 'Girls & Boys', 'Bank Holiday'; December 1993–February 1994: The rest of the album.

'To The End' recorded at RAK Studios; produced by Stephen Hague, John Smith and Blur.

Note: Many of the songs had been demoed before sessions began (mostly at Matrix Studios, London) and some of these recordings were used as the basis for the album tracks.

Producers: Stephen Street; Stephen Hague, John Smith and Blur

Record label: Food

Chart position: UK: 1

Release date: 25 April 1994

> Pete: The summer of 1994 and *Parklife* are completely combined in my memory. I have memories of walking for miles and miles across the fields, listening to a taped copy over and over and over again. Amazingly, I don't think I ever bought a proper copy until well into the next decade.

> Matt: If I had to name one band and album that for me is Britpop, *Parklife* would be the go-to. An incredible collection of songs that sound of the time but also fresh.

The Album

Blur's lengthy third album is quite rightly one of the defining albums of the entire Britpop movement. Released only weeks after Kurt Cobain's death, it picked up on themes of Englishness from where its predecessor, *Modern Life Is Rubbish* left off, building on them to effectively create a zeitgeist in Blur's own image, rather than that of Suede. Where Blur's sophomore effort had been largely a disappointment in terms of sales (and the label considered this continuing musical direction to be a mistake), the emergence of Britpop as a media trend meant that *Parklife* was in a prime position to hit the ground running, and propelled the Food label to huge status: soon to be bought out by major, EMI. With four hit singles, the album went four times platinum in the UK in its year of release, making Blur mainstream stars. The album cover of greyhounds racing at Walthamstow Stadium became an image that transcended the band and acted as a proxy image for the entire era. Blur may have hit number 1, but in mixing Kinksian gentility with a hint of modern ladishness, is it possible they kicked down the door so aggressively that they later wouldn't know how to put it back on its hinges?

'Girls & Boys' (Music: Blur; Lyrics: Albarn) [Single]
This top-5 hit single released on 7 March was inspired by Damon Albarn's holiday in Spain with his girlfriend, Justine Frischmann (more on her later) and the antics of the young British holidaymakers he witnessed there. An out-and-out disco romp, Alex James' greatest-ever bass line, a siren keyboard and (Dave Rowntree's replacement) the drum machine propel the song. The chorus is so damn catchy, it could itself have been picked up by an unprotected Spanish dalliance.

'Tracy Jacks' (Music: Blur; Lyrics: Albarn)
One of Albarn's first Ray-Davies-like character songs (a device that became omnipresent in the following years) tells the tale of a cross-dressing middle-aged civil servant who gets bored with his middle-class life, and bulldozes his own home on a Tuesday morning. How often have we heard that tale? It sounds silly, and it possibly is, but it pumps itself unrelentingly into your brain, and has remained a firm fan favourite: so much so that it was used to promote the band in America.

'End Of A Century' (Music: Blur; Lyrics: Albarn) [Single]
The album's first moment of melancholy beauty (and Blur's greatest since 'For Tomorrow'), Coxon's jaunty guitar pumps are offset by the resignation with which the protagonists are slowly losing the currency of youth. As the album's fourth single, it reached 19 in November 1994. Most agree that 'This Is A Low' would've been a better choice, but despite what 'End Of A Century' claims, it's still something special.

'Parklife' (Music: Blur; Lyrics: Albarn) [Single]
The hit single of *Parklife* was 'Parklife'. Surprisingly narrated by Phil Daniels – the then largely-forgotten star of the mod classic *Quadrophenia* – it's a first-person narrative about all the things seen from the window of a London flat. Though Coxon later claimed it wasn't meant to be a celebration of Englishness but to be sarcastic about it, the genie was out of the bottle. Despite

a memorable video, it didn't perform as well as 'Girls & Boys' in the charts, reaching number 10. But for British youth in the summer of 1994, it was as ubiquitous as Wet Wet Wet was proving to be for their parents.

'Bank Holiday' (Music: Blur; Lyrics: Albarn)
This is a stop-start punk thrash that constantly threatens to fall apart, and elevated by Coxon's guitar and pedal skills, is a joyous, drunken blowout that perfectly captures the wish-I-hadn't-drunk-that hedonism of a British bank holiday.

'Badhead' (Music: Blur; Lyrics: Albarn)
It's time to break out the ballad. A perfect counterpoint to 'Bank Holiday', 'Badhead' sees Damon regretting not only the excesses of the night before, but of all existence in general: 'I might as well just grin and bear it/Because it's not worth the trouble of an argument'. The song also showcases his exceptional arrangement skills: weaving brass, keyboard samples, mellotron and a bared soul.

'The Debt Collector' (Music: Blur; Lyrics: Albarn)
A busked circus-like instrumental much like those on *Modern Life Is Rubbish*, this serves as a palate cleanser, and by rights should've been the album's central point, instead of...

'Far Out' (James)
This somewhat throwaway space odyssey penned by Alex James is totally misplaced as the album's central point. Listing the solar system with a queasy feel and continuing with the circus theme, induces mixed reactions: it's either a bit of fun that doesn't outstay its welcome, *or* it should never have gotten off the B-side list. Either way, the album's huge success meant that 'Far Out' propelled James as a songwriter, and he later went on to further Britpop success with side projects including Me Me Me and Fat Les.

'To The End' (Music: Blur; Lyrics: Albarn) [Single]
Released as a single in May, reaching number 16, this song describes a couple unsuccessfully trying to overcome a relationship bad patch. Featuring lush orchestral strings and French backing vocals by Lætitia Sadier from Stereolab, alternate versions were created that boosted the foreign-language elements for the European market. The song presents Blur at their most romantic, despite the doomed lyric content and the almost 1960s-comedy-soundtrack vibe. Oddly, the song was produced not by Stephen Street but Stephen Hague in order to achieve the epic soundtrack feel.

'London Loves' (Music: Blur; Lyrics: Albarn)
A mid-tempo 'boy/girl-in-London' track, 'London Loves' still shows off some truly off-kilter guitar work from Coxon in full Robert-Fripp-mode. Albarn's

repeated insistence that there's some mystery to be found in speeding cars and speeding hearts is never really explained, but excellent use is made of a radio traffic update in the outro. You can't get much more British than that!

'Trouble In The Message Centre' (Music: Blur; Lyrics: Albarn) [Deep Cut]

Mixing Gary Numan, Magazine, XTC, a Kinks-like chorus and a hint of McCartney's 'Temporary Secretary', this track is cut from a very different cloth to the rest of the album. Call centres, managers and the whole banal world of the British office are here summed up in song form: long before Ricky Gervais finally impaled it in the early-2000s.

'Clover Over Dover' (Music: Blur; Lyrics: Albarn)

With Damon's harpsichord intro and Graham's a fiddly-as-you-like riff, this is a 'cautionary tale' of young love (and possibly suicide) at the White Cliffs of Dover. The song's weaving of British imagery means it can easily be reimagined as the true soundtrack over the closing credits of the movie *Quadrophenia*.

'Magic America' (Music: Blur; Lyrics: Albarn)

Another character song, this time being the tale of Bill Barrett and his simple dream of moving to America. This is Blur's ridiculing reaction to their experiences in the USA, and sums up how Albarn learned the hard way that he didn't really want 'to live in magic America with all the magic people' after their difficult US tour. Though the title offered a useful mocking metaphor for what Britpop was against, this track could easily be written off as filler, despite an enjoyable 1970s-sitcom keyboard solo.

'Jubilee' (Music: Blur; Lyrics: Albarn)

Can this album rock harder than 'Bank Holiday'? Yes, it can. 'Jubilee' – a character song about someone born in 1977 and named Jubilee (As if that were really a thing? Albarn was surely just trying to cram in as much British imagery as possible at this point) – it tells the tale of a young layabout having a hard time with his dad. The brass section is hilariously upbeat, bright and joyous, offering a counterpoint to Coxon's grungy guitar, producing a Roxy Music or Mott The Hoople feel. There's also a fun computer-game solo.

'This Is A Low' (Music: Blur; Lyrics: Albarn) [Single]

This is the standout moment of the entire album, and the point that allows it to evolve from Britpop artefact to modern classic. It weaves all of the album's themes into one sweeping, melancholy and satisfying high point of lowness. Oh, and did we say that you can't get much more British than a radio *traffic update?* We were wrong: this lyric is pretty heavily dependent on a shipping forecast tour around the British Isles – apparently only struck upon due to writer's block, this was a happy accident of conceptual genius.

'Lot 105' (Music: Blur; Lyrics: Albarn)

The album's second instrumental (and another that began life in a soundcheck) is a final return to the fairground theme. Though ultimately unnecessary (Why didn't the album end with ' This Is A Low'?), it does offer an enjoyable outing for Albarn's organ playing before the band join in to bring the house down one last time. Despite going on a bit too long, it rounds proceedings off nicely, acting as a fine counterpoint to 'The Debt Collector'.

Optional Extras

The *Parklife* deluxe remastered version was released in 2012, featuring B-sides and a few rarities. Many of the B-sides are throwaway or even plain disappointing, including more circus-themed instrumentals, a *comedy* rockabilly ('Red Necks') and a jazz interlude ('Beard') – It's been said that the band were already writing for the next album, and weren't willing to use any songs with genuine potential, for B-sides. But there are some gems to be found from the earlier songs. 'Magpie' is a nice Blur-rocking-out number leftover from *Modern Life Is Rubbish*, and while it features no surprises, it does tick a lot of boxes with a slightly psychedelic chorus and lyrics largely by William Blake. 'Peter Panic' is very popular in fan lists and is another character song that sits between early-Bowie and Sid-Barrett-era Pink Floyd. Meanwhile, 'Theme From An Imaginary Film' is an interesting piece originally planned for the Steven Berkoff film *Decadence*. Starting life as an instrumental, words and melody were added on request but ultimately were not liked, leading to its B-side status. It might've been better left as an instrumental.

Edwyn Collins – Gorgeous George (1994)

Recording Sessions: November 1993-April 1994
Producer: Edwyn Collins
Record label: Setanta
Chart position: UK: 8
Release date: 1 July 1994

Pete: Here's an album overshadowed by a hit single if ever there was one. 'A Girl Like You' was absolutely everywhere! You couldn't avoid the damn thing. It got pretty annoying, to be honest, and put me off exploring Edwyn Collins until years after.

Matt: If ever there was an artist synonymous with a song, it's Edwyn Collins. You just couldn't escape this song. It was on pretty much all the radio stations and TV all the time. Although it was Collins' lottery ticket, it probably was a bit of a curse. Some potential fans would've already been sick of the sound of him, whilst others would be disappointed by what a different beast the album actually was.

The Album

As the former frontman of 1970s/1980s Scottish band Orange Juice, Edwyn Collins had experienced some chart success with their single 'Rip It Up' in 1983. But nothing could've prepared the man or his public for the worldwide smash that was 'A Girl Like You', which went on to storm the airwaves for years to come. If that's the only song you know – and it's fair to say that's probably the case for many – then its parent album may not be what you're expecting. Being a more MOR listening experience with plenty of acoustic moments and soul flourishes (the electric piano player should take a bow all of their own), the album weaves all of its elements to make a satisfying and very Britpop experience. However, this is an album that doesn't want to be pigeonholed, and its most telling moments come in its bookends: 'The Campaign For Real Rock' being a laid-back call to arms, while the closer 'This Music Won't Take You Higher', actively baits the most popular alternative styles of the preceding five years.

Standout track: 'Moron'

Key Album: Oasis – Definitely Maybe (1994)

Personnel:
Liam Gallagher: lead vocals, tambourine
Noel Gallagher: guitars, backing vocals, bass, piano, production
Paul 'Bonehead' Arthurs: rhythm and acoustic guitar, piano, production
Paul 'Guigsy' McGuigan: bass, production
Tony McCarroll: drums, production
Recording Sessions: December 1993: 'Bring It On Down' single sessions – The Pink Museum Studios, Liverpool. Producers: Noel Gallagher, Mark Coyle and Oasis. (Includes the recording of 'Supersonic')
January 1994: Aborted album sessions, Monnow Valley Studios, Monmouth. Producer: David Batchelor. Mixed at Olympic Studios, London. Only 'Slide Away' is known to have been used on the album; many (if not all) other tracks being re-recorded.
February-March 1994: Album recorded at Sawmill Studios, Cornwall. Initial mix and additional recording at Eden Studios, London. Producers: Noel Gallagher, Mark Coyle and Oasis
April-May 1994: Additional production/mixing/vocal recording by Owen Morris at Loco studios, Caerleon, South Wales; Matrix Atudios, Fulham, London. Mastered at Clear Studios, Manchester
Producers: Owen Morris, Oasis, Mark Coyle, David Batchelor
Record label: Creation
Chart position: UK: 1, USA: 58
Release date: 29 August 1994

Pete: Oasis arrived so suddenly and so forcefully that at first, I didn't realise they were new. Their rise wasn't just attention-grabbing; it was meteoric. In 1994/1995, it felt like they always had a new single out. Even if you weren't initially sure about them, they sucked you in.

Matt: It is amazing that Oasis managed to sort themselves out to release this. It could've so easily gone in the bin and the band disappear. Luckily, everyone involved persevered. Despite many imperfections, the songs absolutely shine through, on probably one of the strongest debuts in this book.

The Band

Manchester-based childhood friends Arthurs, McGuigan and McCarroll formed Rain in the late-1980s. Initially hiring Chris Hutton as singer, he was sacked and replaced by McGuigan's school friend Liam Gallagher in 1991. Liam's older brother Noel had spent two years as a member of the road crew for Inspiral Carpets, and asked to join his brother's band later that year to use the group as an outlet for his stockpile of songs. Under Noel's leadership, the band's sound matured from a Madchester stereotype into something with greater rock and roll sensibilities. In 1993, the band famously signed with Creation Records after Alan McGee caught them on a bill they shouldn't have even been playing on, and plans to record a debut album, commenced. Despite recording problems, the resultant album and singles proved to be incredibly successful. In 1995, 'Some Might Say' went to number 1; the band replaced drummer McCarroll with Alan White, and they moved on to the second album *(What's the Story) Morning Glory?*, which became a worldwide commercial success. Tension had been steadily growing between the brothers over the years, with split rumours consistently dogging the band. Following two era-defining nights at Knebworth in 1996, the Gallaghers – now fuelled by cocaine and celebrity – continued their quarrelling into recording sessions for their third album, *Be Here Now*: which sold spectacularly, but failed to meet critical expectation. In early-1999, Oasis began recording their fourth album but had to find replacements for McGuigan and Arthurs, who both left, forcing Noel to record their parts. By the end of the year, Colin 'Gem' Archer (formerly of Heavy Stereo) joined on guitar, followed by Andy Bell (from Ride) on bass. The band continued to record and release albums over the next few years, to mixed responses, while being plagued by incidents and ever-changing lineups (White leaving in 2004 to be replaced by Zak Starkey – son of The Beatles' Ringo Starr – who in 2008 was replaced by Chris Sharrock). In 2009, after a series of cancelled gigs, Noel Gallagher announced he was leaving, the remaining members continuing as Beady Eye, releasing two albums before disbanding in 2014. Liam Gallagher then moved on to a solo career, Bell rejoined Ride, and Archer and Sharrock joined Noel Gallagher's High Flying Birds which had formed in 2010. Although various Oasis projects (including a documentary and deluxe album sets) have been released over the last ten years (Liam and Noel now speaking somewhat fondly of each other), it still seems unlikely the band will reform.

The Album

If the creation of *Definitely Maybe* isn't already steeped in legend, it *should* be. Anyone who has heard the early mixes will know that the entire enterprise seemed doomed to fail, and the band – who'd gained so much ground with their first three singles – doomed to be consigned to the also-ran section of Britpop pub quizzes. But that wasn't to be. The tapes were heroically salvaged by producer Owen Morris, who carefully picked his way through a soup of badly-recorded noise, producing an album that went straight to number 1 and became the fastest-selling album in UK history (to that point). It was not undeserved, and *Definitely Maybe* serves as both an early high point for both Oasis and the story of Britpop – adding a much-needed level of guts and glory to what otherwise would've been a movement dominated by the arty-farty aping of sounds gone by. Other Britpop bands could rock, but few were going to roll with it or want superstardom more than Oasis.

'Rock 'N' Roll Star' (Noel Gallagher)

Nailing their colours firmly to the wall, the lead track sets out Oasis' plan in primary colours. They may be from the city where there's 'no easy way out', but – certainly in frontman Liam Gallagher – they're destined to be rock 'n' roll stars. It could almost be laughable if it wasn't delivered with such conviction that it actually all became true. Given the stacks of guitars that Owen Morris removed from original mixes, it may be a surprise to discover that there's still a *lot* left in this – the outro being particularly joyous with its squalling, swirling and spacey guitars, providing a backdrop for Liam to sneer 'Is this rock 'n' roll?' over.

'Shakermaker' (Noel Gallagher) [Single]

Originally released in June 1994 as the band's second single, this pretty much sets the template for Noel Gallagher's ability to – let's say – *borrow* things. A verse from 'I'd Like To Teach the World To Sing' here; a bit of 'Mr. Soft' from the Trebor advert there, plus a nod to his favourite secondhand record store (Sifters in Manchester), the overall effect is somewhat woozy psychedelia in the style of The Beatles. This is no surprise, really, given what later albums would produce. The song narrowly missed out on being the band's first top-10 single...

'Live Forever' (Noel Gallagher) [Single]

...which meant it was left to 'Live Forever' to carry the baton and hit the top 10 (at number 10) in August 1994, just a couple of weeks ahead of the album release. Originally written as a response to Nirvana's initially ironic 'I Hate

Myself And I Want To Die', the relentless optimism of 'Live Forever' meant it became one of the first Britpop anthems. Featuring high notes that Noel would have to later perform live, the song unusually begins with a (rare) Oasis drum solo: but not one that would necessarily bother the greats.

'Up In The Sky' (Noel Gallagher)
An up-tempo (for Oasis) record that probably should've been a single, this starts with a great lead riff from Noel, and some exciting layering from the rest of the band. The riff may get a bit annoying as the song progresses, but its feel-good factor is just remarkable.

'Columbia' (Noel Gallagher)
The album's second-longest song – a lengthy intro dragging it out to a stonking 6:17 – shows how good the band could be at producing mesmerising mid-tempo rock with big choruses. The line 'I can't tell you the way I feel/Because the way I feel is oh-so-new to me' is remarkably charming in its naivety, while the song includes one of Noel's more experimental solos hidden away around the halfway point.

'Supersonic' (Noel Gallagher) [Single]
The band's debut single – with a never-repeated Happy-Mondays-style vocal – is remarkable, as it wasn't even meant to exist, let alone kick off the career of the UK's most successful Britpop band. The plan had been to record 'Bring It On Down', but when the session wasn't fruitful, they decided to flesh out something they'd been jamming on during the warm-up. The song hit number 31 in April, and despite being from a completely different session, sits snugly on the album.

'Bring It On Down' (Noel Gallagher)
Finally recorded in a version the band were happy with, this is the album's fastest song, and – given the tempo range of most Oasis songs – it's little wonder that the band had been failing to record it when they hit upon 'Supersonic'. With Liam's unusually distorted vocals in verse two, the finished piece is a bit like being hit square in the face by a wall of pure Gallagher.

'Cigarettes & Alcohol' (Noel Gallagher) [Single]
Released as a single only six weeks after the album launch, this still managed to push its way further up the top 10, peaking at number 7 – a remarkable achievement, given that this was the fastest-selling album of all time upon release and everyone already had the song. But by this time, the Oasis juggernaut was unstoppable. A relentless, dirty, glam-rock ode to the working-class joys of booze, fags and narcotic abuse, this also proved to be another prime example of *borrowing* – this time from T. Rex, who had originally nabbed it from Chuck Berry – meaning a lot of people were suddenly making a

lot of money from Oasis. This is also the song from which Liam's often-mocked but never-bettered over-pronunciation derives.

'Digsy's Dinner' (Noel Gallagher)

The album's shortest song at just over two and a half minutes, and the most Britpop song they recorded, is also Oasis at their silliest. A song about band-friend Digsy's culinary speciality lasagne probably would've been better left as a B-side. But it does pick up a few points for including a piano solo. Plus, as previously stated, at least it's short.

'Slide Away' (Noel Gallagher) [Deep Cut]

From the short to the epic, this was clearly designed to be the album's farewell statement and a heartfelt farewell to Noel's then-girlfriend. However, rather than building in the bombast, you might expect, the song deploys a surprisingly baggy approach, building on its main groove in a way that feels as if the song is sliding away from the listener. Often quoted by fans as amongst the band's best songs, there are clearly better songs on the album. But that's just our opinion, which Noel's shout of 'Don't know, don't care' answers pretty succinctly.

'Married With Children' (Noel Gallagher)

The album waves goodbye with a chirpy acoustic campfire ditty that bemoans the joys of marital life, or indeed life with anyone, really. It's notable for Liam using a completely different singing style from the sneer he's famed for, and this one he never used again. With its final guitar trill, Oasis had left the building; the Creation label primed for the world stage, and immortality for the Gallagher brothers only one album away.

Optional Extras

The 'Whatever' single – released a few months after *Definitely Maybe* and eventually added to some issues of it as a bonus disc – was designed as an interim release before the follow-up album *(What's the Story) Morning Glory?*. It takes everything great about Oasis and filters it down to a classic single with 'I Am The Walrus'-style orchestration to fully give it a Beatles vibe. It also has better playing all-around. Accompanying the single was the adequate but enjoyable accordion-debuting '(It's Good) To Be Free' and the easily-missed acoustic song 'Half The World Away'. A beautiful, bittersweet, melancholy Noel-sung ballad with restrained organ accompaniment, it later became the theme song for the BBC sitcom *The Royle Family*. In 2014, the album's deluxe remastered version was released, with B-sides, demos, rarities and live songs. Highlights include 'Sad Song' (a similar acoustic number sung by Noel), which, despite the overly simple demo-tape title, is a real hidden gem that should've replaced 'Married With Children' on the album. Other songs of interest include the demo for 'Alive', which unexpectedly has a Foo Fighters 'Everlong' feel to it, despite being written first and featuring a slight Morrissey aspect to Liam's restrained vocal. With a worked out ending, this could've easily been great for the album or as a sterling B-side in non-demo form.

Shed Seven – Change Giver (1994)

Recording sessions: 1993-1994
Producer: Jessica Corcoran
Record label: Polydor
Chart position: UK: 16
Release date: 3 September 1994
Lyrics: Rick Witter; Music: Shed Seven

Pete: Shed Seven are absolute Britpop stalwarts. Though never really an album band, if this book concentrated on singles, they'd be on every second page. I hold a special place in my heart for them, as Rick Witter once gave me a cigarette when they played our hometown and we got past the hopeless security to meet them backstage.

Matt: Shed Seven are *the* Britpop singles band. This is backed up by how their 1999 compilation *Going For Gold: The Greatest Hits* reached a higher chart position than any of their other albums. All this despite Ritter looking like he was 'Riverdancing' in practically every music video.

The Album

There's a fascinating theory that if *Change Giver* had been released a fortnight earlier, Shed Seven could've taken the limelight instead of the Gallagher brothers. Being – somewhat unfairly – everyone's fifth-favourite Britpop band, Shed Seven's solid debut still packs a real template-defining punch for the genre and has aged exceptionally well. A bit baggy, a bit rocky, a bit Smiths-y (see single 'Mark'), and with soaring choruses and four (count 'em!) top-40 singles to show for the album, Shed Seven would reach greater commercial heights as Britpop's star continued to ascend – even if they were never given the credit they deserve for being the creators of some of the 1990s most classic singles.

Standout track: 'Dolphin'.

The Lightning Seeds – Jollification (1994)

Recording sessions: 1993-1994
Producers: Ian Broudie, Simon Rogers
Record label: Epic
Chart position: UK: 12
Release date: 5 September 1994
Written by: Ian Broudie, expect 'Lucky You' (Ian Broudie, Terry Hall), 'Feeling Lazy' (Ian Broudie, Ian McNabb) and 'My Best Day' (Ian Broudie, Alison Moyet)

Pete: I absolutely loved The Lightning Seeds around this time. 'Perfect' really lived up to its name as far as pop singles went. When they did it on *Top Of The Pops,* I got real tingles down my spine and always felt it was underrated next to the other singles on offer.

Matt: This is the point where The Lightning Seeds move from a solo studio project to something much bigger. Broudie had the songs to do it; he just needed to put together a band.

The Album

Following on from the phenomenal *Sense* album, it's fair to say that *Jollification* is a honing of the *perfect pop* template, or – more unfairly – just more of the same. While much of the shimmering production value and the incredible pop choruses remain in evidence, this album is marked more by drawing on a wider set of influences. 'Feeling Lazy' is clearly influenced by The Small Faces' 'Lazy Sunday Afternoon', while 'Telling Tales' is a gentler version of Don McLean's 'Vincent'. It also seems hard to imagine that 'Perfect' hadn't been written after listening to Lou Reed. But what's really surprising is the number of times the album leans into dance music, with many songs incorporating hazy echoes of acid house, while 'Punch And Judy' allows its emotional core to give way to a heavy breakbeat element. It's a wonderful album, and too often overlooked as a key building block of Britpop.

Standout track: 'Change'

Suede – Dog Man Star (1994)

Recording sessions: 22 March-26 July 1994
Producer: Ed Buller
Record label: Nude
Chart position: UK: 3
Release date: 10 October 1994
Writers: Brett Anderson and Bernard Butler

Pete: Despite how much Suede were considered essential-listening at this point, *Dog Man Star* just didn't grab me. I know that makes me a heathen and that I don't deserve to even speak its name, but look what else other bands had offered up since Suede's debut! Was it my fault if lower-hanging fruit had turned my head? Of course I later cottoned on.

Matt: This is such a huge progression from the first album, and has some great songs, but there's something about it that's a little bit flat. Unfortunately, everyone knew of the band's problems, and I'm not sure if that tainted my view of the album. Imagine what it could've been like if the band were all on board and really going for it.

The Album

Magnificently out-of-step with all the other 1994 records – and as a result, often cruelly overlooked – the band took their debut's raw building blocks, and grafted them to the most beautiful, epic, and frankly, pretentious ideas they could find. Though this was guitarist Bernard Butler's last outing with the band – as simmering tensions between him and singer Brett Anderson finally came to a head in every aspect of the band and the recording process – it was one hell of a parting statement and set him up for some wonderful future collaborations. As for Suede themselves, greater commercial success may have been waiting, but *Dog Man Star* would be their artistic high-water mark.

Standout track: 'Heroine'.

Ash – Trailer (1994)

Recording sessions: March-June 1994
Producers: Ash, Tim Russell, Marc Waterman
Record label: Infectious
Chart position: UK: 143
Release date: 18 October 1994
Writers: Tim Wheeler, Ash

Pete: The thing about Ash, is they were essentially the same age as us but seemed to have it all. They could really play, they could write brilliant songs, and they'd been touring while doing their exams. It was hard to not look in the mirror and think, 'What am I doing wrong with my life?'.

Matt: Ash always had a punk DIY ethos – High School band, practised in a garage, self-financed, and their music definitely more rock than indie. Other bands had similar starts, but I always felt there was something about Ash that I could've done too.

The Album

This is not necessarily a great album or even an album at all (Is it an EP? A mini-album? A trailer?), but the debut offering from the Northern Irish trio is by far the noisiest and possibly the least-Britpop record you'll read about in this book. But it showed that bandleader Tim Wheeler had a quite-extraordinary talent when it came to melody, even if it *is* over-squalling guitars and rock drums. Just imagine if you were sixteen years old and discovered you had the ability to write 'Jack Names The Planets', 'Uncle Pat' or the sublime 'Petrol'? Would you use that power for good?

Standout track: 'Petrol'.

Dodgy – Homegrown (1994)

Recording sessions: Late-1993 or early-1994, Rockfield Studios, Monmouth, Wales; The Lab Studio, Liverpool
Producers: Hugh Jones; Ian Broudie (Tracks 2, 5 and 9)
Record label: A&M
Chart position: UK: 28
Release date: 24 October 1994

Pete: One of the great things about Britpop is that every area kind of had their own band. Dodgy – coming originally from Bromsgrove and Redditch – were ours! Whenever I think about them, I feel a touch of hometown pride, especially because – when it comes to singles – they totally knocked it out of the park in the 1990s.

Matt: Dodgy had great skill with multilayered harmonies, as the whole band could sing amazingly. I always think that gave them a unique edge compared to many of the other bands at the time.

The Album

Having built their following through the creation of their Dodgy Club scene in Kingston Upon Thames – well away from the Britpop drama playing out in central London – the Hounslow-three's sophomore album was a beautiful, sun-kissed affair that showed an exceptional talent for fashioning melodic pop by drawing together a vast array of influences (ranging from West-Coast pop to the psychedelia of *Sgt Pepper's...* and 'Itchycoo Park': a trick that also worked well for Crowded House). Standing the test of time partly due to superb co-production from pop-master (and chief Lightning Seed) Ian Broudie, *Homegrown* saw the band take a quantum-leap forward in songwriting that they would continue to better throughout the Britpop years. The album title was also a particularly good pun that played up both the Britpop scene and their extracurricular activities.

Standout track: 'Staying Out For The Summer'.

1995 – Chart battles! TV specials! A Band-Aid-style charity record created by all your favourite indie heroes!

1995 represented Britpop's true cultural high-water mark, with exciting new bands breaking through on what seemed like a daily basis. With Chris Evans joining BBC Radio One in April, it was now possible for *The Evening Session* to rack 'em up, and *The Breakfast Show* to knock 'em down by bringing new groups to huge audiences. This was Britpop's moment to go over the top, both in terms of entering the mainstream and in seemingly losing its marbles.

In a year when the Prime Minister finally got so bored with the sniping from his own benches about Europe, that he entered the Rose Garden and said, 'Come and have a go if you think you're hard enough' (Okay, maybe 'Put up or shut up' were the exact words used), for those that didn't follow the broadsheet soap opera of politics but did have their nose stuck in the *NME*, it was an incredible moment in what had till now been a drab and boring premiership.

Throughout the year, Oasis' successful gate-crashing of the Britpop party had built and built, culminating in early May with the first number-1 of the era (beating Blur, Suede and Pulp to the punch): 'Some Might Say'. The celebratory party – attended by Blur – witnessed the beginnings of a grubby war of words in the smudgy music press (largely due to a girl, rather than any particular chart placement), and despite Blur playing to 27,000 at Mile End Stadium in June, it was clear that the Gallagher brothers had gotten under Albarn's ultra-competitive skin, and touched a nerve.

As the country gently baked in a practically unprecedented heatwave, Albarn finally tired of Mancunians bumping his pint at Camden's Good Mixer, and resolved to do some bumping of his own – repeatedly moving the release date of Blur's latest single 'Country House', in order to make it collide with Oasis' second salvo from their new album: 'Roll With It'. With the date of 14 August locked in and the British media scrambling to cover the best silly-season story they'd had in ages, the Battle of Britpop had begun. It was time for the kids to choose a side. Were they with the working-class heroes Oasis or middle-class art-schoolers Blur?

Though presented by *NME* as a 'British Heavyweight Championship' (complete with mock poster), it was actually an unfair fight. Blur's massive fan base and previous sales figures placed them as the Goliath figure, and – in the real world – Goliath usually tramples all over David. Therefore it should perhaps have been no real surprise that Blur were ultimately victorious in securing the number-1 spot – helped by the BBC Two *Britpop Now* special aired that week with patrician Albarn presenting and playing 'Country House', while showcasing the cream of the crop of the UK's latest bands. (Oasis were noticeably absent by dint of not wanting to bother, while Suede didn't get a look-in due to Albarn's ongoing grudge).

Though a few egos were bruised along the way, this was a fight in which there were only winners. Blur had come out on top; Oasis found themselves with major-player status; a multitude of other bands were pulled from relative obscurity into prominence: thanks to the sudden press attention Britpop was gaining, and a lot of money was made right across the media.

Kudos should still go to all sides for contributing to *The Help Album* (organised by charity War Child to raise funds for war-stricken Bosnia and Herzegovina), which was recorded in a single day and released in September. However, when the dust settled, it all seemed a bit silly really.

What a year to be alive.

The 1995 Britpop explosion is marked in these pages by a mammoth number of releases that seemed too important to overlook. As a period of huge sales (see Elastica claim the title for fastest-selling debut only months after Oasis had claimed it) and even bigger tunes from brand new bands, it's also notable for how many founding-fathers were pulled along in its wake, giving the sense that Britpop was a genuine movement that incorporated a sense of history and cohesion.

Sleeper – Smart (1995)

Recording sessions: 1994
Producers: Paul Corkett, Sleeper, Ian Broudie (Track 3), Stephen Street (Mix)
Record label: Indolent
Chart position: UK: 5
Release date: 13 February 1995

Pete: Aaahh, finally the arrival of Sleeper into these pages! One of the greatest Britpop bands, in my opinion, a group that never seemed to flinch at the fact that pop music is at best a great euphoric adrenaline rush. Like everyone else, I had posters of Louise on my wall. I'm an adult now, though, so instead, I have a framed photo of her on my desk.

Matt: *Smart* always surprised me by how non-Britpop it was in places: often having a much harder alternative-rock edge. It's only Louise Wener's accent, delivery and subject matter that make it so quintessentially British and define the band, but it equally limited them at the same time.

The Album

Landing at the very moment Britpop was going stellar, Sleeper had a huge amount going for them in 1995. With producer Stephen Street, the band had delivered a clutch of great singles ('Swallow', 'Delicious') which had begun to make singer Louise Wener the out-and-out star of the show, throwing the male band members into what became known as 'sleeperbloke' status: a term that would long outlive the band's heyday. However, it was the month before the album's release that truly placed them as part of the zeitgeist, with single

'Inbetweener' telling a tale of suburban ennui, married to some pure guitar pop masterstrokes. Surprisingly, much of *Smart* is actually more indebted to the US alternative, yet – due to Wener's flair for lyrical observation and emotional honesty (just try and listen to 'Amuse' without a lump in your throat) – Sleeper essentially helped *define* Britpop. Though criticism may rest on whether you actually liked Wener's breathy, lusty, vocal delivery, *Smart* still stands as a true indie pop gem.

Standout track: 'Inbetweener'

Radiohead – The Bends (1995)
Recording sessions: February-November 1994
Producers: John Leckie, Radiohead, Nigel Godrich, Jim Warren
Record label: Parlophone
Chart position: UK: 4
Release date: 8 March 1995

Pete: Let's face it, Radiohead just aren't Britpop, are they? Never were, never will be. But at this point, they were at the Britpop party, standing in the corner, only talking to each other, sneering at the hosts, and growling if anyone came too near.

Matt: For me, this is where Radiohead became something special, with vastly improved songwriting, deep lyrics and a consistently great album. This is also where they started producing clever, thought-provoking, powerful music videos – 'Just' had the man lying in the street, confusing passers-by, while the black-and-white, slowed-down/normal-speed dreamlike weirdness of 'Street Spirit' was incredible.

The Album
Beginning with the desolate sound of wind upon a barren landscape (which is about as opposite to Britpop as you could imagine), *The Bends* is not actually as dramatic a reinterpretation of the band's sound as some would suggest ('Bones' in particular still reeks of *Pablo Honey*). But what it certainly did represent was a quantum leap in terms of the band's songwriting. Parlophone's desire for an album's worth of 'Creep'-style material may not have been achieved, but it *was* bettered. As Britpop ruled the airwaves and the alternative became the mainstream, Radiohead offered *The Bends* as an alternative to the alternative. The band's US-style alternative rock was still in place and better than ever ('The Bends', 'Just'), but it was the triple-whammy of slower songs – 'High And Dry', 'Fake Plastic Trees' and 'Street Spirit (Fade Out)' – that really burrowed under the skin, making this record arguably a bigger influence on the generation of bands to follow than 1997's *OK Computer*. Thom Yorke's skill in penning an awkward, bleak and cryptic lyric (with the occasional dash of

schoolboy poetry), had come of age, and Radiohead were clearly destined for huge success.

Standout track: 'Fake Plastic Trees'

Key Album: Elastica – Elastica (1995)

Personnel:
Justine Frischmann: vocals, guitar
Donna Matthews: vocals, guitar
Annie Holland: bass
Justin Welch: drums
Plus:
Dan Abnormal (Damon Albarn): additional keyboards on tracks 4, 8 and 11
Recording sessions: November-December 1992 – 'Line Up', EMI Studios, London
June 1993 – 'Stutter', EMI Studios, London
March-July 1994 – 'Connection', EMI Studios, Townhouse III, Battersea and Konk Studios, Hornsey, London
July-October 1994 – Album sessions, Konk Studios
Note: Some demos were reworked or partially re-recorded during the main album sessions. The album songs also went through a number of mixes by different (well-known) engineers – Westerman (1), Alan Moulder (2, 3, 4, 7, 9, 12, 13), Paul Tipler (5, 10), Bruce Lampcov (6, 14), John Leckie (8), Miti Adhikari (11), Phil Vinall (15)
Producers: Marc Waterman, Elastica
Record label: Deceptive
Chart position: UK: 1, USA: 66
Release date: 13 March 1995

Pete: Say what you like about Blur or Oasis, but in 1995 there simply wasn't a band as cool as Elastica. They may have been very much Britpop, but they simultaneously seemed to be as alternatively hip as The Velvet Underground in 1967. Musically, *Elastica* seems to be the last gasp for Britpop as an arty movement before it all became like a kind of proto-celeb-fest.

Matt: I was too young to know about Wire, so when Elastica emerged, I was blown away with their rockier, punkier sound, clever harmonies and great songs. The infantile vomit noises were just the icing on the cake. 'Connection' has always been an absolute favourite and is so catchy, even my Dad still hums the intro over 25 years after it was released.

The Band

In mid-1992, Frischmann and Welch had left Suede, initially jamming with Albarn on bass, before joining Matthews and Holland to finally form Elastica in October. Soon after, they recorded studio demos, and a tape of further sessions from June 1993 reached BBC Radio One DJ Steve Lamacq, who signed them to his Deceptive Records label, and likely helped them secure a Peel session in September. After the first single release later that year, a further two singles came in 1994, with the band completing a number of high-profile support slots, while Frischmann's relationship with Albarn made newspaper headlines. In 1995, their debut album *Elastica* was released to instant critical and commercial success on both sides of the Atlantic. Unfortunately, the band's influences led to a number of accusations of plagiarism, which were settled out of court, and while these didn't impede Elastica's success, they did knock their reputation.

The following years were difficult for the band, with members leaving (Holland and Matthews), rejoining (Holland), serious drug problems (primarily heroin), new music demoed (but sessions ultimately aborted) and Frischmann's relationship and ultimate breakup with Albarn being a continuing press topic. An EP of demos and rarities was eventually released in August 1999, followed in April 2000 by their second album *The Menace*, which was massively underrated (and underselling). The band spent the rest of the year playing festivals and touring America, but by 2001, they decided to split. In 2017, the debut album was reissued for Record Store Day, and pictures of the band at Abbey Road circulated (except for Frischmann, who now lives in America), leading to reunion rumours which were quickly dismissed.

The Album

It's hard to express what a breath of fresh air Elastica's debut was. But the very fact that it *was*, is somewhat indicative of how Britpop was already becoming turgid as a (perceived) genre. In a sea of 1960s influence (at best) and pastiche (at worst), the three-parts-female group drew from a palette of influences 20 years on from their peers and, frankly, seemed to have a lot more balls. On top of this, they were *actually* cool, not just cool, because they were popular: which is an important distinction.

Dressed in Suede-reminiscent black (singer Justine had been a founder-member, and it could be said she co-owned rights to the look), the band greeted the world with an air of disinterest, disaffection and distance from their peers, simultaneously holding a strong female perspective that had largely been missing. With a sartorial image more reflective of the Velvets or Wire, it was little wonder that when The Strokes landed in the 2000s, it was Elastica that were cited as their closest parallel in cool.

The record's post-punk blasts (yet still with an undeniable slab of raw Englishness) also contrasted startlingly against the increasingly oompahing seaside offerings of Frischmann's then-squeeze Damon Albarn. Incredibly, the whole thing is over within 38 minutes, despite containing fifteen songs of sex, suggestion and remarkably mature emotional sense. Simultaneously jagged, smooth, angular and melodic, the record was nominated for a Mercury Music Prize and has been rightly considered influential right through to today. Of course, any success has its deriders, and many pointed toward Elastica's exceptionally-blatant borrows from Wire and The Stranglers, without ever acknowledging that the band had arguably produced better songs from similar constructs. Some even went for the misogynistic jugular, claiming the entire record had actually been written by Damon Albarn: which is plainly ridiculous. As the fastest-selling UK debut since Oasis claimed that particular crown, the great shame is that – given the band's subsequent descent – the thought of what they could've achieved doesn't bear thinking about.

'Line Up' (Frischmann, Elastica) [Single]

Jagged guitars, chunky bass, and the sound of drummer Justin Welch throwing up: and that's before you even get to the sixteen-second mark. Lyrically, it's the everyday tale of a groupie called – charmingly – Drivel Head, who it's probably fair to say Frischmann doesn't hold in high regard (and given her experiences with two of Britpop's leading frontmen, it's tempting to consider what real-life events might've inspired the song). 'Line Up' is often cited as a prime example of an Elastica *borrow* (Wire's 'I Am The Fly' being the chorus' main inspiration), but realistically, a whole host of groups were being just as blatant, with Oasis being the most noticeable. Here, it just fed into the inevitable backlash that only true brilliance can breed. Issued as a single over a year before the album's release, it reached number 20 in the charts.

'Annie' (Matthews, Jane Oliver, Elastica)

A one-minute-and-fifteen-second-long ode to the band's bassist, and an absolute stonker at that, 'Annie' does more than a thousand late-1970s punk songs did with three times the running time. Foregoing everything deemed unnecessary (intros, outros, solos, bridges), yet still finding time for a pure pop chorus, it may be over before you realise it's begun, but it's still wonderful. Like a dirty aperitif before...

'Connection' (Frischmann, Elastica) [Single]

...the album's catchiest single (which peaked at 17 in October 1994). This is by far the song that defines the band to the masses. Again featuring a borrow from Wire (this time 'Three Girl Rhumba'), it has some wonderful spiky guitar, synth stabs, and a bridge-building to the over-too-soon two-line chorus. The song has had a heck of a life of its own, turning up on TV and in movies as recently as 2019's *Captain Marvel* (though that might've been helped by the film being set in 1995). 'Connection' saw Frischmann's clear-as-a-bell vocals perfectly offset by the dirt that underscored them – full of jagged repetition and lusty 'Hwurghs!' – making something that was simultaneously sexy, sweaty and poppy enough to get the song to number 53 in the US.

'Car Song' (Frischmann, Elastica) [Single]

'You could call me a car lover/'Cause I love it in a motor'. It's cheeky and chirpy – well, as much as Elastica ever get (There's a remarkable touch of the *Carry*

On's at play here, as Frischmann weaves wonderfully wry automobile double-entendres) – with 'Let's go siesta in your Ford Fiesta' and 'In every little Honda there may lurk a Peter Fonda... ooh' vying for pole position (though there are *so many* more). Despite being delivered with tongue firmly in cheek, it's still pretty raw stuff, with guitars sounding like reversing alarms and swooning vocal hooks. Surprisingly – given its incredibly British humour – it was released as a late single in the US, hitting 33 on the Alternative Songs chart.

'Smile' (Frischman, Matthews, Elastica)

Another track clocking in at well under two minutes, this is chugging bombast with a good dose of Englishness ('Peaches and cream, where have you been?'). A song that deals with all the late-night jealousy and recrimination that can come from a late-returning lover, it stands as a lyrical cousin to fellow album tracks 'All-Nighter' and the closer 'Stutter'.

'Hold Me Now' (Frischman, Matthews, Elastica)

Possibly the album's most deliberate post-punk song – with abrasive vocals and guitars that feel as if processed in a meat-canning factory – every element is essentially a pop hook in itself. There's also some genuinely enjoyable linguistic lurching – with lines like 'I can't take the voodoo that you do' and 'It's hard to make a stew when the meat keeps looking up at you' both worthy of acclaim for their originality and flair, despite the emotion on show.

'S.O.F.T.' (Frischmann, Elastica) [Deep Cut]

Starting like a demo, before becoming the record's heaviest song (which is surprising, as the title is supposedly an acronym for 'Same Old F*cking Thing'), 'S.O.F.T.' has an exceptionally laid-back tempo and stripped-to-the-bone instrumentation (Verse one is just bass and vocals) that really shows what an extreme contrast Elastica were to the equivalent walls of sound being created by the Britpop boys-clubs. With sections that explode into screaming anti-lead guitar hooks, its melodic, harmony-rich chorus shows how exceptional the band were at mixing and matching from the post-punk palette, making it easy to see why the album went across so well in America.

'Indian Song' (Frischmann, Elastica)

It seems amazing that of all the bands dabbling in British music's colourful past, it should be Elastica that first introduce a touch of Beatles-style Indian mysticism to Britpop. In fact, it may not even be too great a stretch to blame this song for inadvertently allowing Kula Shaker into the party. Though it's the weakest *song* here – and almost so out of place it might've been better left as an experimental B-side – its chugging drone and touches of harp still created a fine piece of music, but the subdued repetitive lyric chant just doesn't match the song up to its pals.

'Blue' (Matthews, Elastica)

Another fast, punkish song that actually benefits from its proximity to 'Indian Song', as it brings the record back on track. 'Blue' is another high-powered blast that benefits from exceptional new-wave harmonies. Though it's never quite clear what it's about, the suggestive line 'If you want to, I will let you blue' certainly set a fair few pulses racing in indie-boy bedrooms across the land.

'All-Nighter' (Frischmann, Elastica)

Though cut from the same cloth as 'Smile' and 'Stutter', 'All-Nighter' is remarkable in that there's actually an overriding romance that almost echoes similar ground to Blur's 'End Of A Century': in feel if nothing else. Fast and thrashy, Frischmann's tale of frustration in waiting for something 'x-rated' to happen, filling the time with pointless debate and trips to the 24-hour garage, seems like a perfect take on young life in the 1990s – a time before the endless distractions of the internet and mobile phones: when endless waiting seemed to be part of the deal.

'Waking Up' (Frischmann, Elastica) [Single]

This song's liberal borrow from The Stranglers' 'No More Heroes' (last *borrowed* in these pages during 1990's 'Memories Of You' by Inspiral Carpets) resulted in a lawsuit and a thank you for awakening a whole new generation to The Stranglers' body of work. But it also resulted in the band foregoing a hefty chunk of album royalties that doesn't necessarily feel justified given that 'Waking Up' is very much its own beast, adding a remarkable pop shine and a much-more-relatable lyric about underachievement, boredom and the everyday. Reaching number 13 when it was released one month before the album, the line 'Make a cup of tea and put a record on' was hollered on dance floors across the land, despite the fact the song is actually relatively undanceable.

'2:1' (Matthews, Elastica)

With the lyric coming across like a less-on-the-nose Jarvis-Cocker tale of frustration and sadness, the song's instrumental sections also seem to have a peculiar Pulp feel and may even have the album's closest thing to an actual guitar solo. Angular stabs, verse harmonies and raw simplicity make it the album's coldest-sounding song (and almost distressing in feel), while verse two's double vocal is also an inspired and unsettling touch.

'Vaseline' (Frischmann, Elastica)

About the need for a different sort of lubrication to the 'lager, lager, lager' cravings of their male counterparts, 'Vaseline' is an absolute blast of cheek, complete with a 'la la la' chorus that puts it in the same camp as 'Car Song'. Despite the song having a silliness that could've derailed the record, by this point, Elastica could get away with practically anything, including…

'Never Here' (Frischmann, Elastica) [Deep Cut]

...a remarkably heartfelt recollection of a failed love affair. By far the album's longest song (just shy of five minutes), it's actually big enough to swallow several of its counterparts, whole. It's also the album's clear masterpiece, recounting Frischmann's failed relationship with Suede's Brett Anderson. (She remains friends with Anderson, despite this blistering appraisal of their time together.) Despite its running time, 'Never Here' actually feels faster and larger than its individual parts. It should've been the album closer.

'Stutter' (Frischmann, Elastica) [Single]

'Stutter' was Elastica's debut to the world. Released in November 1993 – well over a year before the album – and was popularly considered to be about none other than Damon Albarn. The track acts as a great punky swansong to one of the great albums of the era, yet it's also a sop to the hard-core faithful and could've better suited being a hidden track.

Optional Extras

Surprisingly for such an important album, *Elastica* has no deluxe version, despite there being enough known material to produce one. The 1993 demo is available on YouTube and includes early raw versions of songs that were later re-recorded for the album or B-sides. Further demos from other sessions have been released, including complete songs and sketches, and in a 1995 *Melody Maker* article, producer Waterman referred to a number of different unused mixes, which may or may not make for interesting listening. The rare 2001 CD *The Radio One Sessions* also has recordings of B-sides, which in some cases are better than the released versions. 'Rockunroll' and 'Spastica' are examples of this: both great punky numbers with some fun vocals. 'Brighton Rock' is more difficult – the B-side being a punky ska-type number with enjoyable screeches and more vomit noises – while the *Radio One Sessions* take is far more professional and restrained. Other B-sides include the very Britpoppy 'Pussycat', the chunky guitar rock of 'See That Animal', the overloaded bass of the keyboard-driven 'Car Wash', and finally, 'Gloria', which reworks 'Good King Wenceslas'. All worth seeking out.

Gene – Olympian (1995)

Recording sessions: Autumn 1994
Producers: Phil Vinall, Miti Adhikari
Record label: Costermonger
Chart position: UK: 8
Release date: 20 March 1995

Pete: In Britpop, if you weren't Oasis, Blur, Pulp or Suede, then you needed a *thing* that defined you. Gene's thing was that they were like The Smiths.

115

Actually, they weren't, but I have no doubt that a lot of Britpop kids ended up discovering The Smiths through Gene.

Matt: Gene were already in that lower-tier of Britpop bands and then got a second kicking for ripping off The Smiths: meaning they were often dismissed far too quickly. Pete, they *do* sound like The Smiths (Just listen to the first track!), but the album also includes songs that are part of a larger melting-pot of influences, like The Jam and Small Faces.

The Album

Formed in 1993 from the ashes of baggy band Spin and adding the uniquely-talented vocalist Martin Rossiter, Gene quickly found themselves a place in the music press as ones to watch: no doubt helped by their management team of *NME* journos. But such an observation undermines the quality of the band and their debut album *Olympian*, with its ability to switch from fragile and delicate torch songs to huge fist-in-the-air singles while wringing out every last drop of emotion along the way. Perhaps some of the record's more-rock moments never feel as natural as they should – Gene specialising in somewhat maudlin tales – but this is a wonderful debut, with 'London Can You Wait' at its emotional core. But it's the singles that really shine through, with special praise for 'Haunted By You' and 'Olympian': being some of the very best that Britpop had to offer.

Standout track: 'Sleep Well Tonight'

The Boo Radleys – Wake Up! (1995)

Recording sessions: September-October 1994
Producer: The Boo Radleys
Record label: Creation
Chart position: UK: 1
Release date: 27 March 1995

Pete: The Boo Radleys' true Britpop record! It seems like every album they created placed them as players in some media-scene concoction or other. But the Britpop tag stuck, thanks to the 'Wake Up Boo!' single.

Matt: 'Wake Up Boo!' is the song you think of for this band, where the trumpet and the overwhelming joy are completely to the fore. If you're a trumpet fan, the album will disappoint you. But if you're a pop fan, it moves through every realm imaginable, and covers some you didn't even know existed. It's quite astonishing.

The Album

Having already delivered critically acclaimed perfection in the form of 1993's *Giant Steps*, what else did The Boo Radleys have to prove? Creation's answer was very clearly that it might be nice if they could start selling some records. Which brings us to *Wake Up!*: their fourth album and Martin Carr's supremely successful stab at shifting units. But this is no simple commercial affair coldly created to manipulate the record-buying public. For every pop gem here – and there are plenty – there's also something that adds real weight to proceedings. A record of two distinct halves, the first is power-loaded with singles ('It's Lulu', 'Find The Answer Within') and should-have-been singles, while the second half allows the band to branch out into Beatles-style experimentation ('Martin, Doom! It's Seven O'Clock'). Although the band will always be remembered as the creators of the harmony-laden earworm 'Wake Up Boo!' (which amazingly only ever reached number nine, but has remained a summertime radio favourite ever since), this remains an album of exquisite confidence and capability.

Standout track: 'Find The Answer Within'

Supergrass – I Should Coco (1995)

Recording sessions: February-August 1994
Producer: Sam Williams
Record label: Parlophone
Chart position: UK: 1
Release date: 15 May 1995

Pete: Hailing from Oxford like Radiohead, yet a million miles away sonically, Supergrass just landed like an absolute joy bomb. Although the 'Alright' single would obviously become annoying with time, in the moment, it was just everything that you could've wanted to represent that long, hot, carefree summer when we were finally old enough to start doing some of the things we actually wanted to do.

Matt: Supergrass passed me by for the first few singles. It was only 'Alright' that caught my attention, and I think this was probably more due to the fact that the video seemed to be everywhere and featured a bonkers chopper bike and bed ride around North Wales that seemed like a cross between *The Monkees TV* show and *Last of the Summer Wine*.

The Album

With a scrappy Buzzcocks-like pop-punk energy tied to better musicianship than you could rightly expect from a band so young (singer/guitarist Gaz Coombes was still 19 upon release), *I Should Coco* was a huge initial success, becoming Parlophone's best-selling debut album since The Beatles. Though it has more retro-rock workouts than memory may recall ('Lose It'), and also some truly mature songwriting ('Time'), there's more fun here than you might expect: 'Not Supposed To' even veering on the cusp of being Britpop's first comedy number. But what really shines through is an ability to encapsulate youth in all its glorious small-town innocence ('Caught By The Fuzz', 'She's So Loose', 'Sitting Up Straight'), the eloquence of which ultimately shows the band to be far more than their mutton-chopped caricature would have you believe. The enormous energy of it all may leave you feeling fairground-ride queasy, but it's one hell of a ride.

Standout track: 'I'd Like To Know'

Paul Weller – Stanley Road (1995)

Recording sessions: 1994-Early 1995
Producers: Paul Weller, Brendan Lynch
Record label: Go! Discs
Chart position: UK: 11

Pete: To say Britpop gave Paul Weller a second lease of life is kind of nonsense. He was already on his third or fourth incarnation by this point and was showing no sign of slowing down. However, what Britpop did do, was introduce him afresh to a whole new generation.

Matt: I was a big fan of The Jam and then was utterly baffled by The Style Council, which made me switch off to his solo career. Then, all of a sudden, 'The Changingman' came out, combining ELO with The Beatles and blues rock. It was fantastic, and the album also even made sense of (some of) The Style Council too.

The Album

By the time Paul Weller released his third solo album *Stanley Road*, Britpop had made him one of the most revered elder statesmen of British music. With both Blur and Oasis indebted to The Jam (and not shy about name-checking him in interviews or even turning up on this record: Noel Gallagher playing acoustic guitar on 'I Walk On Gilded Splinters'), the only question was whether Weller's new album would have the tunes necessary to prove the point. Whether it does or not, may rely partly on which elements of Weller's past output you find most appealing. There's a lot here for fans of The Style Council, perhaps less for fans of The Jam, and a lot for those who enjoy their music jammed to breaking point. But this isn't just a by-the-numbers rock exercise – Britrock cornerstone single 'The Changingman' essentially begins the album as a statement of intent: Weller understanding that music covers a very large landscape and that he's earned the right to walk wherever he wants. The mega-ballad 'You Do Something To Me' and the standout soul of 'Broken Stones' placed *Stanley Road* as the commercial high point in an already illustrious career.

Standout track: 'Broken Stones'

Black Grape – It's Great When You're Straight... Yeah (1995)

Recording sessions: Early-1995
Producers: Danny Saber, Stephen Lironi, Shaun Ryder, Gary Kurfirst
Record label: Radioactive
Chart position: UK: 1
Release date: 7 August 1995

Pete: You just didn't see Black Grape coming. I mean, this was Shaun Ryder – a man you felt was unlikely to have ever been at the helm of even one great group. But here he was, back and bigger than ever, with Bez still dancing away on the sidelines. Just joyous stuff.

Matt: Once you got over the fact that Shaun Ryder and Bez were in a functioning state after all the rumours following the messy end of Happy Mondays, you had to compute that this was a really good album, full of great funky, strutting songs, with a fantastic vocal sparring-partner in Kermit.

The Album

Straight in at number one during the great summer of 1995 – at the very point Oasis and Blur were slugging it out in the singles chart – this album offered something completely different to the already-retro Britpop. Though at heart an indie/dance record, these were not the trippy stylings of *Screamadelica* or even like anything the Happy Mondays had delivered: this was a fusion with guts, and was here to bring the party. It was a something-for-everyone record, with beats, raps, rhymes and enough Britpop punches-to-the-air to make it fit the time perfectly while also having little or nothing to do with its peers. Well-received critically (and by the kids), Ryder manipulated a thousand and one drug-addled conversations into lyric form (probably the best mind-mangling poetics of his career), while Kermit's rapping injected hip hop into proceedings, delivering a sonic freshness to an album that still holds up today. In short, this was nothing less than triumphant when any safe bet would've gone for tragedy.

Standout track: 'In The Name Of The Father'

Blur – The Great Escape (1995)

Recording sessions: January-May 1995
Producer: Stephen Street
Record label: Food/Virgin
Chart position: UK: 1
Release date: 11 September 1995

Pete: I remember going to see Blur at the Birmingham NEC on the *Great Escape* tour and just being massively disappointed. I don't think I went to another stadium show for fifteen years. With its big funfair stage props, it just wasn't the visceral experience I wanted, and I got this overwhelming feeling that the whole Britpop thing had become about acts rather than bands.

Matt: This was also the point your parents became aware of Britpop, as it was splashed across the six o'clock news. For me, the album has a lot of good moments, and my opinion of it has mellowed over the years. But at the time, I felt it was very forced and – despite its best efforts – couldn't live up to the expectations set by its predecessors. Although 'Country House' won the Battle of Britpop, the accompanying album lost the war.

The Album

Cited by Albarn himself as one of the two 'bad albums' he's made in his career (the other being *Leisure*), the truth of the matter is that *The Great Escape* isn't really that bad at all. What it *is* – like *Leisure* before it – is a product very much of its time: a distillation of all the things the band felt they had a duty to deliver to their by-now-huge audience. Three albums in three years, and the accompanying pressures of ever-increasing fame, were putting a strain on the group: all of which had reached a crunch point with the Battle of Britpop one month before the album's release. Blur had secured the top spot with the actually-quite-peculiar single 'Country House', so now all they had to do was seal the deal with the third killer album in a row: No pressure, then. Ultimately *The Great Escape* is simply a less-satisfying version of the two albums preceding it, and while it led some to conclude that Blur's think tank was running dry, there's still more than enough going on to make it a great album had only another Britpop group delivered it. Thematically characterised by ever-more-isolated suburban characters ('Stereotypes', 'Charmless Man', 'Mr Robinson's Quango': the list goes on), but delivered with fantastic tunes that offset the subject matter, the record's true high point is the single 'The Universal': which breaks spectacularly from type, by combining the National Lottery's tag line 'It really could happen' with a song about an empty, hollow new century that was now only a few short years away. It may sound bleak, but unlike the other standout 'He Thought Of Cars', it's remarkably uplifting and, well, universal.

Standout track: 'The Universal'

Echobelly – On (1995)

Recording sessions: Early-1995
Producers: Paul Kolderie, Sean Slade
Record label: Rhythm King
Chart position: UK: 4
Release date: 18 September 1995

Pete: I saw Echobelly during the *On* tour. They got helicoptered to our hometown straight from the stage of TFI Friday in London. They were about two hours late, and by the time they came on, I'd met my first girlfriend. So, thanks, Echobelly!

Matt: 'Great Things' was the only Echobelly song you tended to hear, and it's definitely one of the most poppy and catchy songs of the Britpop years. But its alternating chirpy/aloof vocal did eventually grate on me, and it put me off listening to the band for years. It's a real shame, as there are some great songs on this album, and I don't think the singles really did it justice.

The Album

A group that both indie kids and genuine rock fans could get behind, Echobelly boasted the best riffs in all Britpop, yet found themselves underrated through being caught in the mid-1990s media swirl – becoming unceremoniously lumped-in with groups they only had a passing resemblance with, such as Elastica, Sleeper and Lush (Can you spot the similar factor?). They perhaps had Britpop's best vocalist in Sonya Maden, who sang like she had a massive smile permanently on her face, which is pretty remarkable given that, as a lyricist, she was totally unafraid to lift the hood on society and have a poke about, no matter what uncomfortable truths she might find ('Something Hot In A Cold Country'). Like so many groups, Echobelly's fortunes were formed in one perfect single: 'Great Things'. It may not have been ultimately reflective of everything they had to offer, but nonetheless, it was so relentlessly positive that it stands as one of the great Britpop moments and *On* as its perfect home.

Standout track: 'Dark Therapy'

Key Album: Oasis – What's The Story (Morning Glory)? (1995)

Personnel:
Liam Gallagher: lead vocals, tambourine.
Noel Gallagher: lead guitar, backing vocals; lead vocals ('Don't Look Back In Anger'); Mellotron, E bow; bass ('Wonderwall', 'Cast No Shadow' and 'She's Electric')
Paul 'Bonehead' Arthurs: rhythm guitar, piano, Mellotron
Paul 'Guigsy' McGuigan: bass
Alan White: drums
Tony McCarroll: drums on 'Some Might Say'
Plus:
Paul Weller: lead guitar, backing vocals on 'Champagne Supernova'; Harmonica, additional guitar on 'The Swamp Song'
Recording sessions: February 1995 – 'Some Might Say', Loco Studios, South Wales
May 1995 – Album recorded at Rockfield Studios, South Wales
Note: Album sessions were temporarily halted after an argument between Liam and Noel. Mixing took place in June 1995 at Orinoco Studios, South London, and this is when Paul Weller's contributions were recorded.

Producers: Owen Morris, Noel Gallagher
Record label: Creation
Chart position: UK: 1, USA: 4
Released date: 2 October 1995

Pete: An absolutely huge record. Just massive. One of the key records that you point at and go:, 'That's Britpop'. That said, I do remember some initial disappointment; it just wasn't as rock-and-roll as the debut. The opening track was a particular letdown, given we'd previously been treated to 'Rock 'N' Roll Star'.

Matt: This was a far cleaner and more-polished record than the first and combined with some of their best songs, it wasn't so much an album as a moment. The only downside was that every teenager with a guitar would play 'Wonderwall' at every opportunity. That got annoying really quickly.

The Album

For a band often described as having a by-the-numbers approach, the first three Oasis albums are actually quite separate entities. *Definitely Maybe* was a sneering, punkish statement of intent, and the third outing *(Be Here Now)* was the sound of bloated excess writ large. But for *(What's The Story) Morning Glory?*, a much gentler path was trodden – one that might be surprising to new listeners (although it's hard to imagine that there are many left who haven't already sampled its many delights). A very different beast to its counterparts, mostly written on acoustic guitar, this album is also a much more artistic and crafted affair, which is odd given that initial reviews lambasted it for being artless. Needless to say, they changed their tune when the Oasis juggernaut finally became unstoppable, and you couldn't shift a music magazine without seeing the band name somewhere on the cover.

Song elements seep into each other, while strings and pianos are added to the arsenal, producing a record that would place Oasis as the band of choice for stadiums, festivals and even pub sing-alongs. Although clocking in at just over 50 minutes, in terms of material, it's a shockingly-short album. A total of twelve tracks are on offer (two of which are little more than instrumental filler), yet it still feels weighty and important. Following a first half stacked with hit singles, side two is where the band really show what they can do with their chosen form: squeezing every last drop of their ability into some truly standout moments (though this argument admittedly falls a little flat due to 'She's Electric').

Throughout this period, Oasis seemed unstoppable, no matter what befell them. Before recording the album, they'd already lost their original drummer Tony McCarroll – who was replaced with the greater-skilled Alan White. The tour that followed saw a great deal of turmoil within the ranks, as bassist Guigsy jumped ship for a period: ridiculously meaning that stand-in Scott McLeod got pride-of-place in the incredibly popular 'Wonderwall' video. Taking the famous Battle of Britpop in their stride, the losing team proved the truth of the adage about losing battles and winning wars, when the album became the biggest-selling of 1995 – 'Wonderwall' propelling sales that would see it ranked at number five in the all-time UK best seller list: a success cemented forever, when in August 1996, five percent of the UK population applied to watch Oasis take to the stage for two nights at Knebworth in front of 250,000 fans.

'Hello' (Noel Gallagher, Gary Glitter, Mike Leander)
Beginning with a small except of 'Wonderwall', as if to signal knowledge of the monster hit they would soon have on their hands (Did they know? How *could* they know?), the guitars suddenly smash in like the reverse signal of a dump truck here to unload a premium three-minute slab of pure stadium rock on the listener, before we start having to deal with any rubbish about emotions. Upbeat, jaunty and with far more guitars than it knows what to do with, for an opening track, it still never quite feels like it carries enough punch, even with the added weight of the outro section that – thanks to a deft Gallagher borrow – led to Gary Glitter of all people claiming a writing credit. While never capturing the lying-in-the-gutter-staring-at-the-stars majesty of the *Definitely Maybe* opener 'Rock 'N' Roll Star', it's fair to say there wasn't really anywhere else the band could've placed a song called 'Hello'.

'Roll With It' (Noel Gallagher) [Single]
Revisiting 'Roll With It' is a curious experience. After all, in August 1995, was there a bigger song? Well, yes, there was *one*, but all the same, it's bizarre that this was Oasis' contribution to the era-defining Battle of Britpop. While it stands its ground as the album's second song and gives fans another good wedge of what they want before the record takes some more unusual directions, the fact remains that it's the album's weakest song, and *that* includes the two short musical interludes. If you didn't know already, 'Roll With It' charted at number two in August 1995: pipped to the post by Blur's 'Country House'. This meant that for many in the UK at the time, 'Roll With It' defined Oasis: something they moved fast to overcome, with the release of...

'Wonderwall' (Noel Gallagher) [Single]
The battle had been lost and Blur were triumphant, though they didn't know what to do with the spoils of their victory. But what of Oasis? To put it frankly, Oasis were not as big as Blur before the whole silliness happened, but as a result, were now seen as level-peggers. Within weeks of the Battle of Britpop, the parent album was released, selling 345,000 copies in its first week alone, before taking a seat in the album-chart top 10 for a further twelve months. But why? Well, the answer is largely down to the success of 'Wonderwall' – a largely acoustic/chamber-pop ballad (Oasis' first single in this style) – which quickly followed the album and went on to inspire a generation to pick up guitars (then promptly put them down again after realising the song had a

tricky strumming pattern). Although it only reached number 2 (held from the top by singing actors Robson & Jerome: a reminder that the 1990s were far from being all about Britpop), it was the breakthrough that followed the breakthrough, catapulting the album into ever more ridiculous sales figures, 'Wonderwall' becoming *the* song of 1995. The spat with Blur suddenly seemed like nonsense, and the world genuinely became Oasis' stage. Not bad for a song Gallagher claimed he'd never actually finished.

'Don't Look Back In Anger' (Noel Gallagher) [Single]

Finally returning the band to number 1 (though never feeling as big a hit culturally as 'Wonderwall' *at the time*), this single was issued in February 1996 and cemented the fact Oasis were spreading their wings into a form of anthemic sing-along rock that played well both on massive stages and Friday-night pub jukeboxes. Featuring a Gallagher borrow from John Lennon's 'Imagine' (listen closely to the piano) and a lead vocal from Noel rather than Liam, the band's sneer had turned into a soar, and the scene was set for Noel's solo future: though that was a long time down the road yet. Following the horrific 2017 Manchester Arena bombing, the song took on new meaning, not just for the people of Manchester but the nation as a whole: the title and spirit of reconciliation finally making the song a cultural touchstone in its own right. Oh, and if you're wondering, no one knows who Sally is (The band can only agree that Liam suggested it), which probably only adds to its universal appeal.

'Hey Now!' (Noel Gallagher)

This feels like an unbelievably long piece of work. Genuinely – pop it on. Make a sandwich. Go to the toilet. Enjoy a walk. When you get back, *it will still be playing!* But does that make it a bad song? No, not really. But it might've suited being shaved a little. Mid-tempo with a catchy melody and each verse line full-stopped with a simple drum fill, the bridge and chorus combine to create a faintly hazy feeling, while the lyric deals with the healing powers of – you guessed it – time.

'Untitled' (Noel Gallagher)

As if to remind the listener that this is still Oasis, 'Untitled' (technically part of 'Wonderwall' B-side 'The Swamp Song') is a 45-second blast of harmonica-driven blues rock. Nothing much to write home about, perhaps, but artistically, it does help to make the record feel more complete.

'Some Might Say' (Noel Gallagher) [Single]

The album's closest moment to *Definitely Maybe* – which isn't surprising given its proximity and personnel (the last outing for drummer Tony McCarroll before Alan White replaced him) – was Oasis' first number-1 single when released in April 1995, and acted more as a gap filler than as part of the album campaign. An exhilarating piece of rock with Status-Quo-style chugging, solos as catchy as the melody, and a wonderful nonsensical lyric ('The sink is full of fishes/She's got dirty dishes on the brain') with a few decent sneering 'Shi-ine' moments from Liam for good measure, 'Some Might Say' is very much the archetypical Oasis song.

'Cast No Shadow' (Noel Gallagher) [Deep Cut]

For what's essentially a laid-back piece of American MOR rock, this has remarkable depth. Showcasing subtle acoustic guitars, strings and Noel's wonderful soaring backing vocals, the lyric is about The Verve's Richard Ashcroft (We wonder what he made of the line 'As they took his soul, they stole his pride'). It simultaneously showed the levels of artistry Oasis actually could achieve when they wanted to, and paved the way for The Verve's eventual return in 1997 (when they briefly took ownership of Oasis' crown). The famous video for The Verve's monster hit 'Bittersweet Symphony' quite literally depicted Ashcroft as a man who 'walks along the open road of love and life, surviving if he can': coincidence?

'She's Electric' (Noel Gallagher)

You know how we mentioned all those boys who picked up guitars to find they couldn't master 'Wonderwall'? Well, those that decided not to give up entirely, immediately graduated to 'She's Electric' – a much simpler, more poppy and fun song, featuring a nod to the children's TV show *You and Me*, along with some genuine humour: 'She's got one in the oven, but it's nothing to do with me' being a big hit with the dads in the audience. Despite its popularity, it does feel somewhat lightweight, having more in common with the previous album's 'Digsy's Dinner' than anything else on offer here. An argument can be made that it could have derailed the album were it not for the fans' Oasis-can-do-no-wrong' mentality, and the fact it's followed by...

'Morning Glory' (Noel Gallagher)

...the song that should've started the album! Bold and brash, with guitars that stab like knives, it's unbelievably exhilarating stuff, with a brilliant soaring chorus showing both brothers in fine voice. It's so big and overstated that it feels almost like the template for the following *Be Here Now* album, but – and this is a very important distinction – *here*, it's *done right.* As an enormous wall of sound that reminds the listener it's still an Oasis album, the song helps balance a record dominated by its ballads. Though not a single in the UK, it was in Australia and New Zealand, and received significant airplay in America.

'Untitled II' (Noel Gallagher)

Another 40 seconds from 'The Swamp Song', presented as if being played 40 miles away on a small radio that's 40 years old. Its inclusion gives the album a degree of symmetry, and artistically pulls up the whole.

'Champagne Supernova' (Noel Gallagher) [Deep Cut]

The sound of gentle lapping waves, piercing guitar notes, a gentle guitar –
It's time to close on an epic: and what an epic this is! The lyric is somewhat
nonsense yet is delivered with a gravitas (Even the exceptionally obvious
'walking down a hall/cannonball' rhyme does little to damage the overall
feel). This is a seven-and-a-half-minute rock monster, released as a single in
France, Australia and New Zealand, and punctuated with moments of beauty,
plus guitar from The Jam's Paul Weller. The overall effect is that the preceding
album has had a bow put on it, with all the confidence it would take for a
Gallagher brother to wear a bow.

Optional Extras

In 2014, a deluxe edition was released, including B-sides, rarities, demos
and live tracks. The B-sides and a few rarities occupy one whole CD, and it
could be argued that the majority are so good that *What's The Story (Morning
Glory)?* could've been an incredible double album. In fact, half of the B-sides
album *The Masterplan* was made up of some of these songs. Some special
mention should be made of the soft, confidential acoustic 'Talk Tonight',
fan-favourite 'Acquiesce' (with Liam singing verses and Noel on the chorus),
'Step-Out' (with a blatant borrow from Stevie Wonder's 'Uptight (Everything's
Alright)': as a result, relegated to B-side status), the unfairly overlooked
'Underneath The Sky', the 'Good Day Sunshine'-trumpet-heavy 'Round Are
Way' and the majestic 'Masterplan'. The second bonus CD is made up of
rousing live soundcheck renditions and demos featuring Noel mainly. In this
stripped-down setting, 'She's Electric' is a far better prospect. Confusingly,
the included 'Some Might Say' demo is different to what appears on the 1995
Japanese EP. This is a slower, more tentative version, recorded either without
Liam during the 'Whatever' sessions or just by Noel in January 1995 using
The Verve's equipment. Either way, it would've been a nice inclusion on the
deluxe edition.

Cast – All Change (1995)

Recording sessions: Early-1995
Producer: John Leckie
Record label: Polydor
Chart position: UK: 7
Release date: 16 October 1995

Pete: The thing that strikes me about Cast is that, at the time, they felt like
simply another part of everything that was going on. But with the decades that
have passed, you start to hear a song here and there on the radio, and you
realise they were far better than you remember. The singles on this album hold
up especially well.

Matt: It was a shame, but Cast were always in the shadow of The La's, with John Power unable to shake Lee Mavers' legacy or the hope that Cast would be The La's Mark II. The band appearing with simple Merseybeat-style songs was all the critics needed. It's unfair, as these songs are really catchy, and the album is definitely worth revisiting if you dismissed it previously.

The Album

When The La's finally staggered to a stop, seemingly without ever having really started, Lee Mavers' ever-faithful lieutenant John Power finally took matters into his own hands, forming Britpop stalwarts Cast. Proving that the long service to his former group had been anything but a waste of time, *All Change* showed Power to be quite a songwriter – muscling up The La's rattle-and-roll dynamics, delivering a full hour of anthemic and positive indie rock with a side order of gentle psychedelia: Britpop's equivalent to when The Beatles' George Harrison finally got his moment in the sun, unleashing a huge stockpile of superb songs. Though Cast were always considered a second-rung band behind Oasis and Blur, they were still huge, with *All Change* being the biggest-selling debut in the history of the Polydor label, providing two top-20 singles ('Finetime', 'Alright' (Not to be confused with Supergrass song of the same name)), and two top-10 to boot ('Sandstorm', 'Walkaway'): All of which displayed some of the best choruses the 1990s had to offer.

Standout track: 'Alright'

Menswear – Nuisance (1995)

Recording sessions: Early-1995
Producer: Neill Jong
Record label: Laurel
Chart position: UK: 11
Release date: 24 October 1995

Pete: I loved Menswear. I really, really loved them. I don't care what anyone says. They're like the culmination of Britpop; the moment the beast ate itself. A bunch of scamps blagged their way into an extremely good record deal and created what may not be the greatest album ever, but certainly, one that you can point to and say, 'That, right there, is Britpop'.

Matt: I'm surprised you didn't mention that you loved Menswear; really, really loved them. I was always a big fan of the stuttering 'Daydreamer' that in many ways out-Wired Elastica. But where Elastica's influences were often obvious, Menswear would take a band's sound and distil it into an ultimate one-song version. For me, the album walks a tightrope between imitation and emulation. But when they get it right, they really do get it right.

127

The Album

Gloriously bratty, consistently poppy and certainly here for a good time (if not a long time), *Nuisance* is an album that could've probably *never* lived up to the hype. When Menswear formed in 1994 – seemingly by just being in the right clubs and claiming they were a band – the music industry pretty much tripped over itself to secure them. Before they'd even released a single, Menswear had played on *Top Of The Pops* and secured a *Melody Maker* cover, so all they had to do was put out a killer album that would silence their increasingly numerous detractors. While it's fair to say that *Nuisance* never did that, it still has much merit. This record is a glorious moment of self-awareness, openly cribbing from those who had cribbed before them. There's the Elastica song ('Daydreamer'), the Oasis song ('Stardust') and the Blur song (hidden track 'Bones And Red Meat'), all overseen by the wry delivery of suited and booted vocalist Johnny Dean. It's exhilarating stuff; a one-shot *best-of,* even if it only occasionally represents the best of the genre.

Standout track: 'Being Brave'

Key Album: Pulp – Different Class (1995)

Personnel:

Jarvis Cocker: vocals, Vox Marauder, Ovation 12-string, Sigma acoustic, Roland VP-330, Roland SH-09, Mellotron, Micromoog, Synare

Russell Senior: Fender Jazzmaster, violin

Candida Doyle: Farfisa Compact Professional II organ, Ensoniq ASR-10, Korg Trident II, Minimoog, Fender Rhodes, Roland Juno 6, Roland SH-09

Steve Mackey: Musicman Sabre bass

Mark Webber: Gibson ES 345, Gibson Les Paul, Gibson Firebird, Sigma acoustic, Casio Tonebank CT-470, Fender Rhodes, Roland Juno 6

Nick Banks: Yamaha drums, Zildjian cymbals, percussion

Recording sessions: January 1995 – 'Common People', 'Underwear' recorded at The Town House, London

February-April 1995 – 'Bar Italia', 'Monday Morning', 'Pencil Skirt', recorded at The Town House, London

June-August 1995 – The rest of the album completed in July and mixed at The Town House.

Producer: Chris Thomas

Record label: Island

Chart position: UK: 1

Release date: 30 October 1995

Pete: *Different Class* was the moment Pulp exploded as a mainstream band, Jarvis became a celebrity, and I finally had someone I could go to fancy dress parties as with ease. Given all the crazy stuff that went on, I'd say it's only a matter of time before a movie (rather than a documentary) is made about Pulp in this period.

Matt: This was the moment Pulp not only had the songs, but they had the audience: people were listening. 'Common People' was most people's introduction to the band, and it really did give you an idea of them which was only enhanced by the video: which saw Jarvis doing what he does best while being pushed around in an oversized shopping trolley.

The Album

'Blessed are the meek: for they shall inherit the earth' (Matthew 5:5). Did anyone really see it coming? Of course, the signs were there already. Pulp – already on a high from the extraordinary *His 'N' Hers* record (which had only been released in early 1994) – were certainly riding a wave. The eighteen-month interval between albums had seen them triumphantly headline Glastonbury's Pyramid Stage (To say they simply 'stepped up' for an out-of-service Stone Roses, is an understatement, given the strength of the performance), and release the incredible 'Common People' single, which charted at number 2 and was an instant anthem. However, this was no guarantee that *Different Class* would hit number one. In fact, given the exceptionally short amount of time the band had available to write and record following the single's success, the idea that the results should go on to not only be their personal best but also a masterpiece of Britpop, seemed very unlikely. But yes, Pulp had arrived, and by God, weren't they going to tell you where they'd come from. Being twelve tales of sex and social class that consistently side with society's underdogs, *Different Class* is seedy, sexy, nasty, symphonic, sophisticated and natural. The band had reached the zenith of their powers, and even though some tried to keep the crown from them (The *Daily Mirror* 'Ban This Sick Stunt' headline regarding the 'Sorted For E's And Wizz' single was especially memorable), Pulp rose above it all with decency, droll humour and the knowledge that they'd actually created something incredible. They'd already proven themselves musically, but this was the moment to prove themselves in the public eye. It had taken fourteen years, but when they won the Mercury Music Prize, Pulp finally proved that good things do happen to those who deserve it.

'Mis-Shapes' (Lyrics: Jarvis Cocker; Music: Pulp) [Single]

Many would disagree, but the grandeur of *Different Class* is almost undercut by the very first track. Almost certainly the album's weakest song – and a good example of how even the most perfect albums can be derailed by the requirement for just one more possible hit single – 'Mis-Shapes' nonetheless does its job in the context of the record as a soaring distillation of its themes and a rallying call-to-arms for society's bullied outcasts yet to hit their high. Simultaneously air-punchingly perfect ('Just put your hands up, it's a raid, yeah!') and unbearably cringeworthy ('We'll use the one thing we've got more of/That's our minds'), the band wisely made the song a double A-side single with the far superior 'Sorted For E's And Wizz' in September 1995. It preceded the album by a month and matched the success – if not the grandeur – of 'Common People' by reaching number two.

'Pencil Skirt' (Lyrics: Jarvis Cocker; Music: Pulp)

This song feels partly as if it has wandered in from the preceding album *His 'N' Hers* by mistake (which shouldn't come as too much of a surprise, given the two records' relatively-close release dates). 'Pencil Skirt' is a seedy tale of Cocker being 'around when he's not in town', which probably tells you all you need to know. Gasping, wheezy, yet lush and orchestral, the song is constructed around a simple guitar line; a hint of a French feel underscoring the whole piece.

'Common People' (Full Length Version) (Lyrics: Jarvis Cocker; Music: Cocker, Banks, Mackey, Senior, Doyle) [Single]

Arriving at what felt like the peak moment for Britpop as if to draw power from all that preceded it, and cast a long shadow over all that would follow, 'Common People' is the undisputed anthem of Britpop, Britain and the common man, and still has the power to surprise and shock those that believe they already know its every nuance – a stunning achievement for a song that lasts almost six minutes and doesn't seem to even reach first gear until the two-minute mark. A 1980s-influenced, synth-powered, multilayered, inspired-by-true-events story of Cocker at St Martin's College (and the rich girl who will never understand 'how it feels to live your life with no meaning or control', the necessity of cutting your hair to get a job, or the need to 'dance and drink and screw because there's nothing else to do'), the single version was released in May 1995 before much of the album was even written. However, listen closely to Cocker's double-tracking, and you can actually pick out moments of pure joy in his hiccuped delivery, almost as if he knew full well what the band was doing and was loving every second of not only the song's creation but what it would mean for the group from then on. Peaking at number two, life would never be the same for Pulp again. Nor would it be the same for all those that instantly bought into the song's message: which, in later years, even included actor William Shatner, who unbelievably pulled off a mighty-fine version.

'I Spy' (Lyrics: Jarvis Cocker; Music: Pulp) [Deep Cut]

If 'Mis-Shapes' was pure threat, then 'I Spy' is the threat in action. Almost symphonic in structure – comprised of various sections that work together to create something far greater than the composite parts – 'I Spy' begins almost like a soundtrack to a black-and-white art movie, before becoming an epic, orchestrally reminiscent of the Pet Shop Boys' 'It's A Sin'. It even includes a genuinely disturbing spoken-word section that showcases a somewhat nasty streak in Cocker, as he expresses how he'll take revenge on those in the middle classes that have dismissed him through the medium of sex (and, skilfully avoiding dog turds on his bike). The song's most powerful moment comes when, with full orchestral backing, he declares, 'You can take your *Year In Provence* and shove it up your ass'. In all honesty, words can't do it justice.

'Disco 2000' (Lyrics: Jarvis Cocker; Music: Pulp) [Single]

This is a joy – the record's purest and most upbeat piece of pop, despite its slightly angular strutting riff mirroring a tale of woe about being too angular for the girl next door. Lyrically toying with time – a device also used on the follow-up single 'Something Changed' – memories of the past are here mixed with a desire to meet in the future and considerations of how odd it will be to be adults. Released as a single in November 1995, when it reached number 7, 'Disco 2000' did much to cement Pulp in the popular consciousness. Although this is Pulp at their most danceable, the question remains: Is it disco? The answer? A bit, I suppose.

'Live Bed Show' (Lyrics: Jarvis Cocker; Music: Pulp) [Deep Cut]

A musical biography of a bed and all its ups and downs, this song is artistically incredible in concept and possibly even better in delivery. Jacques Brel-inspired French pop, stunning, moody orchestration and observation combine to create a piece that – had it not been created by Pulp, with all their reserves of self-belief – could've so easily been laughed away as pure pomposity and ostentation.

'Something Changed' (Lyrics: Jarvis Cocker; Music: Pulp) [Single]

The terms 'Pulp' and 'charming popular ballad' do not make regular bedfellows. However, at its heart, 'Something Changed' is just that – combining an orchestral, jangly pop sensibility with a mind-bending lyric time twist ('I wrote this song two hours before we met'). For one rare moment, Cocker ponders pure romance rather than pure sex, as the song considers love, destiny and the power of life to always bring with it, hope. The single fully deserved its moment in the sun, reaching number 10 in March 1996: the swansong for both *Different Class* and Pulp as the heart and soul of the Britpop party.

'Sorted For E's And Wizz' (Lyrics: Jarvis Cocker; Music: Pulp) [Single]

When released as a double A-side with the far inferior 'Mis-Shapes' in September 1995, 'Sorted...' almost did for Pulp. The popular press lambasted the record sleeve for being a how-to guide for the nation's youth to store their stash (as if they didn't know already), while the resulting lack of airplay for the song – meaning a surprising amount of airplay given to its counterpart – almost made the band seem like a morally dangerous and artistically-spent force, given they were following the supreme majesty of 'Common People'. But wasn't that always the way with Pulp? Their ability to meld the low into soaring artistic highs is unmatched, and here Cocker recalls the early 1990s rave scene (complete with crowd noises) in a somewhat disappointed tale of drugs and disillusionment, all offset with wonderful humour: 'Mother, I can never come home again/'Cause I seem to have left an important part of my brain somewhere in a field in Hampshire, all right'). With weirdly placed vocal echo and a woozy pop-infused synth, this showed exactly how far Pulp could push the envelope when it came to a pop single.

'F.E.E.L.I.N.G.C.A.L.L.E.D.L.O.V.E.' (Lyrics: Jarvis Cocker; Music: Pulp)

The curious thing about this song is that, musically at least, the instrumentation might have been a better fit for the themes of 'Sorted...'. A six-minute slab of electro-synth and bass that initially feels far more like a comedown than a celebration, at two and half minutes, everything changes, with powerful drums that can still take the listener by surprise (even if you know what's coming), followed by a great fast, dark and disco-infused chorus. An early showcase for the style that would dominate the follow-up album, the song really takes its time – so much so that there's little choice but to repeat the whole thing after the first chorus ends. Listen closely to the backing vocals and there's a moment at the end that shows Cocker to be a far greater singer than many give him credit for.

'Underwear' (Lyrics: Jarvis Cocker; Music: Cocker, Banks, Mackey, Senior, Doyle)

Seedy, powerful, yet slightly unsettling ('There's no way to get out, he's standing far too near'), 'Underwear' originally saw life as the B-side of 'Common People', therefore becoming a strong fan favourite. Enlisting some amusing observations ('If fashion is your trade, then when you're naked I guess you must be unemployed') that offset the subject's genuine unease with what's about to take place when she's joined in the bedroom, the sweeping French orchestration and catchy melody acted as a greater foretaste of what *Different Class* was to provide than the A-side.

'Monday Morning' (Lyrics: Jarvis Cocker; Music: Pulp)

A precursor to some of the themes revisited on 1998's *This Is Hardcore* album, 'Monday Morning', discusses the emptiness of burning the candle at both ends: 'Is this the light of a new day dawning?/No, it's just another Monday morning'. It contains a rather blistering and galloping chorus that make it one of *Different Class*' most upbeat tracks. There's even time for some fun ('Stomach in, chest out/On your marks, get set, go!') and a Blur-esque 'la la la la' section. With some experiment, raucousness and a few revisited musical ideas thrown into the mix, there's a minor feeling of the album marking time before...

'Bar Italia' (Lyrics: Jarvis Cocker; Music: Pulp)

With a melody that feels so natural, it's hard to believe you've never heard it before, this is essentially the sister track to 'Monday Morning', dealing with the comedown from clubbing, yet being unable to go to bed because 'it hasn't worn off yet'. But this is neither downbeat nor epic – instead, being a three-and-a-half-minute country-esque reminder of the standout line from 'Common People': that you 'dance and drink and screw because there's nothing else to do'. The high point comes when Cocker states, 'If we get through this alive/I'll meet you next week, same place, same time', which doubles as a reminder to the listener to check in with the record again: as if we needed it.

Optional Extras

The album's 2006 deluxe edition collects a number of demos and rarities, but not all the B-sides: missing out many of the singles' remixes. A great live version of 'Common People' focuses on electronic noises, including the synth moo. It boils the song right down, firing on all cylinders, cheered on by an animated and enthusiastic Glastonbury crowd. Both 'Mile End' (later on the massively popular *Trainspotting* soundtrack) and 'PTA' are excellent songs. 'Ansaphone' appears in demo form – a simple, stripped-down version of the far-superior B-side: sadly not included. Other demos include the uninspiring 'Paula', the bizarre keyboard demo 'Catcliffe Shakedown', the magnificent disco-inspired fan favourite 'We Can Dance Again', and finally 'Don't Lose It', which explores many of the album's musical ideas. A divisive, thoroughly Pulped live cover of 'Whiskey In The Jar' is also included, followed by a Nick Cave cover of 'Disco 2000', which veers from serious to less-so and back again throughout. At the end comes 'Common People (Vocoder mix)', an effect-heavy version, which adds nothing but fits in well with some of the other oddities.

1996 – Mad for it

The stars had aligned, and the tectonic plates shifted. Take That had called it a day, and even Robbie Williams had bolted for the exit to hang out with Oasis at Glastonbury 1995. The coast was clear for 1996 to be the zeitgeist year for Britpop.

Bands that were previously used to small sweaty rooms with tiny stages now found themselves a part of the mainstream British musical landscape, with both *Top Of The Pops* and Saturday-morning TV appearances calling, while even *Smash Hits* beat a path to their door and knocked off the hinges to get access. Fighting with mad cows and cloned sheep for space in the mainstream press, the music industry acted accordingly – went 'mad for it' and flooded the market with as many Britpop soundalike bands as they could muster at short notice from the nearest pub.

Britpop had settled in and now became part of a celebrity circus, with even those you could usually trust to be more levelheaded, joining the madness – Noel Gallagher collected his Brit award from INXS' Michael Hutchence, with the words 'Has-beens shouldn't present awards to going-to-bes', while Jarvis Cocker stole the show by invading the stage of none other than Michael Jackson.

Meanwhile, a cross-pollination of the arts was taking place, summed up by Chris Evans' new *TFI Friday* show, which chimed perfectly with the age and promoted everything the new culture had to offer, in a positive and occasionally preposterous pro-British light.

Britpop now even had its own movie – *Trainspotting*, released in February, captured public attention and made stars of its lead actors, which was pretty impressive given its violent and depressing subject matter of grim 1980s Edinburgh heroin addicts going through withdrawal or finding their next hit. The film also spawned not one but two huge-selling soundtrack albums that included a veritable who's-who of British music (plus a sprinkling of US acts).

As Euro 96 brought football back into the cultural landscape – softened in image by legally-imposed improvements to stadia, and the Britpop anthem 'Three Lions' (another big win for The Lightning Seeds' Ian Broudie, joined by comedians David Baddiel and Frank Skinner) – the England team put in an unexpectedly strong performance. Though national hearts were broken following Gareth Southgate's penalty kick in the semifinal, New Labour had sniffed the air and were now making overtures to leading cultural players of all stripes to create a sort of Red Wedge for the 1990s generation. Spurred on by Noel's shout-out to Blair at the Brits, the seeds were sewn for what would become known as Cool Britannia.

In short, things were getting big, and nothing came bigger than Oasis' bettering of their own Maine Road Stadium homecoming shows (attendance 40,000) by announcing two nights at Knebworth for a mammoth 250,000 fans. As four percent of the population clambered for tickets, the group secured their place as Britain's biggest band, with August seeing the largest freestanding gig in British history. Their only serious UK challengers now were the new pop group Spice Girls, who released their debut long-player *Spice* the following month.

Yes, the bubble was getting really big, maybe even too big. The only question now was when – and how – would it burst?

The 'new mainstream' nature of Britpop in 1996 is demonstrated by practically all of this chapter's album choices. With no big releases from the key players, it was a moment for second-tier bands (Sleeper, The Bluetones and even Kula Shaker) to soundtrack the summer, flying far higher than they might've otherwise been expected to. Meanwhile, there was even a little room to introduce one more big hitter: the re-emerging Manic Street Preachers finally succeeding in their long-held promise.

The Bluetones – Expecting To Fly (1996)

Recording sessions: 1995
Producer: Hugh Jones
Record label: Superior Quality
Chart position: UK: 1
Release date: 12 February 1996

Pete: To see The Bluetones live at this point meant being greeted with a stage set of spinning police lights. It was so incredibly effective in its simplicity that I still think it's an incredibly cool idea to this day. In a way, it summed up the band, not just because the lights were blue, but because they were dealing with textures, not features.

Matt: The Bluetones for me were always Mark Morriss' vocals – They were so distinctive and well-crafted, they gave an extra level to songs that might've otherwise struggled or come across as slightly generic. Take 'Slight Return' – the music is a nice, jangly slice of pop. But coupled with Morriss' heartfelt vocal, it moves from good to great.

The Album

So here's a pub quiz question for you: Which band knocked Oasis' *(What's The Story) Morning Glory?* from the number-1 spot? The answer: The Bluetones. And while they may have only achieved this Herculean feat for a single week, it was more than enough to secure their place in the Britpop Hall of Fame. Formed in London's Hounslow in 1993, this was no overnight-success story, and accordingly, *Expecting To Fly* has a laid-back air throughout. It shuffles rather than soars; bobs rather than bounces, and in frontman Mark Morris, it has vocals so loungey, they belong in Las Vegas. None of these factors are mentioned as shortcomings. In fact, they're simply building blocks of a record that shows that by 1996, Britpop didn't have to be all balls-out lads-lads-

lads swagger, but could also be delivered with – in the words of the single 'Bluetonic' – 'A little charm and a lot of style'.

Standout track: 'Slight Return'

Key Album: Sleeper – The It Girl (1996)
Personnel:
Louise Wener: vocals, rhythm guitar
Jon Stewart: lead guitar
Andy MacLure: drums
Diid Osman: bass
Recording sessions: Winter 1995-1996, London.
Note: Though little recording information has been found, in May 2020, The Charlatans' Tim Burgess included *The It Girl* as an episode of his lockdown Twitter Listening Party, during which Stewart and Wener shared memories of the sessions, including a picture of demo tapes from Matrix Studios, London (dated 15 December 1995) and Maison Rouge Studios, London.
Producer: Stephen Street
Record label: Indolent
Chart position: UK: 5
Release date: 6 May 1996

Pete: I was really into *Smart. I* genuinely didn't think it could be bettered and thought of Sleeper as kind of belonging to me. I was shocked by how mainstream and pop they suddenly became with *The It Girl. I* didn't feel disappointed or betrayed though; I just thought, 'Awesome, I was right!'.

Matt: *Smart* was really good, but this is definitely their best album. It's certainly the one I return to most often, with the band having a great collection of catchy melodic songs that both complemented – and in turn were complemented by – Wener's vocals. I don't know why I never felt the same way about the third album.

The Band
Wener and Stewart met at Manchester University, and following graduation, moved to London to form a band and look for gigs. Following the recruitment of MacLure and Osman, the band had a number of names before settling on Sleeper. After months of songwriting and rehearsals – plus a touch of media blagging – in 1993, they signed to Indolent Records: a subsidiary of RCA. After three EPs and a tour opening for Blur, Sleeper released their breakthrough single 'Inbetweener', followed by their debut album *Smart* in 1995. The successful follow-up album *The It Girl* was released in 1996, including four top-20 singles. The exhaustive tour led to band tensions, and drink and drug problems ultimately led to Osman's departure. The following album, *Pleased*

To Meet You was released in 1997 (with new bassist Dan Kaufmann) but failed to build on previous success. With the label withdrawing support, tour dates were subsequently cancelled, or the venues downsized. In 1998, the band split – Wener and MacLure continuing to record as part of a new project while Stewart moved into session work. In 2017, Sleeper reformed without Osman or Kaufman. After an initial UK tour, a new album was released in March 2019, and in December 2020, a further *lost* album was released, including material Wener, MacLure and Stewart recorded after the band split. Sleeper continue as one of the great Britpop comeback stories.

The Album

Although the songs that would go on to define the band ('Inbetweener', 'Vegas') had appeared on Sleeper's debut album *Smart*, 1996 was the moment they truly broke through. They had more than paid their dues as a Britpop opening act, and with *The It Girl*, were ready to go over the top for a smash-and-grab invasion of pop territory, enjoying a couple of years of incredible success into the bargain.

But what had changed? Well, Wener's vignettes on the doldrums of suburbia remained intact, as did their already-impressive indie-rock racket and oft-overlooked gift for movie references (The world of gangsters, spies and spooks go through the record like words through a stick of rock). But *The It Girl* also offers greater emotional maturity. Resignation and disappointment abound – perhaps as a result of Wener changing writing partner from former lover Jon Stewart to future husband Andy MacLure – and when brought to the boil greater with a bag of tricks stolen from Wener's 1980s pop adolescence, the result is a truly enjoyable album that turned Louise into superstar poster material for every Britpop-obsessed indie kid in the country. Negative comments about Wener's voice proved to be largely unfounded (only she had the personal honesty to deliver the album's more heartbreaking moments, and if they'd been performed by Celine Dion, did anyone really think they'd work as well?), and *The It Girl* is subsequently a record delivered by real human beings experiencing real thoughts and feelings. The fact that they're having tremendous fun at the same time should not take away from that.

'Lie Detector' (Louise Wener, Andy MacLure)

A single guitar and vocal arrangement place Wener at the heart of the band, the song and the album as a whole. The rest of the band finally catch up around the 30-second mark (What were these blokes doing? Sleeping?), creating a really exciting indie pop post-punk racket backing one of Wener's charming and literate vignettes on suburban life: in this case, about how long-term relationships can still be filled with the agony of distrust. Of all the album's tracks, it's really only here that you feel Wener struggling vocally, and even then, it's in a pounding chorus that's so exciting, it's all part of the fun. A special note should be made of the first outing for what we shall call the

'Sleeper stop' – the music coming to an abrupt end (often combined with a witty lyric), acting as a sort of cheeky wink to the listener. Listen closely: they're all over this record.

'Sale Of The Century' (Louise Wener, Andy MacLure) [Single]

The album's second single nudged its way into the top 10 in April 1996 (a first for the band), just a couple of weeks before the album release. It's a tale about how the shine of new love wears off to be replaced with bitterness ('You said I was cheap/You were the sale of the century' is brilliant). The choppy guitar-led intro leads to a chugging-yet-jaunty verse. But it's the chorus that really grabs the attention, punctuated by guitar lines that your head would require a clamp for to stop bouncing. Blink and you'll miss it, but the song ends with a really curious backwards-sounding outro that feels beamed in from another song, hinting at a depth to Sleeper's musicality which was rarely explored.

'What Do I Do Now?' (Louise Wener) [Single]

On first impression, this could just be an unremarkable album track rather than the album's lead single (It reached number 14). It's a fairly straightforward, mid-tempo, keyboard-led indie-rock outing. But combined with a driving melody and a lyric that's utterly heartbreaking in its description of a relationship going through the motions, you soon realise that Sleeper had stepped up a gear. The line 'Was it when I said I wanted to have children?' and the high keyboard line pull on the heartstrings with whip-like ferocity. Only three songs into the album, and you realise that, while this is pop music, the sheen has been rubbed raw. This may be the album's emotional high-water mark. Even Elvis Costello later recorded a stripped-down version that focussed on the song's rawness.

'Good Luck Mr Gorsky' (Louise Wener)

Highly regarded by fans and band alike, 'Good Luck Mr Gorsky' – titled after Neil Armstrong's legendary moon-landing utterance, is essentially the closest Britpop got to accomplishing its own version of The Beatles' 'Eleanor Rigby'. A simple, stripped-back song with Stewart's delicate guitar work, this tale of stunted ambition and suburban suffocation still has a touch of resigned acceptance and hope at its core. Talking of The Beatles...

'Feeling Peaky' (Louise Wener)

As if there was some mid-1990s rule that you wouldn't be taken seriously if you didn't wear at least one of your influences brazenly on your sleeve, 'Feeling Peaky' is the song that shows a Beatles influence on Sleeper most vividly, which is vaguely surprising given that it's usually only female-fronted bands that Sleeper draw comparisons with. Perky, bubbly, hooky pop with a verse that feels like it drifted in on the Mersey itself, the listener can play spot-The-Beatles throughout, with perhaps the most blatant moment being the 'Lucy In The Sky With Diamonds'-sounding middle-eight.

'Shrinkwrapped' (Louise Wener) [Deep Cut]

Stripped grooves support a soundtrack to the late-night meanderings and concerns of anyone who's ever been in a relationship. Featuring a somewhat-epic chorus – despite the resigned lines, 'I was hatching a thousand great schemes/Maybe I'm too tired to colour them in' – this is another moment that proves Wener is always at her most powerful in the first-person. It's easy to overlook some really great music here, from the verses' gentle build to a beautifully-noisy instrumental section that's the sonic equivalent of the late-night fear. A beautiful tumbling outro, ends the song with the record's most subdued use of the Sleeper-stop.

'Dress Like Your Mother' (Louise Wener, Andy MacLure)

Picking up the pace considerably with some fast indie punk, this song has a touch of Sleeper-by-numbers lurking within its description of domesticity and how people can change with time. But it's still delirious stuff, with a wonderfully cheeky 'Oooh la la' chorus and a pretty hilarious and clear understanding of what Wener thinks about her character's situation: 'It seems to me that you're all dead already'. The Sleeper-stop is again deployed, although, this time, the final takeaway is the line 'You sold your old punk records/Read the book instead'. I'm sure she's not talking about you, dear reader. I'm sure of it. Honestly.

'Statuesque' (Louise Wener) [Single]

The album's fourth and final single was released in September 1996, marking the last time Sleeper would trouble the top 20 (It reached 17). It feels unfair; this should've been top ten at the very least and shows off an unbelievably bold and catchy tune which still feels fresh and full of life. Sharing much of the same musical DNA as Blondie's '(I'm Always Touched By Your) Presence, Dear', the record made its way into *the* Britpop movie *Trainspotting*, for which Sleeper also supplied a cover of Blondie's 'Atomic'. Both 'Statuesque' and 'Atomic' remain key parts of Sleeper's live set to this day.

'Glue Ears' (Louise Wener, Andy MacLure)

This is a song of two parts. Gentle, lilting verses drip with syrup, while hollow, detuned drums pound through choruses that include the record's dirtiest-sounding riff as if it had been ripped from the heart of debut album *Smart*. The overall effect is disconcerting and somewhat disturbing. The lyric offers small images of life as a nightmare – from the man in the rain who looks away, to the dad who 'just recites lines from movies', and – most distressingly – the 'kid in the back is eating flies'. A great, albeit slightly uncomfortable and repetitive outro rounds off the record's least pop moment. Which only makes you more ready for...

'Nice Guy Eddie' (Louise Wener) [Single]

...the record's single-greatest pop moment! Undoubtedly Sleeper's most upbeat moment since 'Inbetweener' – and featuring wonderful electronic undercurrents along with drum-machine-accurate triple-snare flair – this song doesn't have a single second without some ear-catching sound. As a first-person tale of Wener as something approaching a gangster's moll, film references abound, from the *Reservoir Dogs*-inspired title (the band used characters from the movie as holding names for songs during their creation), to mentions of dry martinis and warm chianti. Sexy, sleazy, but also containing some real heart, Wener may 'admit that it all started as a scam', but accepts that 'You were always so polite, I think I loved you', before rounding things off with the track's signature hook.

Following the album release, the single reached number 10. Had it preceded the album, who knows how much higher the song and the band could've flown.

'Stop Your Crying' (Louise Wener)

Despite a good dose of jangling pop, a McCartney-esque bass line and a catchy chorus, this song never feels essential. But what could follow the powerhouse that is 'Nice Guy Eddie'? The main achievement of 'Stop Your Crying' is in acting as a smart placeholder – keeping the Sleeper-ship on course, and preventing the singles from toppling the album. It also features some hooky ska-like guitar stabs, and a string section to anchor proceedings.

'Factor 41' (Louise Wener)

Jerky, quirky and kinky verses break into the album's last gasp of pure pop. Complete with excellent vocal ticks ('You're veryniceinfact') mirroring the joy of the 'little love attacks' that form the lyric's basis, 'Factor 41' also deploys some great descending bass that keeps the whole thing hopping forward. Despite harbouring the record's worst line ('You've done it all, you're very tall'), the song's most intriguing moment comes at 2:10 with a tiny instrumental section that could've gone on 100 times as long to provide the basis for a closing epic. Instead, the band deliver the ultimate Sleeper-stop as Wener states, 'I'm bored of being sycophantic/So get your knickers down': which works just as well and leaves space for...

'Click...Off...Gone' (Louise Wener) [Deep Cut]

It might've been very odd to end on an epic. *The It Girl* is a wonderful explosion of just how genuinely-pop the Britpop beast could be, and this song simply tweaks the template. Stripped-back and hollow, with some cold electronic sounds augmenting a gentle guitar, it shows how good the band were even when only using their most raw building blocks. Click, off, gone – Sleeper's greatest moment in the sun is over. But they had secured their position in Britpop's history, with some style.

Optional Extras

The 2011 *The It Girl* reissue included all the single B-sides, live tracks, remixes, covers and non-album songs. The covers include 'Til Tuesday's 'The Other End (of the Telescope)' – which Sleeper have made their own – and a faithful but uninspiring version of Blondie's 'Atomic'. There are a number of non-album songs worth mentioning, including the 'Denis'-like 'Paint Me', the acoustic synth of 'Room At The Top', the soft verse and jangly chorus of 'She's A Sweetheart', and finally, the soft 'Spies'. The remaining original songs all have moments of interest, but only 'Blazer Sleeves' gives an insight into what happens if Sleeper don't do their signature stop.

Ash – 1977 (1996)

Recording sessions: January- March 1996
Producer: Owen Morris, Ash
Record label: Infectious
Chart position: UK: 1
Release date: 6 May 1996

Pete: The thing I will always remember most vividly about the album *1977, i*s that all summer long, I was suffering from really bad hay fever, and I listened to it repeatedly while reading Arthur C. Clarke's *2001: A Space Odyssey* book series. I find it next to impossible to not combine these elements when I listen to it. It makes me want to sneeze.

Matt: Ash did so well in how they straddled different genres. Essentially, they were punk-pop/rock with a heavy American influence. This meant the rock magazines such as *Kerrang!* were quite happy to feature them, while at the same time, the indie press also found things to like.

The Album

For a band to leap musically from the 1994 mini-album *Trailer* to 1996's *1977* should be considered no small achievement – and the fact this was done while the band had an average age of 19 and were still studying is practically ridiculous. A mammoth leap forward in terms of arrangement and song craft, this debut album proper saw Ash hit a mighty home run, having already laid the ground with the standout singles 'Kung Fu', 'Angel Interceptor' and the unstoppably huge 'Girl From Mars'. But it's the delicacy on show that really astounds, with Wheeler marrying tales of teenage romance to string arrangements by Oasis producer Owen Morris, creating some superb miniature epics ('Goldfinger'). Of course, there's still room for some teenage fun, there being two *Star Wars* sound clips in homage to 1977 (the year the movie was released), a secret track consisting of nothing more than vomit and laughter, and at least one rock-out too many ('Darkside Lightside'): none of which diminish the album's power as an instant greatest-hits collection.

Standout track: 'Angel Interceptor'

Key Album: Manic Street Preachers – Everything Must Go (1996)

Personnel:
James Dean Bradfield: lead vocals, guitars, piano
Sean Moore: drums, percussion, trumpet, backing vocals
Nicky Wire: bass, backing vocals
Richey Edwards: rhythm guitar ('No Surface All Feeling')
Recording sessions: Autumn 1995 (possibly earlier) – 'The Girl Who Wanted To Be God', Real World Studios, Wiltshire.
Autumn-Winter 1995/1996 – The rest of the album (except for 'No Surface All Feeling'), Chateau De La Rouge Motte, Normandy, France.
Winter 1995-1996 – 'No Surface All Feeling', The Big Noise Recorders, Cardiff.
Note: Further orchestration was added to some songs at Abbey Road. Dave Eringa has also stated in interviews that 'No Surface All Feeling' contains parts of the demo recorded with Richey Edwards at House in the Woods Studio, Surrey in January 1995.
Producers: Mike Hedges; Stephen Hague ('The Girl Who Wanted To Be God'); Dave Eringa ('No Surface All Feeling')
Record label: Epic
Chart position: UK: 2
Release date: 20 May 1996

Pete: The thing that always struck me about the release of *Everything Must Go,* was how suddenly the Manics became major players: up there with the likes of Blur and Oasis in terms of popularity. There was no messing about; they were suddenly front-and-centre and enjoying the attention: quite rightly too, given all they'd been through.

Matt: This is the sound of a band that has moved on and matured while still singing about many of the same themes that preoccupied previous albums. But now, they delivered the messages in a more popular format that anyone could enjoy if perhaps not necessarily understand. As a result, it managed to keep many hard-core fans onboard and picked up a multitude of new ones.

The Album

The Manics' fourth album may have been the one that brought them all the success they dreamed of in the era of *Generation Terrorists*, but it came at a heartbreakingly high price. On 1 February 1995 – after his continuing struggles with depression – guitarist Richey Edwards disappeared without trace or real explanation. His loss represented a chasm within the soul of the band, and they seriously considered giving up before the decision was made – with the blessing of Edwards' family – to continue as a three-piece (the door always being open should Edwards return). The resulting album represented a sharp right-turn for a band that had always been abrasive and subversive by nature. With a more mainstream guitar-rock sound than any previous album – but one that fits snugly into Britpop – the group looked different: eschewing their former Clash-style outfits in favour of a style that could only be described as smart-casual. This – combined with the massive success of the album and its singles, Brit awards and Mercury Prize nominations – led some to accuse the band of having sold out. Given all they'd suffered, this was plainly insulting (Admittedly, many of the theatrics were consigned to a previous era (except for Wire), but what was left represented a band that weren't gods, but people doing their best in extraordinary circumstances; trying to come to terms with their past, present and future, in song form. Though Edwards may not have contributed to every song on the record, the emotions that he left behind permeate every moment.

'Elvis Impersonator: Blackpool Pier' (Lyrics: Nicky Wire, Richey Edwards; Music: James Dean Bradfield, Sean Moore)

At face value, this opening song chimes so perfectly with the Britpop mantra that it almost feels designed as a request to join the party. Over acoustic guitar and harp, James Dean Bradfield sings of an 'overweight and out of date' seaside pier, Elvis, and how tawdry it is that American culture infected Britain to such a degree. But when the band start at one and a half minutes, you realise this is actually more subversive. After all, the 1960s British beat-group invasion of the US merely sold their own music back to them, and was Britpop any different? 'It's so f*cking funny, it's absurd', indeed.

'A Design For Life' (Lyrics: Nicky Wire; Music: James Dean Bradfield, Sean Moore) [Single]

What was in many ways the band's big comeback single was released one month before the album landed, charted at number two, and made for nothing less than a true Britpop anthem. Its anti-work sentiment and chorus lyric probably better summed up the last pre-internet generation than any other of the era:

> We don't talk about love
> We only want to get drunk
> And we are not allowed to spend
> As we are told this is the end

The song itself is nothing less than orchestral grandeur with sweeping strings and resigned anger, giving an air of romanticism, making it not so much hopeless as aspirational.

'Kevin Carter' (Lyrics: Richey Edwards; Music: James Dean Bradfield, Sean Moore, Nicky Wire) [Single]

Over staccato chords, shuffling drums and haunting trumpet, the Manics tell the tale of Kevin Carter – a South African photojournalist and Pulitzer Prize winner who took his own life in 1993 after documenting scenes he should never have had to witness. The fact the band managed to turn his tragically-short life story (He was 33 at the time of his death) into a number nine single is a remarkable achievement that chimes with the album as a whole. Most likely the album's weakest single – feeling like two different songs pushed together – it's still obvious why such subject matter would have meaning for the band.

'Enola/Alone' (Lyrics: Nicky Wire; Music: James Dean Bradfield, Sean Moore)

With an exuberant yet bittersweet soft-rock feel, this song deals with the disappearance and loss of Richey Edwards, apparently written after Nicky Wire found photos from his wedding day. As the album's most simple and straightforward song, it's more a diary entry to help the writer come to terms with all that has befallen him. Considered by many to be the album's defining moment, the song may be catchy, but it's also raw and honest in its depiction of coming to terms with loss.

'Everything Must Go' (Lyrics: Nicky Wire; Music: James Dean Bradfield, Sean Moore) [Single]

Released as a single almost two months after the album hit the stands, this song seems custom-built as a response to all those who'd labelled the band as sell-outs following their direction change and subsequent success. Simultaneously asking for forgiveness and daring you to stick the knife in, the clear desire here is that the band wish to 'escape from our history' – and given their recent history, who could blame them for wanting that? With crashing drums, the track driving forward without looking over its shoulder for a moment, the single hit number 5. But this may not be as straightforward as it seems – If you imagine that it's being sung to Richey, then it takes on a whole different meaning: especially in the line 'Look to the future, it makes me cry'.

'Small Black Flowers That Grow In The Sky' (Lyrics: Richey Edwards; Music: James Dean Bradfield, Sean Moore, Nicky Wire)

With an Edwards lyric based around the conditions zoo animals are kept in (where 'chewing your tail is joy'), this song is pivotal in understanding Edwards' mindset before his disappearance. Over a striking harp-led arrangement, the song may be bleak, but it's also beautiful and even elegiac. As the album's central point, it retains the ability to make the listener's hair stand on end.

'The Girl Who Wanted To Be God' (Lyrics: Nicky Wire, Richey Edwards; Music: James Dean Bradfield, Sean Moore)
Featuring sweeping synth strings and drums that recall the first album's programmed sound, this song may not be the album's most memorable, but it's certainly one of its most danceable. Based on the life of American poet Sylvia Plath (who wrote a poem with the same title), there's a symmetry with 'Kevin Carter', in terms of the song's placement on the record, and in Plath also being a Pulitzer Prize winner (albeit posthumously) who passed away at a young age following battles with depression. The opening line, 'There are no sunsets, just silence', is particularly powerful.

'Removables' (Lyrics: Richey Edwards; Music: James Dean Bradfield, Sean Moore, Nicky Wire) [Deep Cut]
As one of the last songs Richey Edwards ever wrote, it's hard to listen to 'Removeables' without believing you can quite clearly see his state of mind in the final months before his disappearance. The chorus lines 'All removables, all transitory/All removables, passing always' seem especially concise in their acceptance and resignation in general. But hindsight is a wonderful – if sometimes tragic – thing, and the difficult subject matter is perhaps why the lyric is set to a particularly-jaunty acoustic clatter: as if to say matching it with anything darker would've been too much to take. Only in the chorus' second half – and when the song simply seems to run out of steam – do you truly get a sense of the emotional weight it carries.

'Australia' (Lyrics: Nicky Wire; Music: James Dean Bradfield, Sean Moore) [Single]
Given the Manics' exceptionally considered and literate lyrics, it's nice when they give you a little light relief. The most bombastic of the album's singles – and containing one of the entire Britpop era's greatest introductions – 'Australia' is pure escapism about running to where you can 'sleep for a while and speak no words'. Let's face it; they'd be deserving of that. An absolutely exhilarating song that's a pure joy from start to finish, the single reached number 7 when released in December 1996: the final shot of the *Everything Must Go* campaign.

'Interiors (Song For Willem de Kooning)' (Lyrics: Nicky Wire; Music: James Dean Bradfield, Sean Moore)
Another Richey lyric – this time about the abstract expressionist artist Willem de Kooning – this is a lament in rock form, for lost youth and vitality as Alzheimer's strips the subject raw ('Say you can remember/Say where is the

tomorrow'). Despite this, it's not a difficult listen, with jabbing chords and funky bass in the verses, a wonderful building bridge, and sweeping choruses full of excellent lead responses. But its finest moment is the instrumental, which recalls the bass-led coldness of Joy Division.

'Further Away' (Lyrics: Nicky Wire; Music: James Dean Bradfield, Sean Moore)

Like 'Removeables', this is a song with sad subject matter set to positively jubilant music. Dealing with simple homesickness ('The circular landscape comes back only with regret') and the passing of time ('The draining away just like an old man's dream'), 'Further Away' has been described as the band's only true love song, though it's anything but soppy. A counterpoint to 'Australia', the lyric details the desire to return rather than escape, and, fittingly, was released as a single in Japan.

'No Surface All Feeling' (Lyrics: Nicky Wire; Music: James Dean Bradfield, Sean Moore) [Deep Cut]

While it's easy to presume this song is the summation of Nicky Wire's thoughts on his bandmate's disappearance, it's surprising to discover it was actually one of the first songs written for the record and even features Edwards on guitar. With the album's quietest moments in its verses and chiming Smashing Pumpkins-esque guitars (as noted on the demo recording) bringing the sweeping chorus to life, this is like a raw nerve being aggravated and acts as the perfect conclusion to an album permeated with loss and all the confusion, heartbreak and hurt that follows it.

Optional Extras

Everything Must Go has been reissued in both 10th and 20th-anniversary deluxe editions, including non-album B-sides; the 10th Anniversary Edition offering additional demos, rehearsals and live songs. The 20th edition includes a live gig and some additional remixes of varying quality, along with unexpected cover versions that were released as B-sides and on the *Lipstick Traces* compilation. The demos and rehearsal versions offer the album songs in low-fi, allowing the listener to hear them without the production and orchestral gloss, which might've made for some more interesting alternative mixes. The non-album songs offer some of the Manics' strongest B-sides. Led by the superb 'Sepia', there are also some of a more tongue-in-cheek nature, such as the domestic subject of 'Mr Carbohydrate', the celebrity relationships of 'Dead Passive', the muzak/1960s film soundtrack of 'Horses Under Starlight', and the flutes and 1960s vibe of 'Dead Trees And Traffic Islands'. 'Black Garden' is built around a funky bass line but does little more, while the repetitive 'Hanging On' and 'No One Knows What It's Like To Be Me' echo the album's more rock moments. The more old-school-Manics-sounding 'First Republic', rounds off the collection.

Ocean Colour Scene – Moseley Shoals (1996)

Recording sessions: 1995
Producer: Brendan Lynch
Record label: MCA
Chart position: UK: 2
Release date: 8 April 1996

Pete: 1996?! How can it be as far along as 1996 when Ocean Colour Scene released this record? It feels like it's one of the blueprint records! I suppose that's down to the retro style of it all – they wanted to sound like these songs had always existed. As a side point, I suppose Ocean Colour Scene were one of *our* bands: coming from up the road in Brum.

Matt: This is one of those albums where everything falls into place. Guitarist Craddock had been working with Paul Weller (who even makes an appearance), and they'd been part of Oasis' massive tour after a request from Noel Gallagher the previous year. They also had a set of great songs, with a lead single that Chris Evans was heavily pushing on arguably the most important and popular radio show in the UK, and on his TV show, *TFI Friday*. They just couldn't go wrong!

The Album

Helped in no small supply by *TFI Friday*'s use of 'The Riverboat Song' as entrance music for every single guest ever, Ocean Colour Scene plugged themselves into Britpop with such force that they leapt straight into the mainstream without passing go, even securing support slots at Oasis' huge Knebworth concerts. This may seem an odd thing to say given that OCS' debut had come four years earlier, but they'd been burnt by their first foray, and now presented themselves as an entirely new band, albeit one whose influences leaned extremely heavily on the 1960s. Unapologetic bluesy mod music for a new generation – with Mick Jagger soundalike singer Simon Fowler – the huge singles taken from *Moseley Shoals* (named after their home suburb in Birmingham) set out an undeniably-bombastic songwriting stall of real quality (Just check out 'You've Got it Bad'), while album tracks like 'Lining Your Pockets' showed they could also be delicate and sensitive when necessary.

Standout track: 'The Day We Caught The Train'

Super Furry Animals – Fuzzy Logic (1996)

Recording sessions: 1996
Producers: Gorwel Owen, Super Furry Animals
Record label: Creation
Chart position: UK: 23
Release date: 20 May 1996

Pete: There's no other band like Super Furry Animals. There's this wonderful story that Alan McGee said he'd sign them to Creation if they sang in English, and they said, 'But we *do* sing in English'.

Matt: Oh absolutely, there's no other band like Super Furry Animals. For 1996, they even had a party tank – a real army tank they bought off an arms dealer, painted blue, fitted with a dance-music sound system and took 'round the festivals. As you do.

The Album

It's hard to be sure what they were putting in the water in South Wales in the mid-1990s, but it's also a fair bet that Gruff Rhys and Super Furry Animals were too busy experimenting with other substances to bother drinking any in the first place. Though you can try to sum up this incredible debut as psychedelic, even then, you're really only scratching the surface, and the very idea that an album as good as this only reached number 23 is preposterous – but then, 'preposterous' would be the band's middle name if it weren't already Furry). Despite this, *Fuzzy Logic* is never bizarre or impregnable; it's just an album that cocks its head and looks at the world from a different angle, and is actually as much enthralled to The Beach Boys as it is to Captain Beefheart. While songs about hooking the hamster up to the electrics ('Fuzzy Birds'), alien abduction ('Hometown Unicorn') and hangin' with Howard Marks ('Hangin' With Howard Marks') may leave some scratching their heads, the singles 'Something For The Weekend' and 'God Show Me Magic' offer wonderful gateway drugs to the album's brilliance.

Standout track: 'Bad Behaviour'

Longpigs – The Sun Is Often Out (1996)

Recording sessions: 1995-1996
Producer: Kevin Bacon
Record label: Mother
Chart position: UK: 26
Release date: 29 April 1996

Pete: I still maintain that *The Sun Is Often Out* is perhaps the single greatest album of the Britpop era. I had a girlfriend once who listened to the album with me and said it sounded dated. That was the end of that particular love affair.

Matt: You were all about the Longpigs, and if you hadn't gotten into them, I think I could've easily missed the band and this album. In fact, I think quite a few people probably did just miss them. Interestingly, Crispin Hunt is now a songwriter and producer for many well-known bands and solo artists from the last 20 years.

The Album

By any definition, it's fair to say that Longpigs didn't really have a fair run of it, and if this album had come out at the point the band initially expected in 1994/1995, they could've been seen as leaders of the pack. Having initially signed to Elektra in 1993 – only for the UK label to close before their debut single was released – the band were saved by none other than U2, who eventually picked them up for their Mother label. Say what you like about Bono, but when it comes to the Longpigs, he'd struck gold (though perhaps not of the financial kind).

Musically a cut above, vocalist Crispin Hunt's ability to jump pitch mid-line was quite unique in the Britpop canon, while Richard Hawley (who later joined Pulp live and enjoyed an outstanding solo career) shepherded the guitar sound into a strikingly loose yet vital force. Despite being an album where almost every song could've been a single, of the five released, only 'On And On' and 'She Said' scraped the top 20: meaning though the record may largely have been only an *artistic* triumph, it was a triumph nonetheless.

Standout track: 'On And On'

Key Album: Suede – Coming Up (1996)

Personnel:
Brett Anderson: vocals
Richard Oakes: guitars
Simon Gilbert: drums
Mat Osman: bass
Neil Codling: keyboards
Recording sessions: November 1995-May/June 1996 – Townhouse, and Westside Studios, London.
Producer: Ed Buller
Record label: Nude
Chart position: UK: 1, USA: 17 (Heatseeker's chart)
Release date: 2 September 1996

Pete: There was a feeling that Suede deserved *Coming Up;* that they'd gotten short shrift and now deserved to take their place back at the top table. Whether this record really achieved that, is up for debate, but it's a great example of a band trying to plug in with the moment for maximum effect.

Matt: This was Suede Mark II (or 1.5), and I actually prefer this version. Yes, they had lost some of the magnificence and inner vitriol, but I feel the band were working together better, and the songs were less conflicted. They had something to prove (that they could cope without Butler) and they really achieved that. It also helped that they were writing catchier tunes.

149

The Album

The music industry can be a fickle business. Suede had essentially created Britpop in their own image, yet, it's fair to say that by 1996 they not only saw their crown slip, but actually be stolen by Blur, who then had it manhandled away again by Oasis. Times had been tough – Suede founder-member Bernard Butler (often seen as *literally* instrumental to their success) had departed during the latter stages of the artistically triumphant (but less-commercially-successful) previous album *Dog Man Star*. This left the remaining members considering what the future meant for them, whilst the press circled and started to enjoy tearing a strip off the group they'd done so much to elevate. Replacing a significant member is difficult for any group, but when Butler was replaced by Richard Oakes (himself a young Butler protégé) and keyboard player Neil Codling (who often seemed surprised to be part of the team), the daggers were out – after all, if Butler is worth two other musicians, then was it really worth carrying on? The answer was undoubtedly 'Yes!', and *Coming Up* proved to be the band's commercial high-water mark – producing a staggering five top-10 singles – introducing Suede to a huge number of overseas markets (including America) and securing a nomination for the 1997 Mercury Music Prize. By embracing the new lineup and aiming their sights firmly at the public's pop jugular, *Coming Up* proved to almost be a project album: as if they'd set out to make the Suede version of a Britpop record and to-heck-with-the-consequences. Listen closely, and you may even find echoes of Blur and Pulp lurking in these songs, and also Oasis in the massive sing-along choruses designed for mass-chanting. Diehards would, of course, complain that this was no longer Suede – by losing the material's previous depth and throwing themselves into the Britpop boom rather than ploughing their own furrow, they'd undercut their own achievements – but they were missing all the fun.

'Trash' (Anderson, Oakes) [Single]

Storming out of the gates, the album's big hitter 'Trash' proved that this time around, Suede weren't all about chasing the dragon but chasing the hits. Four minutes of high-tempo glam with a massive Britpop chorus, the song achieved everything asked of it by hitting number three two months before the album's release. A tie in terms of the band's highest chart position ('Stay Together' had reached the same peak but sold fewer copies), it placed Suede back in the belly of the beast they'd helped create.

But is this trash any good? Well, it's certainly a very enjoyable pop single, but it split the faithful into those loyal to the band and those who missed Butler's six-stringed elegance (though Oakes was an inspired replacement), and anyone expecting *Dog Man Star* part two, were to be highly disappointed. However, in their place, came a whole legion of new Britpop fans for whom this was the zenith of Suede's achievement. Note should be made of the curious similarity between 'Trash' and Pulp's 1995 album-opener 'Mis-Shapes' – Although, Anderson's kooky subjects with their 'tasteless bracelets and the dye in our hair', do seem rather more knowing than Cocker's: as if they're the awkward kids at school that have actively chosen to be the outsiders.

'Filmstar' (Anderson, Oakes) [Single]

The album's fifth and final single was released in August 1997 – almost a full year after the album – and reached number nine. Combining a dirty, weaving, glam-punk riff with a woozy chorus, 'Filmstar' is ultimately powered by repetitive lyrics that hook themselves into the brain, rounded off with some quick lines ('Wash your brain, play the game, again, yeah yeah yeah): a device that would be put to use later on 'She'. Apparently, one of the quickest songs Anderson ever wrote, 'Filmstar' certainly has immediacy, even if it ultimately feels like the record's most guilty pleasure.

'Lazy' (Anderson) [Single]

Three singles in a row! Have that! Although a fair argument could be made that 'Lazy' deploys some fairly Suede-by-numbers work (It is littered with references to makeup, council estates and 'drugging it up' after all), it's still a nice piece of minor pop, which extols the virtues of taking it easy because what's the point of doing anything else? Indicative of the 1990s game that every band were now playing, there's actually something of Blur lurking within the chug of the verses and bass flourishes. The weakest of all this album's singles, but still worthy of its own place in the sun, in April 1997, this *also* hit number nine.

'By The Sea' (Anderson) [Deep Cut]

Making full use of new member Neil Codling on piano, 'By The Sea' is the album's most stunning moment. Coming across like a David Bowie ballad over John Lennon's piano, and including some stunning bass which gives the whole piece wave-like effect, this simple tale of escape for a new life at the coast, is far grander and more beautiful than you'd ever expect. In fact, it's a minor epic, which – had it been swapped with the closer 'Saturday Night' – would've been a perfect album crescendo, with the washed-out repetition of the line 'Into the sea we'll bleed' showing off Anderson's voice at its most stunning.

'She' (Anderson, Oakes) [Deep Cut]

Glam drums! Glam synths! Glam guitars! Glam vocal inflections! This, it's fair to say, is a bit glam, and it's also the album's greatest pop moment. Featuring an excellent quick-line chorus ('She is bad, she is bored, she is bony, she is…') and some fun falsetto 'la la la' backing vocals, you could be forgiven for expecting too little of the track. But it doesn't stop there – by verse two, a string section has begun building and building until the whole thing is unexpectedly pushed into overdrive, transforming into the theme song for a James Bond movie that never was. Given *Coming Up* had one ultimate goal – to place the band back at the heart of the British music scene – how this didn't end up as a single, frankly beggars belief. There's also some really deft Oakes guitar work, which is just that little bit too loud toward the end: as if the group felt it was just too cool to be ignored.

'Beautiful Ones' (Anderson, Oakes) [Single]

Probably the album's best single, this celebration of life (and life in Suede) in all its wonderful madness, is a lot of fun, being simultaneously a Beach-Boys-style list song ('High on diesel and gasoline/Psycho for drum machine) and just rather silly ('Shaking their bits to the hits, oh'). Originally called 'Dead Leg' due to Oakes' threatened punishment if he was unable to pen a top-10 hit, we're delighted to report that no appendages were harmed in the making of this song: it hit number 8 in October 1996. This is so infectious that – as if to hammer the point home – the ending is highlighted by a building 'la la la' section. It feels so unnaturally Suede that you get the impression Anderson just couldn't stop himself from singing along with the pop beast he'd created.

'Starcrazy' (Anderson, Codling)

Like a flipside to 'Filmstar', and about a groupie finding life a lot more boring as life goes on ('Flat on her back in the '80s/In the nineties going nowhere'), this song's protagonist is certainly on the receiving end of one of Anderson's more amusing descriptions ('She's star starcrazy/Electric shock bog brush hair'). Remarkably, this is the first song on *Coming Up* that actually feels like an album track and struggles to match the quality of its counterparts: which is incredible given we're already teetering on the final third.

'Picnic By The Motorway' (Anderson, Oakes)

The verses of the wooziest and disconcerting song have a really nauseous feeling as if you really were drinking in the petrol fumes while enjoying a light lunch on the M25 hard shoulder. Layered with flanged reverb, echo and a field recording of an actual motorway, the song could easily be overlooked if it weren't for a naggingly-catchy chorus – Believe us, even looking at the lyrics 'Hey, such a lovely day, such a lovely day' means it's going to be rattling around the brain box for at least the best part of a morning. With a clear Bowie influence in the middle-eight and a long fade-out, this does stick out a bit like a sore thumb on what's largely an unashamed pop album. But you've got to allow Suede *some* fun, haven't you?

'The Chemistry Between Us' (Anderson, Codling)

By far the album's longest song (7:04), it never quite seems to make enough of its length or reach the grandiose epic levels it's trying to. The song begins promisingly enough in an almost Smiths-like jangle-pop mode. But its somewhat laughable and childlike chorus ('Oh, Class A, Class B/Is that the only chemistry between us?') really does knock the whole thing off course. Not even the supremely-lush outro (mirroring 'She') introduced slowly as if the song itself is giving way is enough to pull it back on track. Ultimately, it wouldn't have hurt to be chopped in half.

'Saturday Night' (Anderson, Oakes) [Single]

Released in January 1997, the third single reached number 6, and actually hit number 1 in Iceland, definitely capturing some of the emptiness that's so significant in that most desolate of months. Despite this, 'Saturday Night' is a lush and uplifting ballad that rounds-off proceedings as a last-dance-style track, with a broadly-optimistic message of where there's life, there's hope: 'It'll be alright, 'cause tonight we'll go drinking/We'll do silly things and never let the winter in'). Featuring sympathetic instrumentation – including Codling's great high organ – the only shame is that this wasn't swapped with 'By The Sea', as both songs may have felt more natural in those places. However, as 'Saturday Night' slowly fades – taking with it Suede's commercial high-point and the beginning of their long, dark Sunday morning of the soul – you can't help but feel glad they had this moment: one that, if it hadn't been for Britpop, might have been denied them.

Optional Extras

There have been two expanded versions of *Coming Up* – a 2-CD/1-DVD set from 2011, and a 20th-Anniversary Super Deluxe 4CD/1DVD set from 2016. Both include a CD of B-sides (with some minor differences in track listing), many of which had been released on the 1997 compilation *Sci-Fi Lullabies*. Additionally, the 2011 edition has a number of demos that aren't replicated on the 2016 CD, plus instrumentals, monitor mixes and alternate versions of album tracks and B-sides. All in all, they make for an interesting listen if you want to see how the band reached the final product, as they offer an alternate version of the album (In fact, with other released demos, you could make a couple of alternate versions). Finally, the 2016 set includes a previously-unreleased 1996 concert. As mentioned, the studio-based B-sides have been released multiple times, and similar to the album, include a mix of softer acoustic piano slow-burn ballads, guitar-led glam rock and some alternative-rock tracks. Due to this eclectic nature, there really is something for everyone, and though you could say that some tracks sound unfinished or lacking, it would've been easy to prune it down to a second album. In our opinion, this would include the gloomy fan-and-band favourite 'Europe Is Our Playground', the piano-led 'Another No One', the introspective 'These Are The Sad Songs', the alternative-rock 'Sadie' and the insistent, aggressive 'Money'.

Kula Shaker – K (1996)

Recording sessions: January-May 1996
Producers: John Leckie, Shep & Dodge, Crispian Mills
Record label: Columbia

Chart position: UK: 1
Release date: 16 September 1996

Pete: I still can't make up my mind whether the advent of Kula Shaker actually represents the moment the wheels fell off Britpop. I enjoyed them, but I could never take the whole thing that seriously. It was like each new band were trying to have a gimmick, and Kula Shaker had dipped their hands into the lucky bag and pulled out mystical Indian stuff.

Matt: Kula Shaker were a psychedelic rock band that found themselves included in the Britpop/post-Britpop scene. Although successful at first, I think public confusion over their sound prevented continued momentum, though it didn't help that there was some media controversy claiming Crispian Mills might've had far-right leanings or that the second album was a mixed bag. My version of *K* included their cover of 'Hush' as a bonus CD, which I think is even better than the Deep Purple version.

The Album

Fronted by Crispian Mills – and of fine acting pedigree, being the grandson of Sir John, and son of Hayley – at first glance, it was conceivable that Kula Shaker were playing a part, using an affected devotion to Indian mysticism as their ticket into the Britpop party. After all, it was one of the few Beatles stones that even Oasis had left unturned, so it seemed only a matter of time until someone used it. But what *was* surprising was that Mills really meant business, and their debut. *K* was a concept album about escaping the 9-to-5 grind and embarking on a voyage of body and mind. The fastest-selling debut since *Elastica*, and an instant UK number 1, *K* delivered a single sung purely in Sanskrit ('Govinda'), another almost entirely sung in Sanskrit ('Tattva') and a lot of peacock sounds. To balance things out, there's also a fair amount of Jimi Hendrix in the mix ('Grateful When You're Dead', 'Hey Dude'), and a touch of The Monkees for good measure ('Smart Dogs'). It should be absurd, and it kind of is (it's still hard to get over the title 'Knight On The Town'), but *perhaps* it's also a bit punk rock in a we-mean-it-man kind of way.

Standout track: 'Tattva'

Part Three. 1997-1999 – The Britpop Bust
1997 – Things, as they say, can only get better

It can be easy to forget that the vast majority of the Britpop story takes place under the Conservative government of John Major. By 1997, the party had been in power for eighteen years and was a tired shadow of the Rottweiler that had torn society in two during the 1980s – now instead being dogged with infighting about Europe and successive scandals involving sexual activity that was anything but back-to-basics.

Since the fall of the Berlin Wall in 1989, America (where in January 1997, President Bill Clinton had just been inaugurated for his second term) had seen a governmental shift toward the centre-left. It was now time for the UK to follow suit. Tony Blair's New Labour project had the wind in its sails, and though most expected a victory, few predicted the scale of landslide they would achieve. Amid a sense of healthy national pride, the celebrations at the Royal Festival Hall on the night of 1 May 1997 stretched long into the late hours. The hangover would be hard to shake off.

Keen to stand on the shoulders of giants, Blair's team had cultivated a strong following in British cultural circles and had actively courted anyone deemed influential enough to fit under the banner of Cool Britannia. Now that they were in power, it was time to say thank you. Having decided it was Oasis rather than Blur that chimed best with their message about being working-class and aspirational, June saw the unbelievable scene of Noel Gallagher, Alan McGee and a host of other pop-cultural figures descend upon Downing Street to meet and greet the new PM, rub shoulders and (potentially, in Noel's case) do naughty things in the toilet.

Unfortunately – as Harold Wilson had found in the 1960s when he associated himself with The Beatles – there's nothing less cool than saying you are. With one simple photograph of Blair and Gallagher shaking hands, Cool Britannia swallowed Britpop into the establishment, and it instantly lost not only its alternative edge but most of its credibility. As a sort of unhealthy post-Oasis laddishness crept into the culture, if you now wanted something that felt both rock and genuinely alternative, you had to hop genres back to dance, where the Prodigy and their album *The Fat Of The Land* provided the only truly dangerous influence on the charts.

Though Blair's popularity would be sustained until the early-2000s – during which time he embarked on a modernising agenda that should be applauded (not least in the arts, where the Department for Culture, Media and Sport, tellingly replaced the Department of National Heritage) – the celebratory feeling was quickly being worn away. If the release of Oasis' *Be Here Now* didn't totally kill the mood (and the disparity between media hype and listener-reaction to that record should *not* be underplayed), then it certainly instantly evaporated on the morning of 31 August when Princess Diana was reported to have died fleeing paparazzi through a Paris tunnel. The sense of shock reverberated through the nation: ironically led by the same media that probably paid the paparazzi to provide the images in the first place. With Britain in extended national mourning, Chris Evans gave up a whole episode of *TFI Friday* to play sad songs, the royal family got a swift lesson in public relations, and Elton John's rewrite of 'Candle In The Wind' instantly became the world's second-best-selling single of all time amid music store scenes that recalled the release of Oasis' *Be Here Now* only weeks before.

Meanwhile, the US was experiencing a musical phenomenon not seen since the 1960s. Spice Girls had released *Spiceworld* – their second number one album – which made them the first British band since The Beatles to have two albums in the US chart at the same time. To top it off, at the Brit Awards, Geri Halliwell's Union Flag dress not only nicked one of the key pieces of Britpop imagery, but effectively rebranded it as a symbol for forward-thinking British creativity, while Robbie Williams' December single 'Angels' pulled the rug out completely. Traditional pop was reasserting itself.

The 1997 album selections mark a parting of the ways. Though there was plenty of classic Britpop on offer from bands such as Sleeper and Supergrass (and what other year truly could've delivered a group like My Life Story?), the heyday was over. As Oasis temporarily lost their crown to a revitalised Verve, Blur took a 90-degree style turn, and Radiohead *really* got stuck in: rewriting the rulebook altogether.

Key Album: Blur – Blur (1997)

Personnel:
Damon Albarn: lead vocals, piano, keyboards, Hammond organ, acoustic guitar
Graham Coxon: guitars, backing vocals, lead vocals ('You're So Great'), theremin, additional drums ('Song 2', 'Strange News From Another Star')
Alex James: bass
Dave Rowntree: drums, percussion, drum programming ('On Your Own')
Recording sessions: June 1996 – Backing tracks, Mayfair Studios, London
June-July 1996 – Vocals (including 'Strange News From Another Star', 'Essex Dogs', 'Beetlebum', 'On Your Own'), plus some synthesizer work, Studio Grettisgat, Reykjavík, Iceland
September-November 1996 – Maison Rouge Studio, London
November 1996 – 'I'm Just A Killer For Your Love', Studio 13, London
Producers: Stephen Street, Blur
Record label: Food
Chart position: UK: 1, USA: 61
Release date: 10 February 1997

Pete: I still remember putting this on for the first time and thinking 'Thank God'. I loved Blur, but there was no way I could've taken another Life-style album. The trilogy of *Modern Life Is Rubbish, Parklife* and *The Great Escape* was enough. Plus, this was an awesome record that completely transformed my opinion of both the band and what I wanted from music. If they hadn't changed so dramatically, I don't think they'd be considered even half as highly now.

Matt: I remember first hearing 'Beetlebum' being played in the common room of sixth form, and the introduction and verse were so different to anything you would expect from Blur, that I didn't believe it was them. Only when the chorus kicked in did it start to resemble a Blur song: it was such a new sound and a brave change.

The Album

The period fans later referred to as the 'Life Trilogy' of Blur albums had come to an end. Admittedly it had been a very rewarding end in terms of commerciality, but there was little else to say in that mode really. Having drained the tank dry of character songs and nods to their favourite 1960s bands, Blur were finally sick of the Britpop beast they'd done so much to raise. With massive sales, had come household recognition (often in the same breath as Oasis) and a feeling in the media that their peak had been reached. However, Blur had reinvented themselves once before, so was it really that surprising they should do it again? Out went the oompah, the 'oi's and the overwhelming desire to shift units, and in came a healthy dose of noisy guitar-led US alternative-rock aggression (Coxon's idea) and alarming emotional sensitivity and fragility (Albarn's state of mind), which combined to create *Blur*: the band's fifth album, and one they were confident enough about to literally pin their name on as an album title. Helped in no small part by the insistent earworm that was 'Song 2', the album became a huge success, finally reaching the American audience that had previously eluded them, and pulling the critics back on side. But what of the Britpop fan base? Well, they were largely pulled along, too, helped by a string of brilliant singles and some even greater album moments. Though there may have been a desire here to destroy Britpop, that was already being done by popular music's never-ending hunger for the thrill of the new. What *Blur* did, was give the band their third persona in three-quarters of a decade and the opportunity to move forward with their reputation and sales intact.

'Beetlebum' (Lyrics: Damon Albarn; Music: Blur [Single]

By 1997, The Beatles were largely considered as territory won by Oasis. Starting *Blur* (and the album campaign itself) with the single 'Beetlebum' was a surprising moment that was seen by many as distilling the entirety of the *White Album* down into one five-minute-long laid-back, fuzzy guitar groove. With a rhythm and drive that actually saw a return to the baggy-esque styling of *Leisure* – but handled with all the restraint and maturity of a band with little to prove but everything to fight for – the single reached number 1, despite a concerned label considering its release as a single as commercial suicide. A song about heroin and Albarn's relationship with Elastica's Justine Frischmann, this is one of Blur's most weirdly sexy moments ('She'll suck your thumb'), as Damon finds the more-mature elements of his voice, which he would employ for the rest of his career. As an example of restraint, it's unsurpassed, and you feel Coxon could go off on one at any moment. But instead, he remains extraordinarily sympathetic to the material, especially during the uplifting and gently-building outro – probably time to let him off the leash though.

'Song 2' (Lyrics: Damon Albarn. Music: Blur) [Single]

If Oasis had 'Wonderwall' as an unexpected mega-albatross, then Blur's equivalent is undoubtedly 'Song 2'. A piece of stupidity that – like the Ramones – displays a raw intelligence in its punk-pop construction and delivery, there can be little doubt that the song's running time of 2:02 and its album position, show a lot of thought and preparation. Of course, you already know it, but when 'Song 2' landed on fresh ears with the album and later as its second single (in April 1997), it was unmistakably the most exhilarating song of the year. Its razor-sharp punky stabbings (Coxon clearly having enormous fun), distorted bass and bounce-off-the-walls 'Woo hoo!' chorus, meant the song just kicked ass, even if it *was* meant as something of a joke to freak out the record execs and as a parody of the grunge or punk scenes. Oh, and where did it place on the singles chart? Number two, of course. It's like the perfect art project.

'Country Sad Ballad Man' (Lyrics: Damon Albarn; Music: Blur)

How do you follow 'Song 2'? Of all the myriad possibilities open to a band as dexterous as Blur, it still surprises the ear to find yourself in the territory of 'Country Sad Ballad Man': a piece of twangy southern Americana that's been so deep-fried, it practically reeks of the heat. The song combines a traditional blues feel with some wonderful San Francisco-style psych-outs (from 3:40), while Albarn revels in vocal styles he's never deployed before. Talking of Damon, the wearily resigned line, 'I had my chances, they had me', must offer a pretty good glimpse into the mind of the man at the time.

'M.O.R.' (Lyrics: Damon Albarn; Music: Blur, David Bowie, Brian Eno) [Single]

Stuttered guitar riffs, beating bass and a drum part that feels like a never-ending build all ramp up the excitement before an absolute explosion is unleashed in the choruses, topped off by an awesome Coxon anti-solo. And we haven't even mentioned the dirty distort of the call-and-response vocals (with a really neat reversal the third time around) that's the antithesis of 1994's 'Girls & Boys'. Sharing a chord structure with the David Bowie songs 'Boys Keep Swinging' and 'Fantastic Voyage' (earning him a credit, although the two songs were originally part of a Bowie experiment to see what could be achieved from the same basic parts, and Blur claimed they were continuing this: as if that would hold up in court!), this is ultimately anything but M.O.R. (Middle of the road). It's unthinkable that this could be by the same band that had delivered 'Country House'. 'M.O.R.' reached 15 when released as a single in September 1997.

'On Your Own' (Lyrics: Damon Albarn; Music: Blur) [Single]

Almost as good as its fellow singles but far more laid-back, this is about how a 'Holy man tiptoed his way across the Ganges/The sound of magic music in his ears', and far more besides. Let's be frank; we've no idea what the song is about. But it doesn't matter, because this is (admittedly noisy) pop music, blipping and droning through various guitar effects, with a backing vocal that (as opposed to 'M.O.R.') is so close to 'Girls & Boys', that Blur could've sued themselves. Charting at 5 in June 1997, 'On Your Own' holds much of the same DNA as Albarn's subsequent success Gorillaz, though his claim that this is essentially one of their first tunes, seems a bit much. This is pure Blur, throwing their toys in the air and seeing where they land, as guitars explode like short-circuiting fuse boards.

'Theme From Retro' (Lyrics: Damon Albarn; Music: Blur)

And now it's time for some art. It's largely instrumental, though there are lyrics that were performed live, but are here rendered all but unintelligible thanks to layers of echo. This is an organ-led piece that – in theory – should be familiar to Blur fans by this point. But 'Theme From Retro' occupies a much darker and more-twisted psychedelic space than the music-hall punk explosions on *Modern Life Is Rubbish*: making this feel like an epic, even if it doesn't actually go anywhere and perhaps goes on a bit too long.

'You're So Great' (Lyrics: Graham Coxon. Music: Blur)

The push/pull dynamic between childhood friends Albarn and Coxon is often cited as one of the band's key strengths, and while *Blur* is certainly the album that began to redress the balance, 'You're So Great' is still the first time Coxon was called on to sing a lead vocal. Despite a stripped-down demo sound (especially vocally), it does have a natural place on this record but would've stuck out like a sore thumb on any preceding album. Though there are no drums, it's far from an acoustic song and acts as a charming and simple album centre point, filled with a yearning hope ('When you tell me it's okay/You're so great and I love you').

'Death Of A Party' (Lyrics: Damon Albarn; Music: Blur) [Deep Cut]

If part of Albarn's intention for *Blur* was to kill the Britpop beast, then this song is possibly one of the nails in the coffin. In fact, it's the song that's responsible for folks referring to the whole darn thing as a party in the first place. Organ-led – like a cousin to 'Theme From Retro' – this is dark and powerful stuff, full of squealing fuzz guitar that leaves a sour taste in the ear, which remains long after the album's more immediate thrills have been washed away. 'Another night and oh well well/Went to another party and hang myself' goes the lyric before the track gently deconstructs with a wonderful breakdown ending.

'Chinese Bombs' (Lyrics: Damon Albarn; Music: Blur)

Meanwhile, at the rock end of the spectrum, 'Chinese Bombs' brings some classic British-style punk, but with a *lot* of added dirt. How can something so wrong feel so *right*? Although American bands are often cited as being an influence on *Blur*, this is really 1977 stuff bordering on Oi!, which helps characterise the record as one that flips drastically between art tracks and more immediate ear-grabbers.

'I'm Just A Killer For Your Love' (Lyrics: Damon Albarn; Music: Blur)

Arty and flangey, with great backing vocals and deft piano holding the whole thing together, this is actually the album's weakest song. There's nothing wrong with it as such – with jazz-like drums and a buzz-ridden guitar fretboard scraping – but with other tracks seemingly covering the same ground ('Beetlebum', 'Death Of A Party'), it's like a jam that went too far, and might've been better placed as a B-side. Unsurprisingly, this was also the test track for the new Blur recording facility, Studio 13.

'Look Inside America' (Lyrics: Damon Albarn; Music: Blur) [Deep Cut]

'Good morning lethargy', declares Albarn, over a fine piece of jangle pop delivered via cheeky guitar and bass with a chamber orchestra no less. The track is a joy despite its world-weary air, and sounds like the soundtrack for the biopic of a Californian group in 1970. Representing the opposite viewpoint to that which inspired the *Modern Life Is Rubbish* album ('Look inside America, she's alright'), this massively underrated song is a minor masterpiece offering a missing link to the previous albums, and with Albarn again in fine voice.

'Strange News From Another Star' (Lyrics: Damon Albarn; Music: Blur)

This is a lo-fi piece, driven by Coxon's acoustic guitar and backed with simple Hammond organ. Any casual listener who was aware of a Bowie co-write on the album might well believe it to be this song. Inspired as much by Ziggy Stardust as by a desire to see exactly how weird the band could make their instruments sound, the often overlooked outro is possibly the track's greatest moment, as the whole thing becomes a sort of sci-fi B-movie death march. It's a real shame it fades out without being explored more fully.

'Movin' On' (Lyrics: Damon Albarn; Music: Blur)

If you hadn't noticed, Blur were moving on. The album's final blast of distorted punk (augmented by squelching synths) is so much fun, it could've easily been another single. 'Hey! This is the music/We're moving on', calls Albarn in a Clash-gone-pop call to arms, suggesting this might once have been considered as a possible album opener. With stabby cheek and some fine let-Coxon-go-crackers moments, the whole thing crashes to an end as if drummer Rowntree has pushed it into reverse.

'Essex Dogs' (includes 'Interlude') (Lyrics: Damon Albarn; Music: Blur)

Beginning as if the song is out of time with itself and every part is trying to catch up, things finally click into place with Albarn's Pulp-ish spoken-word description of a nightmare suburban hellscape. Bass-driven and weirdly nauseating, it may be a distinctly un-pop way to end the album, but have we not just been told quite clearly that the band are moving on? But where were they going? Well, we'd find that out in two short years. What was already certain, was the band weren't going to be playing with their Britpop ball again anytime soon. The album's true ending is 'Interlude': a repetitive building drone. Like 'Country Sad Ballad Man' in reverse, it just makes the whole thing that little bit more unsettling.

Optional Extras

In 2012, a special edition of *Blur* was released, including B-sides, remixes, live versions and rarities. Further demos and alternate versions were also released as part of the *21* box set. Where previous Blur B-side and rarity collections covered earlier in this book included some great additions there isn't much to recommend this time. The alternate and remixed album tracks are often cleaner and more mellow: reducing the abrasion and clearly designed for their expected markets. The 1998 *Bustin' + Dronin'* remix compilation/live album expands on this, and includes the William Orbit mix that led to Blur working with him on their subsequent album and change in sound. 'The Cowboy Song' – from the *Dead Man On Campus* soundtrack – also points at this eventual direction change, with distorted drums, multiple guitar effects, fuzz bass and strange vocals. Other songs expand on *Blur*'s abrasion – the unsettlingly chaotic 'A Spell (For Money)'; the weird cooing song sketch 'Woodpigeon Song' that builds to a noisy fade out; the confused punk of 'Get Out Of Cities'; the woozy discordance of 'Polished Stone', and the droning noise-fests of 'Dancehall', 'Bustin' And Dronin'' and 'Swallows In The Heatwave'. The only song that's less abrasive is the Bowie-esque 'All Your Life' (complete with a 'Nobody Does It Better' piano motif), yet even *this* still falls back on scuzzy guitar and noisy synths. It's possible that some of these songs might've worked better had they been treated more sympathetically and recorded at a different stage in Blur's career: they just aren't up to the layers of noise that drench them here.

My Life Story – The Golden Mile (1997)

Recording sessions:
Early-Mid 1996
Producers: Gary Langan (3, 5-8, 10-12); George Shilling (1, 2, 4, 9)
Record label: Parlophone
Chart position: UK: 36
Release date: 10 March 1997
Songs written by Jake Shillingford (except 'You Can't Uneat The Apple' by Roger Hodgson)

> Pete: My Life Story: Not so much a pop band but an orchestra. An absolutely phenomenal idea that I'm sure could never have made anyone any money. Jake Shillingford is still one of the greatest frontmen I've ever seen live.

> Matt: Plonking a band inside an orchestra is a weird concept, but Britpop seemed to offer just the moment to do it, with a number of bands going down this route. My Life Story didn't stop there, though, throwing in a dash of music hall and a sprinkling of new romance to create a really unique sound.

The Album

With string sections and horns being *de rigueur* in Britpop recordings, My Life Story's recordings did nothing to rock that particular boat. However, while other groups got in session players, My Life Story stood apart by making these players part of the band. A twelve-person monster of a group, you certainly couldn't fault them on the size and scale of their ambition and bombast. The band's second album *The Golden Mile* showed that it wasn't just a gimmick. Featuring harpsichord solos, bubbling chamber pop ('12 Reasons Why I Love Her'), 1960s sentimentality ('Mr Boyd'), vaudeville ('The King Of Kissingdom'), dance breakdowns and Gregorian choirs ('Duchess'), the only thing not to like was perhaps the Marmite voice of frontman Jake Shillingford, who had an uncanny way of sounding like he was sneering at you while being exceptionally sincere. All in all, it's marvellous stuff, and while the full band may not have been built to last (they currently tour as a stripped-down five-piece), they were certainly built to sparkle and shine. There are more than twelve reasons to love them.

Standout track: 'Sparkle'

Supergrass – In It For The Money (1997)

Recording sessions: Autumn 1996
Producers: Supergrass, John Cornfield
Record label: Parlophone
Chart position: UK: 2
Release date: 21 April 1997

Pete: I saw Supergrass on the *In It For The Money* tour, and in a wonderful Supergrass-style moment, I got pulled up by the police for some poor teenage driving. The band were great that night, with a horn section blowing the roof off the place.

Matt: This album was a step up from *I Should Coco* in songwriting. I got this CD at university and thought it was a massive mix of sounds and styles. I enjoyed all of them but thought 'You Can See Me' was a particular highlight.

The Album

Following the truly outstanding success of their debut album two years earlier, Supergrass had made something of a rod for their own back. If *I Should Coco* had been a celebration of youthful exuberance married to raw talent – capped off with the zeitgeist moment of 'Alright' – then where else was there to go that wasn't simply mature and boring? While the album title *In It For The Money* amusingly answers that in tongue-in-cheek fashion, the answer for the band musically was perhaps more of a challenge. With pressure to deliver, and drummer Danny Goffey's duel commitment to his wife's band Lodger putting a strain on recording sessions, the result was an album that certainly feels tainted by a darker edge. That's not to say there aren't rays of sunshine here – in fact, they abound – and along with enough material to keep the faithful happy, there's a joyous display of organ action on 'Going Out' (another point of dispute, as Goffey believed it to be about him), room for a bit of funk ('Cheapskate') and even some steampunk craziness ('Sometimes I Make You Sad'). But it's the underlying brooding that really makes its mark.

Standout track: 'Sun Hits The Sky'

Key Album: Radiohead – OK Computer (1997)

Personnel:
Thom Yorke
Jonny Greenwood
Philip Selway
Ed O'Brien
Colin Greenwood
Recording sessions: September 1995 – 'Lucky', unknown studio (possibly Surrey Sound, Surrey)
July 1996 (Possibly earlier) – Various songs including 'Electioneering', 'No Surprises', 'Subterranean Homesick Alien' and 'The Tourist', Canned Applause Studio, Didcot, Oxfordshire
September and late-1996 (possibly November) – Various songs worked on and completed at St Catherine's Court, Bath
Note: Strings were recorded at Abbey Road in January 1997. Mixing continued at various studios for the next two months. The album sleeve notes audio fixing and

dubbing done at Mayfair, Abbey Road, Air Lyndhurst, Courtyard and The Church Studios, probably in 1997.
Producers: Nigel Godrich, Radiohead
Record label: Parlophone, Capitol
Chart position: UK: 1, USA: 21
Release date: 21 May 1997

> Pete: This may be controversial, and I really do think this is a spectacular album that deserved the attention it got, but Radiohead going mega with a prog album at this point felt like it had a touch of 'Sorry, we were all down The Good Mixer and didn't give *The Bends* the attention it deserved' about it.

> Matt: This is a fantastic album and is probably one of the best of the 1990s. But is it Britpop? Not really, despite having so many shared elements. Even so, it's such a powerful album, and it blew our minds at the time.

The Band

The Radiohead members all met at an independent school for boys in Abingdon, Oxfordshire, and by 1985 had formed the band On A Friday. Despite going to separate universities, the band continued to rehearse at weekends and holidays until 1991, when they all moved into a house. Performing around Oxford, they came to the attention of producer and Courtyard Studios co-owner Chris Hufford, who produced a demo tape and became the band's manager with his partner Bryce Edge.

They were soon signed to EMI/Parlophone for a six-album deal, with the only stipulation being they had to change their name. The debut Radiohead EP *Drill* was released in May 1992, their debut single 'Creep' following in September, and debut album *Pablo Honey* early in 1993. But all the releases failed to make a commercial or critical impact. As 1993 continued, the 'Creep' began to increase in popularity, and by the end of the year, became a massive hit, especially when it was reissued.

The band spent 1994 recording the next album while trying out songs on tour under pressure to produce a successful follow-up. In 1995, their second album *The Bends* was a critical and commercial success, which the band built on with the landmark 1997 album *OK Computer*. They were now faced with the difficult question of where to go next, with tension and unsatisfactory results nearly splitting the band. After 18 months, Radiohead re-emerged with a radical new sound built on diverse and minimal instrumentation. The album *Kid A* and its companion album *Amnesiac*, split fans and critics alike. In 2003, Radiohead released *Hail To The Thief* to a mixed reception, following it with *In Rainbows* in 2006. This was the band's first release out of the EMI contract and was offered as a pay-what-you-want release, leading to a huge debate over the relative merits of this action. Meanwhile, the album itself was critically acclaimed, although its commercial success proved harder to measure.

Since then, Radiohead have largely concentrated on solo projects, although albums released in 2011 and 2016 received continued acclaim despite experimentation with different promotional methods.

The Album

It's amazing that *OK Computer* broke through with as much power and impact as it did. Given the sense of optimism in England only three weeks after the election of the New Labour government – itself steeled by Britpop and Cool Britannia – you could be forgiven for thinking Radiohead had made a mistake. A concept album of sorts – indebted to progressive rock, and an exploration of the stifling effects of capitalism, consumerism and technology on the soul of western civilisation – it was the antithesis of D:Ream's 'Things Can Only Get Better'. In fact, in Radiohead's mindset, things had already gotten worse, and no God, government or self-help guidance stood a chance of doing a damn thing about it. Despite that, this isn't a bleak record. Although certainly antiseptic in nature, it captured all the beauty of the prior album's best moments, painting them in different colours, throwing new shade and light onto some of the greatest questions of our time.

A huge critical and commercial success on both sides of the pond (even winning the Grammy for Best Alternative Album), *OK Computer* finally placed Radiohead as the world-stage players that many fans believed *The Bends* should already have made them. Though *OK Computer* may not have ended Britpop as we knew it in a single blow, it delivered such a mighty wake-up call that it made most of the other music on offer seem slightly silly in comparison and created a template for much of the music that would dominate the next decade.

'Airbag' (Radiohead)

'Airbag' is a song that shows just how far removed Radiohead were from their peers. It's difficult to imagine any other alternative album of the period leading with such a desolate lead line and repetitive drum loop (foreshadowing the next album), even if it's offset by Yorke's excellent vocal. Radiohead are rarely ones to be accused of bombast or ego, but by placing 'Airbag' as the album opener with its line 'In an interstellar burst, I am back to save the universe', there is just a touch of justified self-confidence in what they'd created. Dealing with second chances, rebirth and hope (all brought about through the airbag technology that saves the protagonist's life), there's a fine fan theory that the song should actually close the album due to the song's more-positive subject matter.

'Paranoid Android' (Radiohead) [Single]

This is the most prog that Radiohead ever got, and was an incredible show of self-confidence, given it was released as a single just a few days following the album release. The single hit number three, and launched the band anew to the record-buying public. In its six and a half minutes, the song comprises multiple different sections, many of which don't feel like they have a right to fit together, but together they created something more ambitious than the group had before achieved, or many young music fans had ever heard. The song could be labelled as the 'Bohemian Rhapsody' for a new and disconnected generation, but that doesn't really do justice to a song that references Douglas Adams' *The Hitchhiker's Guide To The Galaxy* (the song title references the character Marvin, and even includes a near-direct quotation) and includes the line 'Kicking squealing Gucci little piggy'. If Radiohead were now gods, then they truly did love their children. Yeah.

'Subterranean Homesick Alien' (Radiohead)
While this song's subject matter may be tried and tested (Hometown boredom and the need to escape), rarely has it been delivered with such forsaken abandon. Over a soundscape of beautiful, twinkling Rhodes piano and guitar effects recalling the night sky, Yorke dreams of being abducted by aliens and returning to tell his friends all about it. The fact that 'They'd shut me away, but I'd be alright' – meaning he'd be even more trapped than at the outset – is quite compellingly bleak.

'Exit Music (For A Film)' (Radiohead) [Deep Cut]
Written as the exit music for Baz Luhrmann's 1996 film *Romeo + Juliet*, the song was so good, they held it back for *OK Computer*. Though thematically on-point with the movie (The lyric tells of two people escaping a father's house at night before 'all hell breaks loose'), the stunning build from acoustic guitar and vocals into Mellotron choir, a buzz-filled crescendo, and the final repeated line 'We hope that you choke', means the track also fits the *album* perfectly.

'Let Down' (Radiohead)
One of the album's most melodic songs – and stunningly beautiful, not least in the rise and fall of the chorus – this song is about being part of the consumer machine and how no one really cares for the human experience within it: 'Don't get sentimental/It always ends up drivel'. Traffic jams, international flight and being 'crushed like a bug in the ground' all demonstrate the suffocation of the spirit. The closing seconds as the song ends under a synthesized sequence, feel rather prescient given that the age of the internet was about to give the song's meaning a whole new level.

'Karma Police' (Radiohead) [Single]
Released four months after the album, the second single reached number 8. The song is essentially a piano/acoustic guitar ballad, augmented by loud drums (much like 'Airbag') and a disconcerting, ghostly vocal wail. Being about the frustration that can only be found in the presence of other human beings and that no matter how hard you try, you remain on the payroll, this a song

for anyone who has ever dreamt about breaking out and breaking heads. The song's stunning video showed Yorke being drowned in a goldfish bowl. His bandmates must've been delighted to have the day off.

'Fitter Happier' (Radiohead)

The album's defining point is perfectly placed at its heart, and is not so much a song as a sonic mood-piece. Against paranoia-inducing piano decay and a loop of ambient TV/radio-static voices, the Apple Mac SimpleText voice reads through a list of frustrations and self-improvement methods, before ending up 'Fitter, healthier and more productive. A pig in a cage on antibiotics'. Part-amusing, part-chilling, it details how, even when we are bettering ourselves, we are merely being entrapped in a different manner, and that all life is ultimately a machine. It's time for some smiles.

'Electioneering' (Radiohead) [Deep Cut]

The album's most exhilarating, joyous and straightforward song is practically punk rock in comparison to all that surrounds it. Like a *Pablo Honey*-era leftover put through the *OK Computer* filter, this is thrilling stuff, with a positively brutal guitar solo recalling The Kinks' Dave Davies in its wilful abandon. Perhaps too obvious to be a single (and possibly out of kilter given its satirical take on politics due to the optimism brought about by New Labour), 'Electioneering' remains a huge fan favourite on an album of fan favourites.

'Climbing Up The Walls' (Radiohead)

As if to bring the listener back following the pure escape of the preceding song, this nightmarish song features chilling ambient sounds and a distorted vocal that only becomes heightened in the instrumental (though it also has a strong melody and chorus). Not a song to be listening to late at night; if you listen hard enough, you feel you can actually hear 'the unborn chicken voices in my head' from 'Paranoid Android' lurking in the mix, and the song ends with a rare anguished scream from Yorke. Although it may not fit perfectly with the album's technology themes, it's still cold and contorted enough to not feel out of place.

'No Surprises' (Radiohead) [Single]

The messages here may be relatively simple (The modern world is a bit scary, and the desire for the simplicity and protection of childhood), but this remains the album's best single. Musically recalling a lullaby, or toy gone wrong, it's the lyric that truly stands out, as they amp-up the suffocation of the modern world ('A heart that's full up like a landfill/A job that slowly kills you/Bruises that won't heal'), before ending with the pleading yet surprisingly cathartic 'No alarms and no surprises (Get me out of here)'. Released as a single in January 1998, it hit number four, despite the majority of the fan base having already played the song into submission.

'Lucky' (Radiohead)

Often forgotten as a single, 'Lucky' remains a fascinating song. Recorded in a matter of hours for the War Child *Help* album in late-1995, it provided the light-bulb moment for *OK Computer*, showing the band a vision of all that their third album could become. Though similarities to 'Airbag' abound – 'Lucky' again being a tale of survival and rebirth – the ambient sounds and guitar recall Pink Floyd's prog era and some of the slower songs from *The Bends*. As for its single status, it was released in France, leaving many in the UK to seek import copies.

'The Tourist' (Radiohead)

The album's final song (or second-last if you follow the fan theory) is a simple, understated guitar ballad that makes the most of Thom Yorke's heroic ability to hold vocal notes with crystal clarity. Its call to 'Slow down, slow down' may have been inspired by guitarist Johnny Greenwood witnessing US tourists on a whistle-stop tour of France, failing to take in the beautiful surroundings, or may have been born from simple observation of life in general. But it's perfectly placed as the genuine closer to an album obsessed with man's place in an increasingly corporate and technological world.

Optional Extras

In 2009, a two-disc collector's edition was released, including single B-sides and songs from a BBC Radio One session (Some versions also included a DVD of videos and TV appearances). In 2017, a 20th-anniversary edition titled *OK Computer OKNOTOK 1997 2017* was released, including the eight single B-sides (excluding live tracks and remixes) and three previously unreleased tracks from the album sessions. 'I Promise' is a shopping list of vows over an acoustic guitar with marching drums; 'Man Of War' has a filmlike (specifically James Bond) quality, while 'Lift' is the star of the unreleased songs, and surprisingly is the catchiest Britpop song Radiohead ever recorded. The remaining B-sides further complement the album, with the shimmering guitar and xylophone of 'Lull', the eerie programmed instrumental 'Meeting In The Aisle', the rock of 'Polythene' and 'Palo Alto', and the simple synth of 'Melatonin', while 'A Reminder', 'Pearly' and 'How I Made My Millions' are more gentle vocal-led exercises.

A special edition of *OKNOTOK* added a cassette of further demos and session recordings ranging from samples, sketches and song ideas to alternate versions. This is a fascinating insight into the album's evolution, including songs that were never further developed and those that were reworked for later albums, such as 'Nude' and 'National Anthem'. Overall, it's not something a casual listener would return to.

In mid-2019, over sixteen hours of recordings from the sessions (clearly the source of the limited-edition cassette) were leaked online after an alleged unsuccessful ransom attempt, and the band soon made them available, with proceeds going to charity. Fans have poured over this archive and produced an online document listing all the demos, rehearsals, live performances and other material.

There are also a number of internet articles on the best bits across this archive collection (search for best Radiohead *OK Computer* outtakes). We will leave this for you to explore if you wish; suffice it to say it's an incredible archive, delving into the mind of the band and its process, but is probably only for real fans.

Oasis – Be Here Now (1997)

Recording sessions: November 1996-April 1997
Producers: Owen Morris, Noel Gallagher
Record label: Creation
Chart position: UK: 1
Release date: 21 August 1997

Pete: Like thousands of others, we listened to *Be Here Now* on the day it came out. We were on a boys' holiday in Newquay and had one copy and one CD Discman. Everyone took a turn to sit and listen to it on headphones, and I just remember hour after hour of everyone's excitement just turning into confused disappointment.

Matt: This album needed to be refined into something better, as it relies on the listener to have the patience to find the best material. Today's listeners are probably more prepared to put in the effort. But on its release – taken in by excessively-positive reviews from music critics frightened to get it wrong again – we were left with an album that's not a patch on its predecessor despite some great moments.

The Album

Released almost one year to the day after Oasis' triumph at Knebworth, it would've been more than fair if Noel Gallagher had called time on the band before the album's release. They really didn't have anything left to prove to anyone. In three short years, they'd ultimately trounced all comers in a tale of unstoppable achievement, and by now, even the Battle of Britpop seemed little more than a hiccup along the way. But it did leave a fundamental question: What exactly do you do when you've become the biggest band in the country? If you're not going to go home, then it's time to go big. And *Be Here Now* is definitely *big*: the single 'All Around The World' even clocking in at a record-breaking nine minutes in length.

Released as 'The biggest album by the biggest band in the world' amid a ridiculous media-storm fanfare, what could've been Britpop's crowning moment ultimately felt more like a victory of style-over-substance. With an unbelievable 71-minute running time, but only twelve songs (and one of them a reprise),

169

this is ultimately a record where the material is enhanced with huge in-your-face production and orchestral punches. By the time you get to 'It's Gettin' Better (Man!!)', you realise it isn't. Despite massive sales and some brilliant touches ('D'You Know What I Mean?' is awesome in its bombast, and 'Fade In' unexpectedly excellent in its reserve), the album just doesn't have many memorable moments. It would be a new decade before the band returned.

Standout track: 'D'You Know What I Mean?'

Stereophonics – Word Gets Around (1997)
Recording sessions: October 1992-February 1997
Producers: Bird & Bush
Record label: V2
Chart position: UK: 6
Release date: 25 August 1997

Pete: I arrived in Wales at the point this record came out, so it was a *big al*bum in my world, and seemed to really sum up what I could see around me in Aberystwyth. It's odd to say after 20-plus years of Stereophonics, but they really did seem to be fresh and offering something new at the time.

Matt: I remember you having this on tape and playing it constantly on a big battered hi-fi stack in the smoky back room of a village pub where we used to go and play pool. Despite the speakers being rubbish, the songs were so catchy they cut through and left a real impression.

The Album
With the extraordinary success of Welsh rock showing no signs of stopping in 1997, it's strange to now look back and think of Stereophonics as a more-provincial band dealing with provincial subjects. Formed in 1992, they had a long road to success that wouldn't be achieved until 1999's *Performance And Cocktails*. But despite this, *Word Gets Around* showed that all the component building blocks were well in place. Kelly Jones – half pub-rocker and half pub-poet – had spent his time in his hometown of Cwmaman, well, honing his observational talents against the whetstone of everyday small-town activity, and finding enough material there for a lifetime. With death constantly walking alongside him – like an episode of *Hinterland* in sonic form ('Local Boy In The Photograph'/'Same Size Feet') – possibly the album's most striking moment is the one time it steps away from this to reflect on the boredom of a London traffic jam ('Traffic'). Occasionally sluggish, but more often than not a great straight-ahead pogo rock record, *Word Gets Around* remains the calling card for all that's truly wonderful about Stereophonics.

Standout track: 'Same Sized Feet'

Cornershop – When I Was Born For The 7th Time (1997)

Recording sessions: Late 1996-Early 1997
Producers: Tjinder Singh, Dan the Automator, Daddy Rappaport
Record label: Wiija
Chart position: UK: 17
Release date: 9 September 1997

Pete: It's difficult to talk about Cornershop in the 1990s without making heavy reference to 'Brimful Of Asha', and I didn't have a clue about them until the Norman Cook remix, despite by that point being a weekly reader of all the music press. Shame on me.

Matt: In addition to the hit 'Brimful Of Asha', Mark and Lard on BBC Radio used 'Sleep On The Left Side' as their background music for years. In 2004 during their last radio show, Mark Radcliffe jokingly apologised to the band that they'd no longer be getting the royalties from it.

The Album

Let's get one thing straight from the off: Do not come here if you're looking for the massive international hit record, UK chart-topper and out-and-out *tune* 'Brimful Of Asha'. You won't find it. What you *will* find is the more delicate indie chugger 'Brimful Of Asha' presented as it was meant to be by Cornershop themselves.

Hailing from Leicester, Cornershop were famously grumpy about the remix, believing that it in no way reflected them as a group, which is fair. On *When I Was Born For The 7th Time* – their third album in a long and continuing career of creating excellent albums – Tjinder Singh showed his exceptional ability to meld indie and electronica with his Indian heritage. Weed-infused grooves, laid-back hip hop, dub soundscapes and good old-fashioned pop choruses all vie for space. Most surprising are 'When The Light Appears Boy' (the last recording of beat-poet Allen Ginsberg) and the Johnny Cash/June Carter-like 'Good To Be On The Road Back Home', which really showed the band making music on their own terms, no matter what superstar DJs might come calling.

Standout track: 'Candyman'

Key Album: The Verve – Urban Hymns (1997)

Personnel:
Richard Ashcroft: lead vocals, rhythm guitar, keyboards
Nick McCabe: lead guitar
Simon Tong: second lead guitar, keyboards
Simon Jones: bass
Peter Salisbury: drums
Liam Gallagher: backing vocals ('Come On'); handclaps ('Space And Time')

Recording sessions: October-December 1996 – Olympic Studios, London
February-March 1997 – Olympic Studios
March-May 1997 – Metropolis Studios, London
May-June 1997 – Olympic Studios
Producers: The Verve, Youth ('Bitter Sweet Symphony', 'Sonnet', 'The Drugs Don't
Work', 'Lucky Man', 'One Day', 'This Time', 'Velvet Morning'); The Verve and Chris
Potter ('The Rolling People', 'Catching The Butterfly', "Neon Wilderness', 'Space
And Time', 'Weeping Willow', 'Come On')
Note: Tracks were rerecorded or overdubbed throughout the sessions, so the
above is based on producer credits. There is also footage of the band rehearsing/
recording at Real World Studios, Bath.
Record label: Hut
Chart position: UK: 1, USA: 23
Release date: 29 September 1997

Pete: Do you remember when 'The Drugs Don't Work' came out? God, that
was a miserable time. The news was filled with Diana on a daily basis, and
suddenly this song turned up that was just heartbreakingly sad. I'm pretty
sure that some cynicism kicked in and I felt like there was some dark record
company art taking place. If 'Bitter Sweet Symphony' had been released in its
place, it would've bombed!

Matt: Though this was released as a Verve album, it's a much-more-
complicated beast: being a split between solo Ashcroft material and actual
Verve songs. But as it happens, it's actually the pinnacle of both, as neither
Ashcroft nor The Verve would produce such a quantity or quality of songs
again.

The Band

Ashcroft, Jones and Salisbury – who were at high school together in Wigan
– met McCabe at sixth form college, forming Verve in 1990 (adding 'The' in
1994). The band signed to Hut the following year and became a critical success
after releasing a number of singles. In 1993, the band released their first album,
A Storm In Heaven, to continued critical acclaim but moderate commercial
interest. The band joined the Lollapalooza tour the following year, but drink
and drugs took their toll, and shortly after the release of second album, *A
Northern Soul,* in 1995, Ashcroft broke up the band. Within weeks, they
reformed with Ashcroft, Jones and Salisbury, followed by Tong, before starting
work on their third album *Urban Hymns,* in 1996.

In early-1997, McCabe also returned to the band and helped complete
the album. The first single, 'Bitter Sweet Symphony', was critically and
commercially successful, but unfortunately, it caused an expensive and
lengthy legal dispute due to it including a short looped sample taken from the
orchestral rendition of the Rolling Stones song 'The Last Time'.

Further singles continued this success, but the band itself was struggling once again. McCabe left in 1998, and the band limped through the remaining tour commitments before splitting in 1999. Ashcroft released three albums over the next seven years, sometimes supported by Verve members, some of whom were involved in their own music. By 2007, the band announced they were reforming – without Tong – and released the album *Forth* in 2008. But tensions resurfaced and the band again split. Ashcroft has returned to his solo career, the rest of the band taking up various musical projects. So far, a further reunion seems unlikely.

The Album

Urban Hymns is pretty much universally accepted as the zenith of The Verve's artistic ability and acceptance. Not bad for a record that shouldn't really exist, considering they called it a day after 1995's *A Northern Soul*. But now they were a more-muscular five-piece, and with replacement guitarist Simon Tong sticking around when Ashcroft's musical sparring partner Nick McCabe got called back in, the band were no longer messing about. They seemed to have something to prove, at least to themselves if no one else. They'd seen their contemporaries become massive stars during the Britpop boom, and while they'd basked in some of that reflected light (Oasis' 'Cast No Shadow' had been written about Ashcroft), it hadn't been on their own terms, and if there's one thing that defines *Urban Hymns*, it's that they wanted to do it their way or not at all.

Other groups had capitalised on market trends by leaning into them (Suede's *Coming Up* being a prime example), but The Verve sought to simply make their masterpiece, and trust that the public would see it as such. It worked. The *Urban Hymns* campaign contained hit singles (including their first number 1), a clutch of gongs including an Ivor Novello award for Songwriter of the Year in 2008, and the adoration of the British public. That such a turnaround was possible not only shows that success in the music industry can turn on a dime and that there is such a thing as right-time-right-place, but that the band itself had discovered a greater clarity of purpose.

This is an epic album full of epics, as much about sonic soundscapes and layers as it is about songs. While it's no surprise that its four most immediate songs were chosen as singles, it's also no great shock to find that much of what made them The Verve is still intact. There are E'd-up space-jam wig-outs, seemingly impossible sweeping guitars, and an almost messianic Ashcroft at the centre, laying hands and compelling his spirit to flow through you. Taken as a whole, *Urban Hymns* is like a vortex of space and time where the rules of science have no meaning. It may only be one hour and fifteen minutes in length, but tune in to its frequency and you can find you've lost a week.

By 2008, the band were gone once more; the only difference was this time they knew they'd fulfilled their promise, on their own terms.

'Bitter Sweet Symphony' (Richard Ashcroft) [Single]

You've heard it before, of course, but sometimes it's still worth just sitting back and taking it all in. Built from a swelling string and percussion loop (deftly borrowed from Rolling Stones' manager Andrew Loog Oldham's orchestral rendition of 'The Last Time': which led to Jagger and Richards sharing writing credits for a considerable period), this was the album's vanguard single, and effectively became the band's calling card overnight, reaching number 2 and seemingly never really going away again. A national (and international) earworm that propelled the fortunes of the band and the album light years ahead of what could ever have been expected, it's still very much a Verve song, with lush guitars and Ashcroft's trademark layered vocals as the song builds and builds. Remarkably long for a single – at almost six minutes long – it's as much a statement of intent as anything, deftly underlined by the iconic video, which featured Ashcroft walking down a city street generally not giving much of a f*ck about what anyone thought of him. Newcomers to the group now had all they needed to know summed up in one neat package. But would the rest of the record live up to such a monster hit?

'Sonnet' (Richard Ashcroft) [Single]

Immediately leaping from the beginning to the end of the campaign, 'Sonnet' was the album's final single but again showed just how singularly bloody-minded The Verve could be. Released in chart-ineligible format – a compromise reached when label and band each wanted different choices – 'Sonnet' was still a huge success, especially on radio, where its chiming acoustic singer-songwriter-like elements really jumped from the speakers; all layered with a wash of guitars, tinkling piano and a gentle orchestrally-building outro. A tale of real-life love in the raw, its album position does much to set the tone. This is not going to be thirteen different takes on 'Bitter Sweet Symphony', for sure.

'The Rolling People' (The Verve)

A reminder that The Verve's space-jam past had not been thrown out in order to sate the market, the opening chorus' declaration of 'Here we are the rolling people, can't stay for long' is at best a lie – this is over seven minutes long, and a song most groups would've saved for an album's final moments. But this is The Verve: practically every song here sounds like an album's final moments. Possibly too much too soon to throw at a listener new to the group, it simply reaffirms the band's intention to approach matters on their own terms, neatly underlined by the last nine seconds, which descends into guitars that sound like radio distortion, and a fade of vaguely-intergalactic noises.

'The Drugs Don't Work' (Richard Ashcroft) [Single]

Just in case that's a bit too much, it's probably best to break out the ballad but take no prisoners while doing so. This is no simple piece of country songcraft, but a heartbreaker full of regret and hope, all touched with a simple fatalistic clarity around the embrace of narcotics: 'Like a cat in a bag waiting to drown/ This time I'm coming down'.

Written about Ashcroft's father dying in hospital – the lyric presumably having a double meaning – the song begins with simple-yet-beautiful guitar and strings, with just a touch of The Beatles 'Let It Be' thrown in for good measure. Coincidentally released at the time of Princess Diana's death – when the national mood was raw and hollow – the single immediately reached number 1. The scene was set for the release of *Urban Hymns* just a few weeks later: a record of true emotion rather than simple Oasis-aping bravura.

'Catching The Butterfly' (The Verve) [Deep Cut]

Six minutes of hazy groove detailing wistful ambition and all its fragility ('I'm gonna keep catching that butterfly in that dream of mine'), this is less a song and more a return to space-jam territory, but in a more subdued manner. A false ending at the four-minute mark simply leads back into the song again like a never-ending snooze in the sun, while the guitar wash recalls the sound of a telephone exchange being pulled apart and put back together. It's interesting to note that the melodic verses have a style that Muse would later put to good effect: albeit with big rock packaging.

'Neon Wilderness' (Nick McCabe, The Verve)

The record's shortest song (2:37) is interestingly credited largely to guitarist Nick McCabe. Like a movie soundtrack, it has cold, unreal musicality and vaguely-chanted, occasional falsetto vocals which arrive in gentle waves as if they're from a different song. As the album centre point or an interlude, it perhaps doesn't feel necessary, but it does actually sound like a genuine urban hymn.

'Space And Time' (Richard Ashcroft)

With this song title, you probably think you know what you're in for: space-jam territory, right? Well, maybe a touch. The final third certainly features an extended musical section, but is more delicate in delivery and clings onto its anchor before slowly deconstructing. Surprisingly, this also has some of the record's most muscular guitar work, especially in the choruses. Jaunty and hooky, yet far from a pop song for sure, this is an immediate and integral part of the record.

'Weeping Willow' (Richard Ashcroft)

Beginning with a shimmering piano chord that gives way to shimmering guitar feedback and a feel that resembles Oasis' 'Cast No Shadow' (but with a touch more menace), this is a moment of epiphany ('There'll be no better day to save me') about those drugs which, as discussed earlier, don't work. Lyrically honest in its simplicity and reliance on co-dependency, the huge melodic chorus and brevity make this one of the album's most Britpop moments.

'Lucky Man' (Richard Ashcroft) [Single]

The third single – released in November and further cementing the album's exceptional success by reaching number seven – may at first glance be a Verve-by-numbers kind of deal. But there's more here than meets the ear. Combining a tinge of country rock with a greater band focus and greater string-section subtlety than the song's counterparts, there's a positivity at work here: as if the song itself is practically reaching for the divine (Listen closely and there's even what sounds like a church organ in the final fading seconds). The string arrangement is interesting, though they rarely burst into the foreground, being like a slower version of those in 'Bitter Sweet Symphony'. Far from being a simple recycling of ideas, they offer an assist to the casual listener, helping to place The Verve as key players by offering a signature trademark to rival Liam's 'Shii-iine' or Blur's horn section.

'One Day' (Richard Ashcroft)

Beginning with a mellow wash of electric piano, guitar and vocals, this is a simple message of moving on, hope and reconciliation, with a hint of classic 1970s rock. If there's one song too many (or one that just doesn't fit) on *Urban Hymns,* then this is probably it, although it does have a certain quiet beauty.

'This Time' (Richard Ashcroft)

Here's something you weren't expecting: Is that Richard Ashcroft rapping? Well, no, not exactly, but this more-muscular vocal – delivered over soulful and even funky guitars – gives the song a chance to spread its wings. Less a rock track and more a low-key piece of 1990s dance music, you expect the electric piano from 'One Day' to make a return at any moment, although you don't really need it when you've got McCabe weaving guitar lines. Given its style, this still manages to fit seamlessly into the record, which, by now, is probably better summed up as Verve-music than any particular style.

'Velvet Morning' (Richard Ashcroft) [Deep Cut]

This is the album's greatest track. Another country-tinged moment, it manages to be effortlessly laid-back and relentlessly driving, with slide guitars putting a gentle haze over proceedings. There's a lot to catch the ear here, not least the chord accents that highlight the melody and micro-chorus 'Another velvet morning for me' power chords. Building to an outro where the band and string section work together (yet not with a standard Ashcroft layered vocal), it's tempting to believe this is the song they actually wanted to release in place of 'Sonnet' as the fourth single.

'Come On' (The Verve) (Includes hidden track 'Deep Freeze' (Richard Ashcroft))

Exactly how do you round off an album when practically every song on it is an epic? You could deliver a *bigger* epic, you could deliver something delicate with shimmering beauty, or you could just get your mates in to trash the gaff. Cue 'Come On' (Could the title be any more Britpop?), which starts out in a bold and Britpoppy baggy style with moments of rock guitar, before crawling to a stop at about two and a half minutes. But the song is far from over, as the band relaunch their attack with their biggest and most muscular space-jam yet, even throwing Liam Gallagher onto the mic to scream, 'This is a big f*ck you! – come on!'. But adding an extra vocalist into a Verve layered-vocal ending doesn't quite create the muscular let's-have-it bravado you might expect. Instead, the record ends on a curiously Happy Mondays/Black Grape vibe, which perhaps doesn't do *Urban Hymns* justice (surely 'Velvet Morning' would've been the moment to stop), but *does* show that – in 1997 – if you had a Gallagher brother on your record, you'd be mad not to get it out into the wild (see also the Echo & The Bunnymen hit 'Nothing Lasts Forever'). A final blast of icy chimes, radio traffic and the sound of a child crying in the secret track 'Deep Freeze', and it's finally time for the rolling people to move on.

Optional Extras

A super-deluxe version of the album was released in 2017, including B-sides, bonus tracks, radio sessions, live versions and a full recording of a (previously bootlegged) gig at Haigh Hall. A deluxe version was also released that only included a live highlights CD as a bonus. Perhaps not much new for a big fan, and over the top or not enough to tempt the casual fan, the material showed that there were demos/recordings made seemingly for two albums: a Richard Ashcroft solo album of ballads and gentle soft rock, and a band album of spaced-out rock anthems. The results were mixed together to form a compromise with the remaining tracks, showing that, in some cases, better songs had fallen by the wayside. Of the B-sides and bonus tracks, there are the funky rock workouts and spacey jams of 'The Longest Day', 'Three Steps', 'Stamped', 'Echo Bass' and 'Monte Carlo'. Then there are the gentle, contemplative ballads and acoustic numbers: 'Lord I Guess I'll Never Know', 'Country Song', 'Never Wanna See You Cry', 'The Crab' and 'So Sister'. Also included are a couple of oddities: the dub-ish version of 'Bittersweet (MSG)' and the slick folk-rock of 'This Could Be My Moment', which doesn't really work. Furthermore, a number of tracks that were leaked and confirmed as session outtakes were originally planned for the deluxe album but removed at the last minute (supposedly over a dispute regarding writing credits). These are a mix of ideas and album demos plus extra songs with working titles. Again, there's a mix of softer, confessional songs ('Sweet & Sour' and 'Tina Turner') and rockier numbers, though these are split between groovy instrumental jams ('Wednesday Madness', 'King Riff 2') and jangly indie rock and pop ('Jalfrezi', 'Oh Sister', 'All Ways Are Maybes'). It's a shame these weren't included in the deluxe version, as they would've been a nice bonus for fans who thought they had everything.

Speaking of everything, there are a number of demo bootlegs that have been available for years, including a number of released songs from this album and subsequent Ashcroft solo albums (including the future single 'A Song For The Lovers'), plus some additional tunes that never went any further. These are for true fans, as the songs themselves are not outstanding, and the sound quality leaves a lot to be desired, but they do include two instrumentals: the lounge-bar groove of 'One Before Dinner' and the folk-rock of 'Jerusalem'. 'Misty Morning June' is a jangly pop song, while 'A Little Bit Of Love' has a rockier sound that draws comparisons with weaker Oasis songs. Finally, there are two versions of one song – 'It Takes Two' and 'Open The Skies' – the latter being more polished but less interesting; the former making the most of the Hendrix-like guitar. For a band struggling with internal conflict, they were incredibly productive.

Sleeper – Pleased To Meet You (1997)

Recording sessions: 1997
Producers: Stephen Street (with Cenzo Townshend on 'Motorway Man')
Record label: Indolent
Chart position: UK: 7
Release date: 13 October 1997

Pete: Even given my genuine love of Sleeper, what struck me most clearly about *Pleased To Meet You,* was just how out of kilter it seemed with where music tastes suddenly seemed to be. Radiohead were suddenly in vogue, and (I really hate saying this) what Sleeper had to offer just didn't seem as important.

Matt: I'm going to go a step further and say that at the time this was released, Sleeper were actually irrelevant. If they'd released the album six months earlier and were marketed as a band moving away from Britpop (like Blur), this could and should have done better. Unfortunately, that didn't happen, and the band were arguably one of the first casualties of the scene, despite this actually being a strong album when taken on its own merits.

The Album

Sleeper were smart-enough cookies to see the way the wind was blowing by 1997, and with their third album, they made a strong bid to bounce from the Britpop bubble into a longer career. *Pleased To Meet You* boasts better songwriting, better vocals and better instrumentation than its predecessors, yet it doesn't quite hold together as an album due to its more-eclectic nature.

Combining Pixies-style alternative rock ('Please Plcase Please'), ambient indie-dance ('Breathe') and electronica ('Motorway Man') with a whole host of other musical excursions from the template, there's still enough classic Sleeper bombast here to please the faithful. While it's clear they wanted to create as great an album as possible, the writing was on the wall when the label released only two singles: 'She's A Good Girl' (which reached 28) and the Blondieesque 'Romeo Me' (39): which is a shame when 'Firecracker' was screaming out to be pushed over the airwaves. Having already lost bassist Diid Osman early in 1997, Sleeper split the following year. Though they did return to the fray as heroes in 2017 – releasing two further excellent albums – they deserved better than to become another Britpop casualty.

Standout track: 'Because Of You'

1998 – The times they are a-changing...

It was only one year since the general election, but it already felt as if things were getting worse. Although Blair certainly achieved the seemingly impossible with the Good Friday Agreement (a deal between the UK and Irish governments, plus the main political parties in Northern Ireland) – effectively bringing an end to the troubles that had for so long divided so many – not everyone felt the dawn of a new day was shining upon them.

As the March edition of *NME* asked the question, 'Ever had the feeling you've been cheated?' and Chumbawamba's Danbert Nobacon took more direct action by hurling water over John Prescott at the Brit Awards, it was clear that the Cool Britannia brand was already a thing of the past. Most of the big Britpop players had now joined the London elite, and seemed too busy living it up as celebrities to worry about being common musicians anymore, while the New Deal For Musicians (brought about through pressure from Alan McGee and Clint Boon, among others) showed just what a disparity there was between the kids and their heroes.

As labels saw the way the wind was blowing and began to cull their rosters, the desire as ever in the music industry was for cheap new blood and a fresh take on old ideas. A generation of bands who'd grown up in the 1990s were now coming of age, and with the vast amounts of Britpop money still washing around the industry, they were signing deals and delivering their own take on all that had come before them.

Although the summer months did bring some mid-1990s-style fun (the real World Cup '98 anthem clearly being 'Vindaloo' by Fat Les, which, featuring Keith Allen and Alex James, made for a far better song than the official track or even 'Three Lions '98'), Britpop as a cultural force was gutted and spent. Traditional manufactured pop had fought back, and was once again ascendant, with Robbie Williams and Spice Girls flying high (even if Ginger did leave in May), while younger talent hit the airwaves in the form of Billie Piper: who at age 16, became – with 'Because We Want To' – the youngest British solo artist to hit number 1.

Luckily, Wales ignored the memo, with Cardiff now taking over from London as the new home of British guitar pop.

For Britpop, this was the year that its ongoing legacy began to make itself known. The album choices for 1998 include bands such as Embrace and Catatonia, who now took centre stage with their own enthusiastic takes on the preceding decade's music, while Pulp returned to give us the inside gossip on what the lifestyle had really been like.

Key Album: Catatonia – International Velvet (1998)

Personnel:
Cerys Matthews: vocals
Mark Roberts: guitar
Owen Powell: guitar

Paul Jones: bass
Aled Richards: drums
Recording sessions: 1997 – Tracks 1, 3, 4, 6-12 at Monnow Valley Studios; track 2 at Rockfield Studios; track 5 at The Big Noise Recorders
Producer: TommyD, Catatonia
Record label: Blanco y Negro
Chart position: UK: 1
Release date: 2 February 1998

Pete: Living in Wales, I was already pretty well-acquainted with Catatonia, and had even seen them live. I really liked them and already owned their first album, but was totally blindsided when 'Mulder And Scully' became such a big hit and the band leapt into the mainstream like they did.

Matt: It wasn't just 'Mulder And Scully' that was a big hit, 'Road Rage' was also heavily played. These were the first opportunities many people had to hear the band, and a lot was made of Matthews' strong singing accent and enunciation that often dragged the words, making her delivery unique.

The Band
Mark Roberts was part of the Welsh-language band Y Cyrff throughout the 1980s, initially on guitar before also becoming vocalist. Finally releasing their debut album in 1991, the band realised they'd run their course, and split later that year. At the same time, Roberts met Matthews and they began going out, writing songs together, then forming Catatonia (originally called Sweet Catatonia). Throughout 1992, the band – now including drummer Stephen Jenkins and bassist Guto Pryce – played live and recorded demos. This led to interest from Crai Records, who in 1993 signed the band that now included Paul Jones on bass, Dafydd Leuan on drums, and Clancy Pegg on keyboards. Their debut EP *For Tinkerbell* was released in May, and received critical acclaim from the *NME* and Radio One DJs. The band then signed with MRM management, leading to Pegg's departure and the single 'Whale' on the Rough Trade label.

In 1996, Catatonia signed with Blanco y Negro Records and began recording their debut album for immediate release. During this time, Leuan left the band and was replaced by Richards, while the relationship of Matthews and Roberts collapsed. As the first album had consisted of re-recorded songs and new material, Catatonia were quickly able to return to the studio to work on the follow-up, which, when eventually released in early-1998, became their most successful album: *International Velvet*. The band spent the rest of the year touring and writing songs for their third album: released in 1999, again to great commercial success.

A planned tour of America was delayed supposedly because of Richards' appendicitis and then cancelled by year-end after a miserable tour of Australia,

Japan and New Zealand, where rumours around Matthews' mental and physical health were growing. By 2001, the band had regrouped and released their fourth and final album *Paper Scissors Stone*, which the critics mauled, and with Matthews entering rehabilitation for depression, drinking and drugs, the band called it a day. All of Catatonia have continued to be involved in music, with Matthews being the most successful, releasing a number of albums.

The Album

Catatonia were almost too late. By 1998, the Britpop party was winding down, Noel Gallagher-influenced songwriting was taking centre stage, and in the press, the 'pop' element was increasingly being substituted for 'rock'. But Catatonia didn't care. Maybe the party was over, the best nibbles nibbled and all the good booze drunk, but with *International Velvet*, they knew they had a classic Britpop album on their hands, and they not only wanted in, they were determined to have a damn good time when they got there.

Though Welsh bands weren't uncommon in the Britpop framework, it was certainly unusual to have one fronted by anyone as sassy and truly special as Cerys Matthews – a one-woman tornado of energy, who endeared herself to all as the movement's crossover-Queen bar none (Older generations could even be heard whispering in hushed tones of the new Shirley Bassey they'd seen on TV). Meanwhile, the kids were just pleased to see someone still having some damn fun and not just crying about their glamorous-looking lives down a microphone.

International Velvet reached number one and even got nominated for the Mercury Music Prize, while its singles took the charts by storm. It goes to musical places you might not expect, mixing indie guitar-pop, tearjerker ballads, and even elements from the underground dance scene – all tied together with the guts-and-glory whiskey-and-cigarette-smoke delivery of Matthews' non-apologetic Welsh accent. Though Catatonia released two more top ten albums – which both deserve praise – *International Velvet* was a last gasp for Britpop in its purest form.

'Mulder And Scully' (Cerys Matthews, Mark Roberts) [Single]

With cheeky guitars and a zeitgeist-capturing lyric (name-checking the lead characters of the hit US show *The X-Files*), this could've so easily just been the Britpop novelty single of the month. The fact that it wasn't was due to a few factors. For starters, the single release came only days before the album, which proved how much the band had to offer, while the name-checking is simply a mischievous shorthand, the song actually being about a doomed relationship. But the greatest reason is that it's simply a brilliant song, with a huge sing-along chorus, a middle-eight where the vocal really flies, and a fine experimental guitar workout in the outro.

Reaching number three on release, and sticking around on the radio for the rest of the decade and beyond, the song delivered the band fully-formed to the wider public and paved the way for Cerys Matthews to become a star in her own right.

'Game On' (Cerys Matthews, Mark Roberts) [Single]

Released in November 1998, this jangly acoustic-led indie ballad was the album's final and weakest single, but still catchy. Only reaching number 33 (causing some concern at the label), the song talks (ironically) about achieving destiny, with the bold claim 'I know that I could never fall from grace/I'm far too clever'. However, as the album's second track, it's a perfect counterpoint to 'Mulder And Scully' and shows the band has far more in its arsenal than one simple novelty pop track.

'I Am The Mob' (Mark Roberts, Catatonia) [Single]

With big crashing chords and bold vocals appropriating thematic elements from *The Godfather*, 'I Am The Mob' is huge fun and a real big hitter. Reaching number 40 on release, the song received a scandalous lack of airplay when some of its lyrics were considered a touch less than family-friendly: 'I'm gonna put a bullet between your knees'. This still doesn't stop it from being the album's greatest adrenaline rush, with stop/start verses, punky guitars and a huge chorus. It's hard to imagine any other band of the time pulling off this mixture of fist-pumping delivery and slight silliness (The band Kenickie perhaps?), but at a point when music was becoming terribly serious again, what was not to like?

'Road Rage' (Cerys Matthews, Mark Roberts) [Single]

Following up the 'Mulder And Scully' single was always going to be a challenge. Luckily, they had a song just as big, just as catchy, and – importantly – just as capable of turning a common phrase to their advantage. Though the title did cause some controversy (It had been lifted from a description of the horrendous Lee Harvey murder: a move for which Matthews contacted Harvey's mother to apologise), the song itself is a masterpiece of indie pop. The verse's low-key trip hop elements added a slightly futuristic element, while the wonderful building bridge and monster chorus kept the kids singing all the way to the multi-layered outro. Nominated in the Best Song category at every major event (including the Ivor Novello awards), 'Road Rage' hit number five in May 1998, and moves between three keys. To think they'd peaked with 'Mulder and Scully'!

'Johnny Come Lately' (Cerys Matthews, Catatonia)

The album's first non-single comes across more like a leftover from the debut album *Way Beyond Blue*. With swooning guitars and a melody in the style of The Sundays, Matthews begins the song in her highest register, giving the pained regret a delicate fragility.

'Goldfish And Paracetamol' (Cerys Matthews, Paul Jones)

This slightly weary tale of unfulfilled acceptance is best described as a piece of trip-hop fusion that's perhaps an experiment too far. Utilising programmed drums – bringing club-dance elements into the mix, giving the whole piece space to breath – the greatest moments come in the final minute when a single horn section gives way to a fine piece of song deconstruction.

'International Velvet' (Mark Roberts, Catatonia) [Deep Cut]

With a chitty-chitty-bang-bang groove before cheeky ska guitar stabs make everything more contemporary, the title track is surprisingly not the album's defining moment. The four minutes and 23 seconds have all the Catatonia elements you'd expect – including Welsh language verses and a big, bold chorus which features the couldn't be more Catatonia with its line 'Everyday when I wake up, I thank the lord I'm Welsh.' The end is particularly fun, as the song dissolves into a wonderful pub chant.

'Why I Can't Stand One Night Stands' (Mark Roberts, Catatonia)

This sparse waltz is less a song and more an emotional sketch: the equivalent of leaving a note on the fridge as a reminder against self-destruction. It's touching stuff, and makes for a fine central point on the record, even if it doesn't ever feel truly necessary to the album as a whole.

'Part Of The Furniture' (Cerys Matthews, Mark Roberts)

This is a song of many different parts. Delicate verses give way to big rock moments and even a muscular ending that allows Matthews' voice to fly over squalling and grunting guitars, making the listener vaguely wonder if they're still listening to the same song.

'Don't Need The Sunshine' (Owen Powell, Catatonia)

This is the album's most jangle-pop piece of sunshine. Almost childlike in its classic pop sensibility, it's still Catatonia at its heart, meaning any such expression is going to come with caveats: 'But you *don't* need the sunshine/ You *don't* need the good times'. For something so pure, the song uses its campfire sing-along simplicity to deliver some remarkably grown-up ideas, including emotional self-awareness ('And I don't mind your lies so keep on talking') and brutal face-in-the-mirror honesty ('I decided that the answer could not be bought across the counter').

'Strange Glue' (Owen Powell, Catatonia) [Single]

The greatest of all the singles, it's amazing to discover that this swooning ballad is actually an attack on the band's US label, who'd failed to support the band and were now considering dropping them: 'When faced with my demons/I clothe them and feed them and I smile/Yes I smile as they're taking me over'.

Containing the album's best lyric and a melody that feels as old and natural as the wind, 'Strange Glue' far transcends its subject matter, with a number of lines that tear at the heartstrings: 'Oh the end of the night never comes too quickly for me, and I smile'). It's a really beautiful song even if it wasn't meant to be, and its August 1998 chart position of 11 at least did it some justice. As for America? Sadly, it never did fall under Catatonia's spell.

'My Selfish Gene' (Mark Roberts, Catatonia) [Deep Cut]

It's 2:00 a.m. in a Swansea Club. The local mobsters have all gone home. The janitor sweeps away the night's debris. Yet two of the house musicians are playing one last song. In a spotlight that catches the cigarette smoke, Cerys Matthews drapes herself over the piano and begins to sing the story of her life. Though lyrically light, the song tells you all you need to know about the frustrations, resentments, desire and hope that made *International Velvet* a possibility in the first place. Despite never being intended for the album, and included to replace 'That's All Folks' (a future B-side; ordered from the album by the record label, due to the subject matter), it's an incredible moment and the perfect way to add real gravitas to the last record to truly put the pop in Britpop.

Optional Extras

In 2015, a deluxe version of the album was released, including a bonus disc of B-sides, remixes, alternate versions, live performances of the singles and non-album tracks. Though few in number, they are a mix of anthemic guitar songs ('Jump Or Be Sane', 'I'm Cured') and organ-led folk songs ('No Stone Unturned', 'Blow The Millenium (Part 2)'). Some of these are next-level epics with harmonic and atmospheric guitars, such as 'Mantra For The Lost' and the controversial 'That's All Folks'. Even though this would've been a great album closer, perhaps the simpler 'My Selfish Gene' was the better choice.

The Bluetones – Return To The Last Chance Saloon (1998)

Recording sessions: 1997-1998
Producer: Hugh Jones
Record label: Superior Quality
Chart position: UK: 10
Release date: 9 March 1998
Writers: Chesters, Devlin, Morriss, Morriss

> Pete: In terms of managing to break out of the bubble and continue a career of immense longevity and critical success, The Bluetones really are one of the few great bands to find their way out of Britpop. It may not be a view shared by many, but I rate this album far more than the debut.

Matt: Wisely moving away from the Britpop sound with their second album, The Bluetones were now exploring a genre further south of their original West Coast influences. I did feel it lacked a catchy single, though.

The Album

Released only two short years after their debut number one album *Expecting To Fly*, and charting at number 10, many now suspected the Bluetones' day was already done. It's even possible the band felt the same given the album title. But The Bluetones were smart enough to understand that while fashions may change, excellent songwriting will always stand the test of time, and *Return To The Last Chance Saloon* showed just how much they still had to offer.

If Britpop was largely about looking backwards at the past greats of British music, and repackaging them for a 1990s audience, then this is a great example of a group simply setting fire to the blueprint and carving out their own future. A semi-concept album of sorts – full of Sergio Leone soundscapes and images of the old West – even some of its most Britpop moments are cut from a more transatlantic cloth (check out the exceptional single 'If…'), which may summon Rudyard Kipling, but also has a couple of sneaky steals from Glen Campbell's 'Wichita Lineman'. Of course, there's enough standout moments here to keep the casual listener happy – 'Solomon Bites The Worm' being an underrated Britpop classic; 'Sky Will Fall' nothing less than a Bond theme in waiting, and 'The Jub Jub Bird' showing that even The Bluetones could rock out. But this is a record best enjoyed as a whole.

Standout track: 'If…'

Key Album: Pulp – This Is Hardcore (1998)

Personnel:
Jarvis Cocker
Nick Banks
Candida Doyle
Steve Mackey
Mark Webber
Recording sessions: November 1996-January 1998 – Two main session blocks took place at The Town House, London (March-May 1997) and Olympic Studios, London (June-August 1997), with mixing occurring during/after sessions. There was also a later session at an unknown London studio from November 1997 to January 1998.
Strings on 'Dishes', 'This Is Hardcore', 'A Little Soul' and 'Seductive Barry' recorded at Whitfield street, London 1997.
Note: 'Help The Aged' and 'Northern Soul' were recorded during abandoned album sessions at The Town House, London, in November 1996. Both were overdubbed in 1997, with 'Northern Soul' becoming 'Glory Days'. In 2020 and

2021, a specialist music-memorabilia auction site sold a number of mixing session cassettes, which give various dates throughout 1997.
Producer: Chris Thomas
Record label: Island
Chart position: UK: 1
Release date: 30 March 1998

Pete: This is actually a better album than *Different Class*. It feels like they've stretched themselves in every possible way, pushing themselves to create not a concept album, a cohesive musical statement. Come on, tell me I'm wrong. Prove to me I'm wrong.

Matt: I'm not going to. This is what Pulp had been building up to over the last couple of albums: an epic soundtrack to all aspects of life. A really cracking record.

The Album

The three years following Pulp's *Different Class* had taken their toll on the band and – elevated to the status of national celebrity – Jarvis Cocker in particular. Being a national figure – with exploits such as his Michael Jackson stage invasion at the Brits making him known to everyone – was hard for Cocker to come to terms with, and the lifestyle and its associated substances had worn him down. Never one to shy away from a self-aware lyric, it's no surprise that Pulp's sixth album would reflect this mood. But for many, it was still a bit too dark to stomach after what was a family favourite. Although detractors would class this album as one hour and ten minutes of claustrophobic wheezing (Blur's 'Death Of The Party' writ large), there were also those who felt the band had stepped up, delivering an album truly phenomenal in its songwriting, scope and extremely high production values. More gritty and disturbing than previous Pulp fare – with cover art that caused minor controversy when adverts on the London Underground were targeted with slogans accusing the cover of demeaning women – this definitely wasn't *Different Class* part two, but it did stand in a class of its own.

Though the party may have been over, Pulp could hold their heads high, having produced three albums in a row that documented the best of the road toward Britpop's heyday and aftermath.

'The Fear' (Lyrics: Jarvis Cocker; Music: Pulp) [Deep Cut]

With drawn-out lead guitar backed by menacing chords, Pulp are not messing about. A song that genuinely sounds like the post-big-night-out-fear incarnate, this was especially difficult to listen to in 1998 when – if you were young and lucky enough – most days incorporated an element of that very feeling. Always articulate, it's a sonic exploration of the exhilarating highs of success and the crushing lows of depression that can follow it. Covering panic attacks and loneliness, this self-proclaimed 'horror soundtrack from a stagnant waterbed' deserves special kudos for also incorporating the magician Paul Daniels' catchphrase 'You're gonna like it, but not a lot'. Chilling.

'Dishes' (Lyrics: Jarvis Cocker; Music: Pulp)

If 'The Fear' is about dealing with celebrity status, then 'Dishes' expands on the theme, reflecting on the simple truth that a celebrity is just a person and one with household chores to complete at that. When Pulp hit with *Different Class*, the 32-year-old Jarvis Cocker was slightly older than your average pop star, so it's only right he should've shown his burgeoning midlife crisis in sonic form. Though the verses may be dark and reflective, the choruses are in contrast a gentle, lilting pop, with excellent guitar hooks and chiming synths. Though many cite the line 'I'm not worried that I will never touch the stars/'Cause stars belong up in heaven' as the standout, for us, it's still got to be the part-comic-epiphany of the opening and closing line 'I am not Jesus, though I have the same initials'.

'Party Hard' (Lyrics: Jarvis Cocker; Music: Pulp) [Single]

The most industrial-sounding song Pulp would ever undertake. With a factory-floor rhythm, chainsaw guitars and Bowie-esque vocals, 'Party Hard' is essentially the night before 'The Fear': a night in which Cocker realises something may be amiss with his lifestyle. There's no real subtext here, with lines like 'Entertainment can sometimes be hard/When the thing that you love is the same thing that's holding you down' and 'Why do we have to half-kill ourselves just to prove we're alive?', but it's exhilarating stuff, with Niles-Rogers-esque funk chords and even a robotic tongue-in-cheek 'Baby, you're driving me crazy' thrown into the mix. The album's fourth single, it reached a lowly 29 in September 1998. Although Pulp would place slightly higher again come the turn of the century, symbolically, this slice of noisy death-disco sealed their fate.

'Help The Aged' (Lyrics: Jarvis Cocker; Music: Pulp) [Single]

A truly peculiar choice of single, and doubly so when you realise it was also the lead single. Charting at 8 in November 1997 (four months before the album), fans could certainly be forgiven for being confused about what to expect from the new record. Mixing the skeleton of a classic Pulp song – as Candida Doyle's simple keyboard line provides the backing for Cocker to eulogise about the inevitability and despair of ageing – it was clear the band were heading into darker territory and were not afraid to throw off some of their pop-star clothes in order to embrace the night. Despite the song featuring a mammoth uplift in its middle-eight, this counterpoint to 'Glory Days' ultimately makes you feel like *that* song should've been sent out to fight.

'This Is Hardcore' (Lyrics: Jarvis Cocker; Music: Pulp, with Peter Thomas) [Single]

Over six minutes in length – and including a sample of The Peter Thomas Sound Orchestra's 'Bolero On The Moon Rocks' – with simple keys and a superb stripped-back arrangement, the title track not only feels massive but clearly displays the sheer breadth of ability in both the band and producer Chris Thomas. With more sonic space than Pulp are used to, this still feels exceptionally claustrophobic, as Cocker reflects on pornography and the person. Begun as a sonic experiment to escape the confines of traditional song structure, this is closer to ambient-dance than indie pop and all the more remarkable for it. There's also some disturbing humour to be found, not least in the closing moments when Cocker states repeatedly, 'Then that goes in there/Then that goes in there/Then that goes in there/And then it's over', just at the point that a seedy saxophone joins the throng.

Another odd choice for a single – despite its obviously stunning sonics – it reached number 12 three weeks before the album launch.

'TV Movie' (Lyrics: Jarvis Cocker; Music: Pulp)

Beginning with acoustic blasts over an electronic hum, this is actually not as dark as you may be expecting. A positively chirpy love song with piano, strings and even a whistle solo, you can actually hear some true yearning in Cocker's voice when he repeats 'So please say you're going to stay' and asks 'Is it a kind of weakness to miss someone so much?'. Given the welcome relief it brings from the album's predominant dark mood, the only real issue is that this gem of a pop song isn't longer.

'A Little Soul' (Lyrics: Jarvis Cocker; Music: Pulp) [Single]

The album's third single is a painful autobiographical tale that successful musicians have repeated since The Beatles first came to prominence: one of estranged fathers coming out of the woodwork when their children experience success. Cocker may have forgiven his dad, but that doesn't stop this acoustically-led and lyrically nuanced song from being full of sadness, regret, pity and pain: all held together remarkably sprightly given the subject matter.

'A Little Soul' reached 22 in June 2008 and proved that – unlike his old man – Cocker really was overflowing with soul.

'I'm A Man' (Lyrics: Jarvis Cocker; Music: Pulp)

This feels something like a continuation of 'A Little Soul', as Cocker takes time out to 'start to wonder what it takes to be a man'. Despite an upbeat chorus, some great stuttered moments, extraordinarily-noisy guitar riffs in the middle section, and the biggest drums ever heard on a Pulp track, here this does feel like an album track, whereas on any other Pulp album, it could've been a potential single.

'Seductive Barry' (Lyrics: Jarvis Cocker; Music: Pulp)

Yes, it's a rotten title. Or is it? While arguments persist over whether this is the most Pulp song title ever or just a bit rubbish, what's undeniable is that it's an eight-and-a-half-minute monster that only *Pulp* could really deliver while keeping a straight face. Drawing the listener in with a disturbing synth and bass wash (with female vocals by Neneh Cherry) and 'I don't know' elements recalling a chant or mantra, the overall effect is less sexy and more unsettling, and the string arrangement during the final minutes is spellbinding.

'Sylvia' (Lyrics: Jarvis Cocker; Music: Pulp)

If 'Seductive Barry' knocked you slightly off centre, 'Sylvia' is here to remind you that Pulp definitely still know how to knock out a pop song. With quiet verses and a massive pop chorus worthy of anything from *Different Class*, it's a tale not directly of Sylvia, but of someone who reminds Cocker of her existence and how those feelings get muddled along the way. Featuring some classic Pulp character detail such as 'Her father's living with some girl who's a year younger than her' and 'I've not seen her for a long time', there's also room for greater introspection, as Cocker wonders to what extent he's the same as all the other men who hang around beautiful women.

'Glory Days' (Lyrics: Jarvis Cocker; Music: Pulp, with Anthony Genn) [Deep Cut]

Brilliantly continuing the theme of 'Common People' in its celebration of the everyday triumphs and crushing banality of real-life ('We were brought up on the space race/Now they expect you to clean toilets'), 'Glory Days' is a master class in mixing grand, driving pop with smart lyrics, and was a prime candidate for a single that should've been. Though the key change doesn't feel necessary, it does get us to a wonderful moment for all those who have noted a title-share with Bruce Springsteen: check out the guitar riff at 4:10. Never let it be said that Pulp don't know what they're doing.

'The Day After The Revolution' (Lyrics: Jarvis Cocker; Music: Pulp)

The album's closing song is a rousing call to arms for the everyman and a simultaneous swipe at the New Labour project (a theme Cocker was playing with on various B-sides at this time). ''Cause the meek shall inherit absolutely nothing at all', Cocker sings while pointing out that 'Although nothing looks different, a revolution took place'. Although a fair argument could be made for 'Glory Days' being a better album closer, 'The Day After The Revolution' retains a thematic resonance in its disappointment and self-awareness. Plus it gives Candida Doyle the chance to hold on to her final chord for ten minutes straight. Have you listened to all ten minutes waiting for something to happen? Thousands did, and thousands realised the joke was on them. It's exhausting to listen to, but that's kind of the point.

Optional Extras

The album was originally released in two versions: one having an additional CD of live tracks from Pulp's 1998 Glastonbury appearance. It's an entertaining show, but isn't quite as special as their 1995 appearance. In 2006, a deluxe album edition was released with a second CD of outtakes, B-sides, demos and alternate mixes. 'Cocaine Socialism' is an early version of the better 'Glory Days', while 'It's A Dirty World' was a late arrival to the sessions, and sounds like a confusing mash of songs and jamming. The B-sides allowed the band to explore different musical styles but were unlikely album contenders, with the stomping rock of 'Like A Friend', the French-café loop of 'The Professional', the 1980s electropop and vocoder of 'Ladies Man', the country drum loop of 'Laughing Boy', and the scuzzy punk anthem with distorted trumpet: 'We Are The Boyz'. 'Tomorrow Never Lies' was originally offered to the James Bond film *Tomorrow Never Dies*, and though there are similarities to the more-rock Bond themes, it wasn't accepted but could've been an interesting new direction.

Then comes a series of tongue-in-cheek demos that sound like a band in a bit of a creative lull, experimenting with instruments such as the Mellotron. Presumably, some of these demos were using working titles ('Can I Have My Balls Back, Please', 'My Erection'). Two of them are more-structured songs ('You Are The One', 'Street Operator'). Though they have classic Pulp elements, they do sound uninspired when compared to 'This Is Hardcore (End Of The Line Mix)' – an extended version of the violin-centred instrumental section from the original song, that's beautiful and highlights the strength of the album tracks compared to what else was being written.

Key Album: Embrace – The Good Will Out (1998)

Personnel:
Danny McNamara: lead vocals
Richard McNamara: guitar, backing vocals
Mike Heaton: drums, backing vocals
Steve Firth: bass
Mickey Dale: keyboards, string arrangements (Additional musician)
Recording sessions: 1997-1998 – Various sessions recorded at Beaumont Street Studios, Huddersfield. Produced by Dave Creffield and Embrace.
'All You Good Good People' and 'Come Back To What You Know' recorded at Hook End Studios, Oxfordshire. Produced by Youth.
Note: Additional recording is known to have taken place at a studio in Nottingham, Whitfield Street Studios, London, and Metropolis Studios, London. Steve Osbourne also did additional production on 'One Big Family'.
Producers: Youth, Steve Osbourne, Dave Creffield
Record label: Hut
Chart position: UK: 1
Release date: 8 June 1998

Pete: I know a lot of people who really derided Embrace at the time this was released. The claim was always made that they were just copyists, but I still don't buy that at all. If anything, they seemed more willing than most to put in the work to try and realise their vision.

Matt: Embrace are a band that emerged too late in some respects, but when they did, they had some really good songs that maybe weren't groundbreaking but offered something that other bands had moved away from. They probably kept the flag flying for this music style much longer than might've happened otherwise.

The Band

Brothers Danny and Richard McNamara formed Embrace in West Yorkshire in 1990. Initially using a drum machine, Heaton was soon appointed on drums. Although they played some gigs, they focussed on writing songs, only settling on the name Embrace in 1992. By 1996, bassist Steve Firth had joined, and they started recording. These demos were used to find a manager which then facilitated the recording of the single 'All You Good Good People' for Fierce Panda in 1997. This led to a label bidding war, Embrace ultimately choosing Hut. Two EPs followed before the debut album was released in 1998 to critical and commercial success. At the same time, Mickey Dale – who worked with the band on their debut – was made an official member. In 2000, the band's second album was unable to replicate the success of the first, and they quickly recorded their third album, *If You've Never Been*, in 2001. A further two albums were released before the band went on hiatus in 2006. By 2013, Embrace had started touring and recording again, releasing *Embrace* in 2014 and *Love Is A Basic Need* in 2018.

The Album

Like seemingly all-new bands that came to prominence in the Noel-Rock Britpop afterglow, Embrace arrived beating their chests and proclaiming themselves the saviours of music while promising (stealing a phrase here) to live forever. But for all the bombast, there were some soft hearts beating in those McNamara brothers' chests, and ultimately it was this that connected with the fan base. Which is not to say *The Good Will Out* doesn't have its fair share of upbeat moments. With vocals often taken by guitarist-brother Richard, there are plenty, and it may surprise those who think they know the band to hear just how many are bolstered by football-chant backing from The Bricklayers: the collective name for anyone who was nearby and fancied a bit of a shout. It's just that these aren't the songs that stick with you. For every 'One Big Family' or 'I Want The World', there's a 'Fireworks', a 'Retread' or a 'My Weakness Is None Of Your Business' – all of which made it clear that these brothers – despite their influences – were actually cut from fundamentally different cloth than their Mancunian counterparts. Yet what do we say about the influences? Well, they're certainly clear enough – Oasis, The Beatles, The Verve and even The Charlatans all played their part in creating Embrace, but was that something to deride the group for?

Let's put this in context. The band in West Yorkshire in 1990, and slowly but surely they worked painstakingly to create their own sound: all at the same time the Britpop bubble built, boomed and burst around them. To have not been influenced by it would've involved burying their heads in the sand. When bands such as Coldplay or Electric Soft Parade cited exactly the same influences just a couple of years later, it was hailed as almost innovative, simply because the year no longer started with a 19. It also misses the point – as inspired as Embrace might've been by what had recently come before, they were also genuinely aiming to take the sound to another level: something they did with remarkable skill and success. *The Good Will Out* may be a record about breaking up (and – on its three final piano-led songs – moving forward), but it's also a huge album – a one-hour slab of orchestral rock-and-roll balladeering, as big (if not bigger) than any brought to the table previously. Critics claimed that singer Danny's voice was not as big as the material he'd created, and while it's fair to say it divided opinion, it was also free of affectation and raw with the emotion he poured into every lyric.

'Intro' (Danny McNamara, Richard McNamara)

An orchestra prepares, the tension builds. We've been promised something special, and there are nerves on both sides of the curtain.

'All You Good Good People' (Danny McNamara, Richard McNamara) [Single]

Released twice in 1997 – first on super-indie Fierce Panda, and then on Hut as part of an EP, this is six minutes of pure orchestral bombast, with huge symphonic sweeps and a football-chant chorus that essentially acts as a call to arms to embrace Embrace as there's nothing better on offer:

All you good good people listen to me
You're just about done with the way that you feel
'Cause nothing rings home enough to dig your heels in

Like the rest of the album, this is ultimately really a relationship song but delivered with such guts and glory that it feels like you have to decide whether you're in or out. The answer is, you should be in. This is brave take-no-prisoners stuff and totally open to ridicule. But the band really do go for it, even mimicking the orchestral tuning buildup from The Beatles' 'A Day In The Life' as nothing more than a bridging tool to the outro. To put that in context, Embrace are stealing the climactic closing moments of the greatest song of the greatest album ever recorded, just to get them back to the chorus: That takes some balls.

'My Weakness Is None Of Your Business' (Danny McNamara, Richard McNamara) [Single]

Less bombastic by far, but showing that the band can deal with more delicate material, the piano-led and more emotional song was the album's third single, reaching number 9 due to its more subtle – but still huge – chanted chorus and trumpet support. With a touch of Richard Ashcroft ('Hallelujah you're the one/ Come back now'), there's a fascinating 'la la la' moment ripped straight from the 'na na nas' in The Beatles' 'Hey Jude': not the last time this album would wear that song's influence on its sleeve. Given that *The Good Will Out* is not only a title but a theme for the record, this is notable for the alternative lines 'Because my weakness is none of your business/But bad will always collect', showing that there are other outcomes available.

'Come Back To What You Know' (Danny McNamara, Richard McNamara) [Single]

A song about clinging to doomed relationships and the damage it can do, this is again delicate terrain, meaning that when the choruses hit, they do so with the force of a punk rock explosion. Okay, maybe that's going a bit far, but it really shows the band's power to build a song seemingly from nothing until going full-pelt hammer-and-tongs. Expressing an emotional depth that was way beyond their male peers ('Coming back to what you know won't mean a thing/Everything that you've done, keeps you from me'), the song proved to be Embrace's biggest chart smash to date, hitting number 6. Though all the singles have their own merits, it's this one that actually feels the most perfect.

'One Big Family' (Danny McNamara, Richard McNamara) [Single/EP]

With the album's nastiest guitar riff and most alternative sound, this song has 'single' written all over it. With the vocal taken by guitarist Richard McNamara – who has a remarkable, actually-in-tune Shaun-Ryder-esque style – this is not just the most danceable song on an album not known for indie-disco hits, but also the most aggressive. Peaking at number 21, it really was a narrow miss for greater success and remains a highlight.

'Higher Sights' (Danny McNamara, Richard McNamara)

With a stripped-back opening which (for Embrace) rather hilariously means they're augmented by just the one horn section, this is one of the album's shorter songs, and one of its most romantic: 'Then we'll dance/Those plans we make won't last'. The band are marking time here, perhaps, despite the anthemic chorus. Maybe not the most necessary of inclusions, 'Higher Sights' may well have had high hopes, but was always going to suffer on an album that places it six songs in as the first album-track proper.

'Retread' (Danny McNamara, Richard McNamara)

'Retread' is a song for all of Embrace's detractors. For all those that compared them to a retread of Oasis or The Verve, it's hard to imagine Ashcroft or Gallagher ever singing the lines 'Now I feel so insecure/I can't save something I feel so much for/Won't you stay and a leave a light for me?' with the feeling necessary to make them believable. Equally, for all those that questioned Danny McNamara's voice, he really pulls out the stops when it comes to the sustained notes. While this is still clearly Embrace territory (indeed, the brothers credit it with being the first song they wrote that supplied a blueprint for the type of band they wanted), it starts with an acoustic guitar and gently builds into something more epic and orchestral. The lyric is also notable for being the first use of the album title phrase 'The good will out' on the record – but not the last.

'I Want The World' (Danny McNamara, Richard McNamara) [Deep Cut]

The second biggest rock moment after 'One Big Family', and once again featuring brother Richard on vocals, this is a full-on Happy Mondays blast, but with bigger, bolder, more-squalling guitars than ever, plus an up-front organ. In fact, it's worth imagining how great the Happy Mondays' Shaun Ryder could've been singing this track.

'You've Got To Say Yes' (Danny McNamara, Richard McNamara)

Opening with another lead guitar riff backed with some cool organ giving it a surprising alternative edge, this song shows Danny too can deliver a Happy-Mondays-style vocal: which rather begs the question, why did Richard get the prime rock cuts? With massive, exhilarating, chanting choruses, this is pretty raw stuff. A song calling on a partner to not give up on a relationship ('You've gotta say yes/How can you have doubts?') – even for a band as emotionally heart-on-sleeve as Embrace – the lines 'Cause you, you know better/'Cause you're hooked and your f*cked without me', seem rather strong.

'Fireworks' (Danny McNamara, Richard McNamara) [EP]

It would be remiss of us to not point out this song's similarity to The Verve's 'The Drugs Don't Work'. But our hats have to go off to Embrace here. On an album filled with exceptional orchestral moments, this song delivers the most outstanding musical section using only a piano and a cello: combining on the intro to spine-shuddering effect. While it does share a fair amount of DNA with The Verve, they *are* strong genes, and deserve to proliferate. A song of regret for how a relationship fades, this was the band's second single, and their first to hit the top 40: reaching 34 in May 1997. Luckily, no one told Richard Ashcroft.

'The Last Gas' (Danny McNamara, Richard McNamara)

Beginning and ending with guitar distortion, this is very much Embrace in their groove-rock mode, with Richard McNamara channelling The Charlatans' Tim Burgess (Check out the verse, 'It's the way I feel/It's the way I feel/I'm in your hand, do as we planned/Show me the way you kneel'). It really does make you wish The Charlatans had created some songs with this kind of backing. It's also close in spirit to Oasis at their most full-on, with big 'ba ba ba' chorus backing vocals. It perhaps does rely on its influences a bit much, but as the last gasp of the album's big rock moments, it's still great stuff.

'That's All Changed Forever' (Danny McNamara, Richard McNamara)

The first of three piano-strong ballads that close the record and deal with moving on, here we are treated to an introduction that rivals 'Fireworks' for the album's most beautiful moment. Notable again for Danny defying his vocal critics (check out the falsetto at 2:30), it seems hard to imagine any of the band's forerunners being as willing to express themselves. The second outing for the band's signature phrase ('No more worries and doubts, the good will come out'), this is essentially a love song about choosing to move on while looking over your shoulder and learning from past experience.

'Now You're Nobody' (Danny McNamara, Richard McNamara) [Deep Cut]

A song of two halves – the first being a lyrically-light vocal section and the latter purely musical – this is best described as what it might've sounded like if Simon & Garfunkel had been invited to guest on The Beach Boys' *Pet Sounds* album. This, of course, means it's really quite special, even if it doesn't feel like it's been crafted from exactly the same materials as the rest of the record. The subdued horns in the expansive instrumental – and the final moments that sound like a child's toy being wound down – also make for unexpected touches.

'The Good Will Out' (Danny McNamara, Richard McNamara)

Following the lead set by 'My Weakness Is None Of Your Business', the title track shares a huge amount of its DNA with The Beatles' 'Hey Jude' (Imagine what might've happened had Embrace gone nuts for 'Helter Skelter' instead). Starting with a piano and taking a full seven minutes to build and fade away, the most striking moment comes at the halfway point when the female backing vocals join the fray and you just know it's going to go off – the tension builds, and suddenly we're released into a full-on Beatles soundscape. Despite this, the defining moment for the band's signature phrase isn't actually as bombastic as you might expect: the time for that is done. The album is done. The breakup is over. With hope in his heart for a new dawn tomorrow, Danny McNamara is moving forward with his life and healing.

Optional Extras

Unfortunately, there's no deluxe version of the album, but it would be interesting to see what might be included, as the band recorded a number of demos prior to recording the album. What *is* available comes from the single B-sides and EPs. Many of these remixes, orchestral versions, alternate versions, live tracks and unreleased studio tracks appear on the 2005 B-sides collection *Dry Kids*. Of the unreleased studio tracks, the majority are either acoustic guitar or piano ballads – Highlights include the Lennon-esque 'The Way I Do', the Americana of 'Dry Kids', the stripped-down 'Free Ride' and the retrospective acoustic 'Love Is Back' with its gentle moaning chorus. 'Feelings I Thought You Shared' is a light country number with a trumpet solo leading to a big-band outro, while 'Don't Turn Your Back On Love' is a full-on guitar number with church-organ accompaniment. Some of the earlier EP recordings are far more rocky, with the Oasis-sounding 'You've Only Got To Stop To Get Better' and the wailing 'Blind': also available in a less raw version on the B-sides collection.

Theaudience – Theaudience (1998)

Recording sessions: 1997-1998
Producers: Mike Hedges, Ian Grimble, Billy Reeves, Peter Collins, Sophie Ellis-Bextor, Patch Hannan, Nigel Butler, Angie Dial, Dean Mollett
Record label: eLLeFFe, Mercury
Chart position: UK: 22
Release date: 17 August 1998
Writers: Reeves (tracks 1-12, 14), Butler (4, 12), Smith (5), Sweeny, Jones, Alexander (10), Mollett (13)

Pete: I really felt – and still do – that Theaudience brought something fresh to the table. No one else had created an album like this in all the years of Britpop, and I don't think it's too big an exaggeration to say they laid some of the groundwork for acts such as Amy Winehouse, as well as the standout star Sophie Ellis-Bextor herself.

Matt: Theaudience were a dark, gothic pop band with Britpop parallels who could turn their hand to a number of genres. Sometimes disjointed, they're an interesting what-if in terms of how they might've approached a follow-up album.

The Album

Formed by guitarist Billy Reeves for a bet to prove just how easy it was to land a record deal (given the sheer amount of cash floating around alternative music in 1996), Theaudience (all one word because almost *all* Britpop bands had one word titles) were a far better band than their origin story might suggest. Combining alt-indie with genuine pop-soul, their ace in the hole came in the form of the distinct vocals of soon-to-be-solo chanteuse Sophie Ellis-Bextor. Featuring some killer – albeit unusually-titled – singles ('If You Can't Do It When You're Young; When Can You Do It?', 'A Pessimist Is Never Disappointed'), the band's tales of youth and struggle carried a certain aloofness amidst the vulnerability, providing an air of genuine cool. Certainly, some songs feel unnecessary – 'Bells For David Keenan' being the prime example – but there's so much promise on show that the only real shame is that, in 1999, Theaudience gave up on their audience by splitting up.

Standout track: 'Harry'

Manic Street Preachers – This Is My Truth, Tell Me Yours (1998)
Recording sessions: August 1997-June 1998
Producers: Mike Hedges, Dave Eringa
Record label: Epic
Chart position: UK: 1
Release date: 14 September 1998
Writers: Lyrics: Nicky Wire; Music: James Dean Bradfield, Sean Moore

Pete: I was in Wales the day the Manics scored their first number one, and it made the BBC Wales news, as you'd expect. It was hilarious hearing a newsreader say the words 'If you tolerate this, then your children will be next'.

Matt: For me, this is where the band went too far into big anthemic numbers with pretentious titles and lyrics. The lead single 'If You Tolerate This…' is a prime example, and though the Manics have always been a wordy band with powerful lyrics, I felt it just didn't seem to fit together. Luckily, not all of the album and follow-up singles had the same effect.

The Album
The incredible popularity of *Everything Must Go* in 1996 (released a decade after they first formed) offered the Manic Street Preachers a template for success. Now that they'd achieved their destiny and were as big a band as they'd always promised the faithful they would be, it seems childish to pick at them for playing it safe and not changing course for the follow-up. Frankly, they'd waited too long for such a moment, and it was time to capitalise. While there's a faint whiff of Oasis' bloated *Be Here Now* about how this album simply builds on its predecessor's highs, the Manics really did have the bit between their teeth. A number-1 album which also contained their first chart-topping single, *This Is My Truth, Tell Me Yours* may not feel as vital as previous long players, but there's a lot of gold to be mined from its hour length: not least from Nicky Wire's excellent literate lyrics (the first time he'd carried this duty alone). With four stunning singles that cemented the band as one of the

big players (even if they don't get mentioned enough alongside Blur, Oasis, Pulp and Suede), the only point of criticism is for 'The Everlasting', which feels a touch 'Britpop-by-numbers': Wire stating he wanted to rival Blur's 'The Universal' and Oasis' 'The Masterplan'. But all can be forgiven for any record that contains 'My Little Empire'.

Standout track: 'You Stole The Sun From My Heart'

1999 – Millennium Mania

As the countdown began to close in on the 20th century, there was an air of deflation. Though the economy was doing well and unemployment in the UK was at an all-time low, the mood of 1999 was curiously downbeat, as if the millennium bug was something you could actually get sick from.

In the UK, London had been unexpectedly terrorised when 23-year-old antisocial loner David Copeland planted three bombs. Internationally, the world was shocked by America's Columbine High School massacre – a senseless act that the right-wing media found scapegoats for in alternative acts such as Marilyn Manson and Eminem.

Britpop felt long-dead. It had now become a cover-all term for a type of backwards-looking retro music, rather than the optimistic forward-thinking scene it had been in 1993. With safe-feeling pop music like Britney Spears, B*Witched, and comeback-queen Cher clogging up the charts, the UK alternative responded with the New Acoustic movement: spearheaded by the *NME* with the acronym NAM. It may have roped together various Noel-rock groups, but ultimately it was just too chin-stroking and beardy to be considered as something the kids could really get behind. Most of them were now on Napster anyway, using the new file-sharing platform to listen to the music they actually wanted, for free (albeit after several hours' wait).

The year and the century were seen out by Tony Blair singing 'Auld Lang Syne' arm-in-arm with the Queen at a half-filled Millennium Dome.

It felt knackered. But it had been a very busy decade.

Though 1999 may not have been a classic year for British music, this chapter's albums represent some of the best to be found in the post-Britpop world. From the huge-selling offerings of Travis and Stereophonics, to the Britpop bubble-breaking of Supergrass and Blur, it may not have been as exciting culturally, but that didn't mean there wasn't still some genuine quality on offer.

Key Album: Stereophonics – Performance And Cocktails (1999)

Personnel:
Kelly Jones: vocals, guitar
Richard Jones: bass
Stuart Cable: drums
Recording sessions: October 1995-October 1998 – Various sessions, including Courtyard Studio, Oxford ('Roll Up And Shine'); Real World, Bath ('Roll Up And Shine', 'The Bartender And The Thief', 'Just Looking', 'I Wouldn't Believe Your Radio', 'T-Shirt Sun Tan', 'A Minute Longer', 'I Stopped To Fill My Car Up'); Parkgate Studio, Sussex ('Hurry Up And Wait', 'Pick A Part That's New', 'Half The Lies You Tell Ain't True', 'Is Yesterday, Tomorrow, Today?'); Rockfield Studio, Monmouth ('She Takes Her Clothes Off', 'Plastic California')

Producers: Bird & Bush
Record label: V2
Chart position: UK: 1
Release date: 8 March 1999

Pete: It's a fine album, but it wasn't what I was expecting. I'd bought the single 'The Bartender And The Thief', and I was primed and ready for *Word Gets Around* part two. When the band suddenly went mega, I was thinking, 'Surely some people must end up buying the first record and realise this is a misstep?'. Goes to show what I know.

Matt: For me, this is a consolidation album. The first had built a strong core-following, but this was the album to reel everyone else into what they were missing, and add a number of festival sing-alongs to their already strong arsenal.

The Band

Kelly Jones and Cable had been in a number of bands, both together and apart, before Richard Jones joined them around 1989. By 1992, the band had begun writing and gigging in earnest: at one point under the name Tragic Love Company. It wasn't until 1996 that the band changed their name to Stereophonics (originally with a 'The') and demo tape which was gathering interest and airplay. Soon the band were signed to V2 records, and began recording their debut single, and album *Word Gets Around*: released in 1997 to critical and minor commercial acclaim. The 1999 follow-up *Performance And Cocktails* met with a more mixed critical reception but was far more commercially successful. The band continued to release a new album every two years, again with mixed reviews, but generally gained good sales, until 2010 when they took a short hiatus. During this time, Cable – who'd left the band in 2003 – passed away, and his replacement Javier Weyler also left. In 2013, the band re-emerged with new drummer Jamie Morrison, and a new album. Returning to a new-album-every-two-years schedule, Stereophonics are now one of the most successful Welsh rock acts and are currently recording album number twelve.

The Album

Stereophonics second album is perhaps not what you remember. Often recalled as an album of acoustic ballads (Has any other band in this book made such use of the drum brushes in place of sticks?), it's certainly true it has its fair share, and that many made it into the public consciousness as hit singles. It also comes with a fair amount of up-tempo rock, while a good few tracks straddle the two.

Where their debut *Word Gets Around* was essentially an exercise in indie rock, this offering aimed directly at the middle of the road. It worked. A huge commercial success, *Performance And Cocktails* was the UK's fifth-biggest-selling album of 1999, delivered five high-charting singles, and set Stereophonics on the road to becoming one of the biggest acts of the next decade. While there's very little here that could be deemed alternative or even edgy, Kelly Jones had clearly moved on as a songwriter. Turning his ever-keen observer's eye away from the vignettes of small-town Welsh life that had defined their debut, he now looked out to the wider world that touring had brought the band into contact with. Here, we witness slithers of the mundane given crystal-clear clarity, film scripts presented as songs, and even a few chunks of world-weary wisdom. Though Jones' skill with a lyric, raspy voice and ear for a catchy melody are all key factors, it's actually the music that surprises the most on this record. At a moment when you couldn't seem to get musically arrested without a full orchestra behind you, this album was notable for being largely free of ornament, just the stripped-back sound of three people in a room playing simple, catchy rock. Though the critics didn't seem to agree with the record-buying public (many critics making misjudged comparisons with Oasis), by delivering the goods with an impressively straight bat (although a rugby analogy may have been more fitting at this point), the band had found their audience and were not going to apologise for it.

'Roll Up And Shine' (Lyrics: Kelly Jones; Music: Stereophonics)

Starting with the hilariously drawled line, 'Why don't you take a look in my mouth?', the album's first song (which includes the album title in its third line) is a big 1970s rock opening with driving and tinny verse guitars, squealing classic rock riffs and an anthemic chorus. A song all about being in Stereophonics, by those that know best what it's like to be in Stereophonics, the defining line is 'So why don't you take a look around?', which – delivered over stop/start power chords – is essentially Kelly Jones setting out his song writing stall as an omnipotent observer of all human nature, and asking the listener to check out his wares.

'The Bartender And The Thief' (Lyrics: Kelly Jones; Music: Stereophonics) [Single]

On Stereophonics' debut album *Word Gets Around*, Jones proved himself as a deft observer of small-town life, injecting empathy, understanding and heartbreak into moments that would normally go unnoticed. With this song, we see for the first time that his canvas has expanded. Rather than tell simple stories of simple folk, he was now capable of delivering miniature feature films in song form. Of all such songs on the album, this is the best and certainly most exhilarating example. The album's fastest song and an absolute rock juggernaut to boot. The protagonists meet one night while robbing a church: 'The bartender and the thief are lovers/Steal what they need like sisters and brothers'. Though it may not have the same emotional weight as many of the other songs, it's huge fun, and it reached number three in November 1998: whetting the appetite for the album's release five months later.

'Hurry Up And Wait' (Lyrics: Kelly Jones; Music: Stereophonics) [Single]

The drum brushes are out, and it won't be the last time. The album's shortest song and the final single (reaching 11 in November 1999), this is a beautiful acoustic-led piece about all the tiny wasted moments in life: 'Wait for a break so you can take a little something that'll make your next break come along a little quicker'. Based around a title that The Beatles would've referred to as a Ringo-ism' (see 'A Hard Day's Night'), Jones' voice never soars like you feel it might, as the song slowly builds and electric guitars join the fray. Instead, the melody feels as exhausted and resigned as the moments he's describing. Quite rightly, the song simply fades away.

'Pick A Part That's New' (Lyrics: Kelly Jones; Music: Stereophonics) [Single]

A bit like a self-help book in song form, this again details some of life's more mundane moments ('People drinking on their own/Push buttons on the phone'). But it tackles the subject with more upbeat positivity. A jangling guitar riff and power-chord chorus accompany the key message that 'You can do all the things that you like to do/All around, upside down/Pick a part that's new', before in the outro challenging the listener to actively be that change: 'So what's new to you?'. Issued as the album's third single, reaching number 4 did not set Kelly Jones off on a new career as a modern-day guru, but it did help to cement the fact that Stereophonics were becoming genuinely big players.

'Just Looking' (Lyrics: Kelly Jones; Music: Stereophonics) [Single]

Of course, commercialism and capitalism have been dealt with in these pages before, but they haven't been tackled with the same level of desperation ('There's things I want, there's things I think I want') or the keenly-observed knowledge that aspiration itself can be a key driver: 'I'm just looking, I'm not buying/It keeps me smiling'. Featuring delicate guitar work that ultimately bows before a powerful chorus, this is probably the most incessantly catchy of all the singles (It hit 4 in February 1999, shortly before the album's release). Special note should be made of the instrumental breakdown section (It took a *lot* of building to get to a point where you could consider breaking it down again), which leads to a euphoric build. This is also Jones' best vocal delivery of the record, moving from gentle restraint to a belting chorus.

'Half The Lies You Tell Ain't True' (Lyrics: Kelly Jones; Music: Stereophonics) [Deep Cut]

Beginning with sounds that resemble the song being crowbarred in from another record, 'Half The Lies You Tell Ain't True' (another Ringo-ism) is exhilarating big-rock posturing with chugging riffs that wouldn't be out of place on an early Manic Street Preachers album. Unusually, the lyric is more centred around Jones himself and his frustrated attempts to get to the truth of another's character ('I'm gonna find out/I'm gonna find a piece of you') as if his observational powers have momentarily fled him and he's pretty peeved about it, even resorting to name-calling ('Under size, a naked fake/That's a face that fits for two). Who cares? – If you were in a mosh pit in 1999, you would've been going wild.

'I Wouldn't Believe Your Radio' (Lyrics: Kelly Jones; Music: Stereophonics) [Single]

The fourth single – which reached 11 in August 1999 – is a surprisingly low-key affair. In fact, it wouldn't sound at all out of place if it were being busked on the streets of Cardiff, with its acoustic guitars and a three-piece drum kit (including another outing for Cable's brushes). Believe it or not, even an accordion joins the mix at one point, as if a fellow street entertainer decided to join in before being kicked away. Driven by a rolling drum pattern, this song continues the themes of 'Just Looking', but with the world-weary air of anyone that sings for their supper: 'You can have it all if you like/And you can pay for it the rest of your life'. With more than a shade of Oasis thrown in, this even includes the occasional Gallagher-style nonsense lyric, which is surprising for Jones.

'T-Shirt Sun Tan' (Lyrics: Kelly Jones; Music: Stereophonics)

A song of sex, sweat and failure, this is another small-scale story with a big chorus driven by rock guitars and blistering vocals. Of all the rock numbers on offer, it's the least satisfying as it chugs along, but there are still some neat moments of realism that deliver a smile.

'Is Yesterday, Tomorrow, Today?' (Lyrics: Kelly Jones; Music: Stereophonics)

A song about the compulsion to make lists and how in doing so, you're simply putting off actually doing the things you're making the lists about. This is a delicate country-tinged ballad with room enough big rock guitars to emphasise the descending melody lines. Though it's about hitting rock bottom ('picking up ripped cigarette boxes hoping that one remains') and making plans to 'come back again', it's still hopeful stuff, with a great middle-eight, simple piano and a delicate outro. It's a fine piece of craftsmanship, even if it's not as memorable as some of its counterparts.

'A Minute Longer' (Lyrics: Kelly Jones; Music: Stereophonics)

A heartfelt ballad about not wanting to leave the pub (yes, really, although we suspect Jones may also have had larger concerns in mind), this is one of the album's weakest moments, with drum brushes and acoustics back out in force, and electric piano thrown into the mix. By the end, there has been a 'Crash back to date' – presumably meaning an alcohol-induced hangover the next morning.

'She Takes Her Clothes Off' (Lyrics: Kelly Jones; Music: Stereophonics) [Deep Cut]

The defining trait of the debut album *Word Gets Around* was Jones' excellent ability to deliver tales of small-town life as if they were entire novels in song form. This is a song exactly in that style, as if he's proving to himself he can still deliver them. Though it doesn't necessarily keep with the album themes, this is the doomed tale of the life and death of former carnival queen Porta Bubble Joan, who wanted to 'be another Marilyn' but is now middle-aged and desperate. This is a genuinely affecting piece – like a scene from Jones' own version of *Under Milk Wood* – and definitely stands as an album highlight.

'Plastic California' (Lyrics by Kelly Jones. Music by Stereophonics)

A theme that 1990s bands often utilised was their experience of the United States. In fact, it was exactly this subject that Blur used to kick-start the entire Britpop movement as a marketable form with *Modern Life Is Rubbish*. But the Stereophonics' line on such matters is far more non-committal ('Some love, some hate'), as if they're far too savvy than to accidentally ostracise one of the world's largest markets. Mid-tempo rock and with a difficult album placing (What can really follow 'She Takes Her Clothes Off'?), there's still space for some wry observations: of which 'Plastic California looks like Blackpool' and 'All the beautiful people make it true/But you look as good as you' are the best.

'I Stopped To Fill My Car Up' (Lyrics: Kelly Jones; Music: Stereophonics)

An incredibly simple piano ballad that is left completely unadorned for the first minute and a half, the album's final moment is another filmic piece, detailing Jones stopping for fuel one night and returning to find a man in his car with a gun. With an air of director Quentin Tarantino in its mixture of realism ('I paid the lady no change and then it started to piss down') and fantasy ('I just made up this story to get your attention/Makes me smile'), there is perhaps a slight suggestion that the album should've concluded on a grander statement. But maybe that would be to miss the point. *Performance And Cocktails* is an album of small moments, writ large by being immortalised in song.

Optional Extras

In 2010 *Performance And Cocktails* was released in both deluxe and super-deluxe versions, the latter including a CD of B-sides and one of rarities, while the deluxe was simply highlights of its bigger brother. The rarities CD is actually a little misleading, as it consists of live versions of album tracks (and one B-side) played at radio sessions and various venues on tour, and although they're solid versions, outside of the studio, the simplicity of some of the songs is obvious. The B-sides consist of more live versions, more radio sessions, a number of covers and some non-album tracks, including a demo and an alternate joke version of 'I Wouldn't Believe Your Radio' with Cable doing his best Tom Waits impression. The three original non-album tracks are a mixed bag, with a nice acoustic folk-like tune reminiscing about the good old days ('In My Day'), an unnecessary instrumental jam with a curious monologue provided by engineer Marco Migiliari ('Postmen Do Not Make Great Movie Heroes'), and the simple unfinished feel of demo 'Nice To Be Out'. The best B-sides are the covers, and it's a brave band that try their hand at such big names and well-known songs, even if they are a strong influence. Featuring Kelly Jones and a guitar (plus occasional minimal added instrumentation), he runs through faithful versions of tracks by Neil Young, The Rolling Stones, The Kinks, Bob Dylan, Nirvana and The Tragically Hip. On the whole, these are really good ('Angie' and 'Sunny Afternoon' in particular), but some don't quite make it ('Something In The Way' and 'Positively 4th Street'). Overall, this is one of the few deluxe versions reviewed for this book that doesn't really bring much to the table.

Key Album: Blur – 13 (1999)

Personnel:
Damon Albarn: vocals, piano, synthesizers, acoustic guitar, melodica, backing vocals ('Coffee & TV')
Graham Coxon: guitars, banjo, saxophone, lead vocals ('Coffee & TV'), co-lead vocals ('Tender'), backing vocals
Alex James: bass, backing vocals, double bass ('Tender')
Dave Rowntree: drums, percussion
Recording sessions: 19 July-19/20 November 1998 – Various sessions held at Studio Sýrland, Reykjavík, Studio 13, Sarm West Studios, Mayfair Studios, London
Note: Recording dates of June-October 1998 are widely used and its probable work did start earlier than July (as listed in several articles). Studio 13 engineers have stated 'Trailerpark' was worked on first (and it was debuted at live shows in June 1998) and also pre-production work before sessions moved to another studio. The *21* box set states that a jam of 'Battle' was recorded at Mayfair Studios on 11 August 1998.
Producers: William Orbit, Blur
Record label: Food, Parlophone
Chart position: UK: 1, USA: 80
Release date: 15 March 1999

Pete: Often referred to as 'the breakup album', this is simultaneously the drugs album *and* a weird sort of conceptual affair in which Damon starts warbling 'Space is the place' whenever there's a couple of minutes to kill. It's wildly experimental, and 'Tender' doesn't even seem to belong on the record. You know what?: it may be my favourite Blur album.

Matt: This is a difficult album, with long, drawn-out pieces that take the listener through a depressing journey of samples, sketches and bits of songs.

Described like that, it shouldn't work, but it does! You do have to be in the mood for it, though.

The Album

Having effectively already changed musical direction twice in their career – once following their debut album *Leisure* to effectively create the Britpop sound, and again with *Blur* in 1997 to try and destroy it – by their sixth album, Blur decided that constant musical reinvention was the key to longevity, and took a sharp left turn. Hiring producer William Orbit rather than their long-standing producer Stephen Street, the band set about forging new ambient noise-filled soundscapes – an experimental panorama filled with electronica, Americana, noise and pop – for an album that would prove they had what it took to continue their career, despite concerns outside the camp that to change the formula further would *end* their career.

Thematically, the album is a double-edged sword: sharp and unpleasant. In 1998, Albarn had split with long-term partner Justine Frischmann of Elastica. Having gotten together in 1992, their relationship had risen and fallen with the tide of Britpop itself, the pair being seen as innovators of the genre, the star celebrity couple and two of its personal casualties. As hard-drug-use permeated Elastica and stalled any plans for further releases until the new decade, it also seeped into the Blur side of the relationship, adding another strain to the oft-stretched relationships inside the band itself. The last album for fifteen years to feature all four founders as active members, *13* wasn't so much the end of the party (They'd already done that in 1997), but the stepping stone to a new future.

'Tender' (Lyrics: Albarn, Coxon; Music: Blur) [Single]

Sounding initially like an Alan Lomax field-recording of a solo blues guitarist from the early-20th-century, the seven-and-a-half-minute 'Tender' is a steadily-building love song, including the stripped-down four piece gospel choir, blues solos and Coxon taking the lead vocal on the choruses. American-sounding but in no way a pastiche, this is rightly considered one of the band's defining achievements, and the song reached number two in February 1999: catching both the band and public by surprise (Let's face it, eight minutes of gospel didn't really have 'hit' written all over it). Still, it connected with fans and the radio-listening public, even if it doesn't necessarily feel like it connects with the album as a whole.

'Bugman' (Lyrics: Albarn; Music: Blur) [Deep Cut]

Taking up the now much-watched song two position of a Blur album, and essentially trying the same trick but through the musical blender of William Orbit, 'Bugman' actually bugs out. Noisy fun, with misfiring samples, chainsaw guitars and a breakdown section that appears to feature Coxon playing six solos simultaneously, this is closer in spirit to what was achieved on the preceding album *Blur* (as well as harking back to 'Trouble In The Message Centre' from *Parklife*), and manages to be a fun piece of pop, despite the fact it crumbles into itself and begins again in almost backwards form before Damon begins a falsetto of 'Space is the place': which for many signifies the record's true start. Taken as a whole, this might all sound a bit mental, and that's because it is.

'Coffee & TV' (Lyrics: Coxon; Music: Blur) [Single]

With juddering chords and quirky, awkward lyrics ('Do you feel like a chain store?/Practically floored', it begins before dreaming of escaping this 'big bad world'), this may not have been Coxon's first time on lead vocal, but it was his first time as singer on a Blur single. Delivered in deadpan style (It takes Albarn's backing vocals to lift the choruses), there's a strong sense that Coxon doesn't really want to be here, let alone singing – which is partly true, as he feared the song accidentally becoming a hit and him, therefore, being tied to it forever. Presented to the world with one of the all-time great videos (a milk carton goes in search of the lost child (Coxon) on its side), the song was a hit, of course, representing *13* at its most pop. However, charting at only number 11 in June 1999 meant it wasn't so substantial as to cause the guitarist too many sleepless nights.

'Swamp Song' (Lyrics: Albarn; Music: Blur)

Sharing a title with Oasis, and also being a groovy, grungy, Mississippi blues riff, 'Swamp Song' mixes the album's twin themes of love and drug abuse. With a second verse that's pure joy – featuring falsetto backing vocals and Albarn really enjoying seeing just what his vocals can do – the choruses stand in contrast due to their industrial sound and Damon screaming 'Stick it in my brain!'. By the conclusion, it's positively manic, and only anchored by the 'la la la' backing vocal.

'1992' (Lyrics: Albarn; Music: Blur)

With a lilting melody, woozy drums wash and buzzing bass, '1992' details the year that Albarn's relationship with Justine Frischmann began. This is a song of two distinct parts – the first half in the style of the early standout track 'Sing'; the second a haunting soundscape reminiscent of Radiohead's work on *OK Computer*. Lyrically oblique, the message may be hard to pin down, but the desolate mood is transcendent.

'B.L.U.R.E.M.I.' (Lyrics: Albarn; Music: Blur)

Changing tack spectacularly for an out-and-out punk-rock romp, this is direct and to the point – being a potted history of Blur and the music industry as a whole (E.M.I. being their ultimate record-label bosses). Accepting the fact that pop music is by nature cyclical and everyone is 'using the loop of another pop group', it also looks to a future when 'a teenage maniac will bring it all back':

as if predicting much of what would follow in the 2000s indie scene. Featuring some daffy duck-quack vocals, its blast of energy gives way to a hauntingly beautiful electric piano.

'Battle' (Lyrics: Albarn; Music: Blur)

Again hinting at Radiohead through the cold feel and use of ambient sounds, 'Battle' isn't so much a song as a soundscape that occasionally collides with vocals. Coxon's guitar attempts to make it recognisable as a tune one-third of the way in, but ultimately, this is Blur making full use of their new producer: throwing the pieces into the air and seeing where they land. Despite feeling like it's beamed in from another planet, the final minute pushes the envelope further, with a prog-like interlude based around another song altogether.

'Mellow Song' (Lyrics: Albarn; Music: Blur)

Again a song of two parts, the opening section is genuinely mellow, and with its picked acoustic guitar, may be the closest the band ever got to really producing something that could be deemed as a ditty. Lyrically dealing with substance abuse to cope with a breakup ('Shooting stars in my left arm, an alcohol low), the conclusion feels like William Orbit has begun a timer counting the song down to a gentle musical implosion.

'Trailerpark' (Lyrics: Albarn; Music: Blur)

With heavily distorted drums and off-kilter organ before what sounds like a jam session, the oft-repeated line 'I lost my girl to The Rolling Stones' has been taken by many as a direct reference to Frischmann's drug use, rather than her running off with Charlie Watts in the only music story of the 1990s to not make the tabloid press. Followers of Albarn's subsequent career may note how much 'Trailerpark' sounds like a Gorillaz track, although it fits wonderfully on *13*.

'Caramel' (Lyrics: Albarn; Music: Blur)

A sickly-sweet soundscape that echoes its title, 'Caramel' is a yearning mood piece that can be read as a desire to recover from heartbreak, drug abuse or both simultaneously: 'I've gotta get over/I've got to get better'. Quite what working on a song like this must have felt like for Albarn – given its gnawing hooks, unsettling vibe and almost eight-minute length – isn't worth considering, but hopefully, it delivered some form of resolution and release.

'Trimm Trabb' (Lyrics: Albarn; Music: Blur)

Trimm Trabb are a brand of trainers, and Albarn owned a pair. But this song is not about that. Instead, it's a dissection of the prevalent late-1990s lad culture, which Blur had played their part in creating. As with many Blur albums, this seems like the one-song-too-many, though it remains a fan favourite due to the pure guitar power that Coxon unleashes at the halfway point.

'No Distance Left To Run' (Lyrics: Albarn; Music: Blur) [Single]

As the album's third and final single – released in November 1999 – it's nothing short of shameful that it only reached 14. There's a gentle blues riff and resigned, disintegrating vocals which call time on the Albarn/Frischmann relationship without bitterness (okay, maybe there's a *touch* of bitterness), and the return of the gospel choir halfway through simply adds to the heartbreak. Ultimately hopeful for the future rather than hollow, this song is a beautiful piece of music and massively underrated.

'Optigan 1' (Lyrics: Albarn; Music: Blur)

Ending the album with an organ instrumental (created using an Optigan optical organ, hence the title), this almost circus-like piece recalls the Life trilogy, but is here presented through a William Orbit filter. A repetitive loop, *13* concludes on a cycle, as if love, life and all that it contains are ultimately part of a great coil spinning through the cosmos: which, of course, they are. For Blur, the decade and their heyday were over, but new adventures were yet to come. As they knew only too well, pop bands don't really die, they simply phase into new stages.

Optional Extras

In 2012, a deluxe version of *13* was released, the second CD containing the single B-sides which were made up of non-released songs and remixes (including individual band-member versions of 'Bugman'). In addition, there was a demo included on the Japanese album issue and the 2000 'Music Is My Radar' single.

The *21* box set had a further three rarities made up of a B-side and alternate versions of album songs. Previously there had always been a wealth of material for B-sides and the deluxe album editions (if sometimes of mixed quality), but this time it seems there was not much additional material. 'French Song' is an instrumental collection of song bits, while 'Mellow Jam' is pretty much what it says it is: a repetitive mellow jam with a pleading vocal. 'All We Want' is minimalist, choppy pop, while 'So You' is probably the best track, with a dirty groove and heartfelt vocals. The other extras include a full version of the spacey instrumental 'Beagle 2' (written for the Mars spacecraft of the same name), and a great full and fun version of the *Parklife* track 'Far Out': now a rocky, bouncy number. Conversely, the 'I Got Law' demo was later slowed down and reworked from a solo cheesy keyboard and drum machine number into the more well-known Gorillaz track – 'Tomorrow Comes Today'. The non-album 'Music Is My Radar' single splits fans between the fuzzy dance-jam track of the title song and the wistful, gentle soul of its B-side 'Black Book'. In the end, this is a disappointing collection.

Catatonia – Equally Cursed And Blessed (1999)

Recording sessions: 1998-1999
Producers: TommyD and Catatonia

Record label: Blanco y Negro
Chart position: UK: 1
Release date: 12 April 1999

Pete: Catatonia were so big by this point that they were essentially a mainstream band, weren't they? I'd even go as far as to say they didn't even seem cool anymore, which is a bit much given how good this record actually is.

Matt: This was effectively the difficult follow-up album for Catatonia, and I think it shows. Even the title seems prophetic in terms of what happened over the next year. The album shies away from the instant catchiness of the previous one, and requires the listener to put some real effort in.

The Album

If you want to understand just how phenomenally successful Catatonia had become in the late 1990s, then you need look no further than the album charts. When *Equally Cursed And Blessed* was released (beating ABBA to the top spot, no less), both of their other albums were also to be found in the top 40. The whirlwind had been diverting. In 1998, singer Cerys Matthews had scored another hit, guesting with Space on 'The Ballad Of Tom Jones', which she would then follow up at Christmas 1999 with an actual Tom Jones duet. In short, Matthews was now a household name: the acceptable face of the alternative *and* a *bona fide* member of the tabloid-hunted glitterati. It should therefore be no surprise that some of the album's strongest moments reflect the madness that surrounded the band ('Post Script') and the need to escape from it ('Valerian'): both notably Matthews compositions. Catatonia still knew how to have a good time, though. 'Storm The Palace' is positively punky (for Catatonia), while 'Karaoke Queen' may be one of the worst songs the band ever wrote, but effortlessly does the job it set out to do: shows the necessity of hit singles, no matter how lightweight they may be. *Equally Cursed And Blessed* may not be as stocked with hits as its predecessor was, but it was more than enough to keep Catatonia flying high for one more album before they split in 2001.

Standout track: 'Bulimic Beats'

Key Album: Travis – The Man Who (1999)

Personnel:
Fran Healy: vocals, guitar, piano
Andy Dunlop: guitar
Dougie Payne: bass
Neil Primrose: drums
Recording sessions: June 1998-July/August 1998 – Chateau de la Rouge Motte, Normandy, France; Abbey Road, London. Produced by Mike Hedges ('Turn', 'Why

Does It Always Rain On Me', 'She's So Strange'), plus a possible fourth song.
August/September 1998-January 1999 – Various sessions held at a number of
studios, including RAK, Mayfair, Roundhouse, and Angel. Produced by Nigel
Godrich.
Note: Album credits list 'Writing To Reach You', 'The Fear', 'Driftwood', 'The Last
Laugh Of The Laughter' and 'Slide Show' as being recorded at RAK studios at one
or more sessions in September and November 1998. Healy has also stated that
'Writing To Reach You' was the first song recorded with Godrich. 'As You Are' and
'Luv' were recorded at Mayfair Studios, possibly later in the year. Mixing sessions
also continued into 1999.
Producers: Nigel Godrich, Mike Hedges
Record label: Independiete
Chart position: UK: 1, UK: 39
Release date: 24 May 1999

Pete: I was a massive fan of the preceding *Good Feeling*. It was so much
fun. While I did notice at the time that there were untapped depths in the
songwriting, I never expected *The Man Who* to be what it was when I bought it
on the day of release. I wasn't so much disappointed, but I was confused as to
why they'd given up on the rock side of things. Of course, I was wrong.

Matt: This is an incredibly clever and well-made album, with songs that
combine a huge chunk of The Beatles and their solo work with a sprinkling of
Bowie and the best of the Britpop bands. On top of this, the change in musical
direction signified that taken by many bands that followed and had a massive
impact. I think *The Man Who* heavily dictated the sound of the early 2000s.

The Band
Around 1990, Dunlop joined a local band formed by brothers Chris and
Geoff Martyn in Lenzie, Scotland, and Pickford later joined on drums. After
their singer left in 1991, fellow Glasgow School of Art student Fran Healy
successfully auditioned. By this point, the band were called Glass Onion,
and in 1993 they released their debut EP of the same name. Despite local
cult status, a record deal eluded them until a 1995 demo was sent to Sony.
Impressed by one of the songs, the band were invited to play a showcase gig,
and on the strength of this, secured a publishing deal. At this point, Payne
(who'd been introducing the band on stage) was recruited to bass, and the
band moved to London, with both Martyn brothers leaving the group. The
band started writing and recording songs for their 1997 debut album *Good
Feeling*. Despite positive reviews, important support slots and celebrity
endorsement, the album didn't sell well.
    The band returned in 1999 with the more melodic second album *The Man
Who*, which was met initially with severe criticism for the change in direction.
However, when ~~The~~ third single, 'Why Does It Always Rain on Me?' hit big,

the album and band's career skyrocketed. Travis' third album *The Invisible Band*, continued this success. While on tour in 2002, drummer Primrose dove headfirst into the shallow end of a swimming pool, breaking his neck and almost dying from the spine damage. This led to the band almost splitting up, but thankfully, Primrose made a full recovery and in 2003, they were able to release the new album *12 Memories*. The band recorded and released their next two albums quickly in 2007 and 2008 before Healy released a solo album in 2010. In 2013, Travis returned with their seventh album *Where You Stand,* and have since released two further albums, the latest in 2020.

The Album

It could've been career suicide. While the 1997 debut *Good Feeling* had been a rowdy, upbeat and glam-infused rock album that was generally positively received by critics and built the band a committed fan base, *The Man Who* saw the group change tack to classic songwriting, ballads, introspection and heartbreak. Although clearly masterful and downright beautiful, the initial reaction was mixed, bordering on poor, and though the album entered the charts at number 5, Travis looked set to face the chopping block next time the accountants at the label got their red pens out. All that changed with the exceptionally-catchy third single 'Why Does It Always Rain On Me?', which brought them a huge amount of coverage when it heralded an abrupt change in the weather at Glastonbury 1999. The turnaround was stark and dramatic, pushing Travis into the mainstream seemingly overnight, pushing the album to number 1 and making them true contenders for the crown as the nation's favourite band. The end-of-year poll plaudits were numerous, and a Best Album and Best Group win at the Brit Awards (and a pair of Ivor Novellos for songwriter Fran Healy in 2000) sealed the deal. The band had been right to stick to their guns, creating a timeless portrait of love, life and the fragile beauty of simple existence.

'Writing To Reach You' (Fran Healy) [Single]

The album's first single is also its finest. It not only redefined the sound of a band best known for good-time rock into something more fragile and classic, it repositioned singer Fran Healy as a lyricist of note. A song written directly to an audience who may or may not be listening (and when the album was released, the odds-on bet was that they wouldn't be), it's a yearning ballad (with some excellent noisy guitar predating Coldplay's early hits) that's resigned, thoughtful and perhaps just a little bit fed up. The line 'The radio keeps playing all the usual/And what's a wonderwall anyway?' is particularly noteworthy, given the song shares the same chords as the Oasis hit.

Although 'Writing To Reach You' hit number 14 when released two months before the album, it genuinely seemed that Travis would not be reaching their audience.

'The Fear' (Fran Healy) [Deep Cut]

Essentially an acoustic country piece played on electric guitars; this is not a song that deals with the drug-induced psychosis so often detailed in late-era Britpop. Instead, it's about relationships reaching their autumnal stages and potentially ending. Surprisingly placed so early in the album, the song ultimately decays into a minute-long wash of static, ending suddenly and displaying a darker edge to the group.

'As You Are' (Fran Healy)

Indebted melodically to the John Lennon songs 'Oh My Love' and 'Across the Universe', 'As You Are' may be built around subtle verses detailing loneliness, but tips into classic Travis rock templates with a vocal build and yells recalling some of the fun found on the band's debut *Good Feeling*. Although it never goes far enough to make it seem out of place on *The Man Who*, it's good to see some of that DNA still present.

'Driftwood' (Fran Healy) [Single]

This is another song showing the lyrical dexterity Healy was now capable of. 'Driftwood' not only directly presents life as like being buoyed upon a river with little choice but to go with the current, it also employs a device whereby each line seems to segue into the next as if in one long stream of consciousness: 'Rivers turn to ocean, oceans tide you home'; 'Pillars turn to butter, butterflying low'. Never judgemental, the gentle sentiment and lilting refrains meant the single fared slightly better, reaching 13 when released a week before the album.

'The Last Laugh Of The Laughter' (Fran Healy) [Deep Cut]

Effectively the central point on what feels like quite a short album, this is a stunningly sad song that manages to combine emotive verses, almost church-like backing vocals, and a somewhat incongruous jolly piano line. With some lyrics sung in French ('My life', 'My whole life', 'Life's like that', 'On the last page of the chapter', in case you were wondering), this is a song about endings and therefore might've been better placed as the album closer, or being twice the length given its ability to generate a feeling of hollow desolation tinged with hope.

'Turn' (Fran Healy) [Single]

As the album's last single, it may come as a surprise to learn that – on paper – this was the album's biggest hit, buoyed on by the success of 'Why Does It Always Rain On Me?'. Though 'Turn' is the least satisfying of the singles and feels a touch contrived, it's still soaring stuff and has the album's biggest chorus. Very much the template for the following record, it also offered a big sing-along moment that proved especially successful in live settings, with its hopeful lyric about the importance and power of change.

'Why Does It Always Rain On Me?' (Fran Healy) [Single]

Featuring far more cello than you may remember, this is ultimately the album's big hit, no matter what the charts say. Sad yet joyous, downbeat yet bouncy, it was this song alone that turned the tide for both the band and album alike. A number-10 hit in August 1999, the song picked up considerable unexpected media attention when the band summoned a Glastonbury downpour during the song's opening bars on what was otherwise a fairly clement weekend of weather. Being the song that pushed Travis into the mainstream, 'Why Does It Always Rain On Me?' has gone on to transcend the band, being their most recognisable aspect.

'Luv' (Fran Healy)

A fairly straightforward harmonica-led song about a relationship getting rocky and realising you're still in love, this features atmospheric guitars in the style of The Verve, and a Beatles-like chorus that shows the song as a form of diary or self-help: 'Singing this song, singing along/Makes it easier for me to see you go'. Although highly regarded by fans, this is one of the album's weaker songs, which may partly be due to it coming after two songs that helped define the listening tastes of 1999.

'She's So Strange' (Fran Healy, Adam Seymour)

With shades of The Bluetones' 'Bluetonic' and Bowie ('the cats were all sniffing glue' obliquely recalling 'Ziggy Stardust'), this picks up the pace a touch. An acoustic piece about a girl who raided the petty cash and ran away for a new life in (of all places) Birmingham, this feels more like a character sketch than a song; coming and going as if it's a late-night dream of someone that flitted in and out of Healy's life.

'Slide Show' (includes 'Blue Flashing Light') (Fran Healy)

Also dreamlike and wistful, like a lost memory, is the album closer, 'Slide Show'. Beginning with a field recording of people getting in a car, Healy may state that he feels he's about to cry, but it's ultimately a positive song about finding a new start on a beautiful day, and is supplemented by an extremely tasteful chamber orchestra.

With lyrical references to the Manic Street Preachers ('Cause there is no design for life'), Beck ('There is no devil's haircut in your mind') and Oasis ('There is not a wonderwall to climb or step around'), it recognises that all the elements which make up an existence are important building blocks for the soul. A perfect way to round off an album of exceptional beauty, there's still room for one more song: the tucked away and remarkably clattery 'Blue Flashing Light'. Though it doesn't have any real place on the record and features some slightly bad language, it's actually one of the finest hidden tracks of the decade and shows that Travis still know how to let loose when they want to.

Optional Extras

A deluxe album was released in 2019 and includes a second disc of bonus tracks, including B-sides, covers and live cuts. The covers are an eclectic (and competent) selection, from The Ronettes 'Be My Baby' to The Band's 'The Weight', via Joni Mitchell and a tongue-in-cheek take on Britney Spears' '…Baby One More Time'. The Travis songs are a mixture. Rockers include 'Green Behind The Ears', 'Village Man', the stomp of 'Yeah Yeah Yeah Yeah', the glam 'High As A Kite' and the pub-rock 'Rock 'N' (Salad) Roll'. There are also gentle acoustic numbers, including 'Only Molly Knows', 'Where Is The Love' and the Jeff Buckley-esque 'Days Of Our Lives'. 'Coming Around' is the great in-between single released after the album and was heavily influenced by The Byrds. This single's B-sides also cover a variety of genres, including the 'Ob-La-Di Ob-La-Da' reggae ska of 'We Are Monkeys', the folk of 'Just The Faces Change', and The Shadows-sounding 'The Connection'. Overall, it's an interesting collection of songs, but none of them would have added anything to the album.

Muse – Showbiz (1999)

Recording sessions: April-May 1999
Producers: John Leckie, Muse, Paul Reeve
Record label: Mushroom
Chart position: UK: 29
Release date: 7 September 1999

Pete: When I first heard Muse, a small part of me labelled them as Radiohead copyists. But I was still blown away by how massive they sounded. Nothing I'd heard had ever seemed so big, especially from a three-piece. The bass alone had a phenomenal impact.

Matt: I've always associated Muse with the 2000s, and you forget that this album was actually released in 1999 and that some EPs preceded it. Muse have gone on to be a massive live attraction and produced some great albums. This one only hints at their potential.

The Album

If Oasis had inspired a crop of also-rans in the mid-to-late-1990s, then that baton had now been passed to Radiohead. While there's little doubt that this first Muse album is heavily indebted to the boys from Oxford, it's by no means a copy-and-paste attempt to cash in. Marrying the delicacy of *The Bends* to a much more muscular rhythm section, *Showbiz* also features nods to Elastica's Annie Holland in its bass-driven arrangements ('Cave', 'Sober'), while in the quite exceptional soaring vocals of singer/guitarist Matt Bellamy, there's more than a touch of Suede-like histrionics at play.

Formed in Teignmouth in 1994, like Embrace you can hardly fault Muse for their influences. The period had not only given rise to incredible music, but it had also shown how alternative bands could conquer all before them. By cherry-picking the best the 1990s had to offer and injecting some stadium-rock high theatrics into the mix, ('Falling Down', 'Showbiz') Muse created a sound that was both unique and long-lasting, setting them up for an incredibly long and successful career at the top.

Standout track: 'Muscle Museum'

Supergrass – Supergrass (1999)
Recording sessions: 1998-1999
Producers: Supergrass, John Cornfield
Record label: Parlophone
Chart position: UK: 3
Release date: 20 September 1999
Writers: Supergrass, Rob Coombes

Pete: The X-Ray album! This is like welcoming back an old friend. It's amazing how many great singles were pulled from this record alone – for most groups; they would be enough for a whole career!

Matt: This album sounded like a mash-up of 1970s bands, creating a real melting pot of songs and styles, but with a Supergrass finish. The slightly cheesy 'Pumping On Your Stereo' also had a fabulously bonkers Muppets/ *Labyrinth*-style video which I loved.

The Album
If Supergrass' second album had shown that the band were young, virile and talented enough to outlive the Britpop bubble – albeit in a darker form – the band's self-titled third LP is something of a settling of the waters. In the four years since the chart-topping *I Should Coco*, they'd matured significantly, looked inside themselves (quite literally due to the x-ray style cover) and made the decision to simply be the best band they could possibly be. Though certainly more upbeat than their sophomore offering, and with a clutch of hit singles to show for it, this was no return to the Buzzcocks-at-100-miles-per-hour version of the band, instead showing the groups versatility. There's glam ('Pumping On Your Stereo'), folk ('Shotover Hill') and even the closest a Britpop band ever really came to writing a Christmas song ('Jesus Came From Outta Space'): even if the latter really is rather silly. With singer/guitarist Gaz Coombes slowly morphing into a one-man Jagger/Richards, there are some excellent retro nods to be found here, too, not least in the proggy 'Eon' and the pastoral 'Mama And Papa', which feels as if it's been plucked straight from The Kinks' *The Village Green Preservation Society*. Supergrass had bounced out of the Britpop bubble. Now there was little else for them to do but 'just keep moving'.

Standout track: 'Mary'

Afterword

This is the next century...

What a decade it had been. The 1990s had witnessed the birth, boom and bust of Britpop: arguably the most exciting, vibrant and sensational period British music had witnessed since the 1960s. It was a time when homegrown indie guitar music from towns and cities across the UK went mainstream, pop stars were cut from the most unlikely of cloth, and British culture made its voice heard with some incredibly bombastic choruses.

Looking back – and this may simply be the rose-tinted haze of youthful reminiscence at work – the 1990s feel like an era of relative innocence where optimism and opportunity flourished. The new century – kick-started by the devastating terror attacks on America in September 2001 and their long-lasting international reverberations – had at the time seemed like it would never really be reached, and we could simply go on living in that golden age forever.

In retrospect, like all trends, the Britpop heyday might have been relatively short. However, in terms of impact, did those days ever really end?

The decade that followed witnessed the natural ebb and flow of music industry fashions. While many of Britpop's biggest hitters continued into the 2000s, it did not belong to them. As a new wave of British talent developed their own rockier version of the 90s sound – with groups such as The Libertines and Arctic Monkeys at the fore – it was natural for groups such as Blur, Pulp and Suede to ultimately go on hiatus and their members explore other musical directions or extra-curricular activities. Only Oasis (and to a lesser extent the Manic Street Preachers) can be said to have continued their drive for glory through this period, becoming a world-class stadium act before finally snapping under the weight of inter-Gallagher conflict in 2009.

Perhaps it was simply the fact that the 90s kids grew up, got jobs and had some money in their pockets, but it was the 2010s that added the twist to the Britpop tale. Maybe it shouldn't have been a surprise that many of the bands should suddenly join the package tour bandwagon (after all many of the 60s and 70s groups that had inspired them had been on the circuit for decades in various guises), but it was still remarkable that many (Sleeper, Shed 7) managed to combine this with the creation of new music that had the ability to gather attention and bother the charts. Meanwhile, individuals such as Damon Albarn, Brett Anderson, Jarvis Cocker and the Gallagher brothers all became cultural figures in their own right – seemingly now more influential than the bands through which they made their names – although their bands can still make the headlines when they become active.

Whether this trend will continue or simply be a marketing blip centred around album anniversaries is yet to be seen. Certainly, it's unlikely that any individual band will capture the zeitgeist again in the way that took place during the Britpop boom. However, right now, it seems that despite 20 years having passed since it was supposed to have finished, it's still possible to be part of the Britpop party.

Writing this book has allowed us to do just that: relive, reminisce and rediscover. We hope it has done the same for you.

On Track series

Level 42 – Matt Philips 978-1-78952-102-3
Aimee Mann – Jez Rowden 978-1-78952-036-1
Joni Mitchell – Peter Kearns 978-1-78952-081-1
The Moody Blues – Geoffrey Feakes 978-1-78952-042-2
Mike Oldfield – Ryan Yard 978-1-78952-060-6
Tom Petty – Richard James 978-1-78952-128-3
Porcupine Tree – Nick Holmes 978-1-78952-144-3
Queen – Andrew Wild 978-1-78952-003-3
Radiohead – William Allen 978-1-78952-149-8
Renaissance – David Detmer 978-1-78952-062-0
The Rolling Stones 1963-80 – Steve Pilkington 978-1-78952-017-0
The Smiths and Morrissey – Tommy Gunnarsson 978-1-78952-140-5
Steely Dan – Jez Rowden 978-1-78952-043-9
Steve Hackett – Geoffrey Feakes 978-1-78952-098-9
Thin Lizzy – Graeme Stroud 978-1-78952-064-4
Toto – Jacob Holm-Lupo 978-1-78952-019-4
U2 – Eoghan Lyng 978-1-78952-078-1
UFO – Richard James 978-1-78952-073-6
The Who – Geoffrey Feakes 978-1-78952-076-7
Roy Wood and the Move – James R Turner 978-1-78952-008-8
Van Der Graaf Generator – Dan Coffey 978-1-78952-031-6
Yes – Stephen Lambe 978-1-78952-001-9
Frank Zappa 1966 to 1979 – Eric Benac 978-1-78952-033-0
10CC – Peter Kearns 978-1-78952-054-5

Decades Series
The Bee Gees in the 1960s – Andrew Mon Hughes et al
978-1-78952-148-1
Alice Cooper in the 1970s – Chris Sutton 978-1-78952-104-7
Curved Air in the 1970s – Laura Shenton 978-1-78952-069-9
Fleetwood Mac in the 1970s – Andrew Wild 978-1-78952-105-4
Focus in the 1970s – Stephen Lambe 978-1-78952-079-8
Genesis in the 1970s – Bill Thomas 978178952-146-7
Marillion in the 1980s – Nathaniel Webb 978-1-78952-065-1
Pink Floyd In The 1970s – Georg Purvis 978-1-78952-072-9
The Sweet in the 1970s – Darren Johnson 978-1-78952-139-9
Uriah Heep in the 1970s – Steve Pilkington 978-1-78952-103-0
Yes in the 1980s – Stephen Lambe with David Watkinson

978-1-78952-125-2

On Screen series
Carry On… – Stephen Lambe 978-1-78952-004-0
David Cronenberg – Patrick Chapman 978-1-78952-071-2
Doctor Who: The David Tennant Years –
Jamie Hailstone 978-1-78952-066-8
Monty Python – Steve Pilkington 978-1-78952-047-7
Seinfeld Seasons 1 to 5 – Stephen Lambe 978-1-78952-012-5
James Bond – Andrew Wild 978-1-78952-010-1

Other Books
Babysitting A Band On The Rocks – G.D. Praetorius 978-1-78952-106-1
Derek Taylor: For Your Radioactive Children –
Andrew Darlington 978-1-78952-038-5
Iggy and The Stooges On Stage 1967-1974 – Per Nilsen 978-1-78952-101-6
Jon Anderson and the Warriors – the road to Yes –
David Watkinson 978-1-78952-059-0
Nu Metal: A Definitive Guide – Matt Karpe 978-1-78952-063-7
Tommy Bolin: In and Out of Deep Purple – Laura Shenton 978-1-78952-070-5
Maximum Darkness – Deke Leonard 978-1-78952-048-4
Maybe I Should've Stayed In Bed – Deke Leonard 978-1-78952-053-8
Psychedelic Rock in 1967 – Kevan Furbank 978-1-78952-155-9
The Twang Dynasty – Deke Leonard 978-1-78952-049-1

and many more to come!

Would you like to write for Sonicbond Publishing?

We are mainly a music publisher, but we also occasionally publish in other genres including film and television. At Sonicbond Publishing we are always on the look-out for authors, particularly for our two main series, On Track and Decades.

Mixing fact with in depth analysis, the On Track series examines the entire recorded work of a particular musical artist or group. All genres are considered from easy listening and jazz to 60s soul to 90s pop, via rock and metal.

The Decades series singles out a particular decade in an artist or group's history and focuses on that decade in more detail than may be allowed in the On Track series.

While professional writing experience would, of course, be an advantage, the most important qualification is to have real enthusiasm and knowledge of your subject. First-time authors are welcomed, but the ability to write well in English is essential.

Sonicbond Publishing has distribution throughout Europe and North America, and all our books are also published in E-book form. Authors will be paid a royalty based on sales of their book. Further details about our books are available from www.sonicbondpublishing.com. To contact us, complete the contact form there or email info@sonicbondpublishing.co.uk